I0813009

IMAGES
of America

THE SEBAGO LAKE AREA

WINDHAM, STANDISH, RAYMOND, CASCO, SEBAGO, AND NAPLES

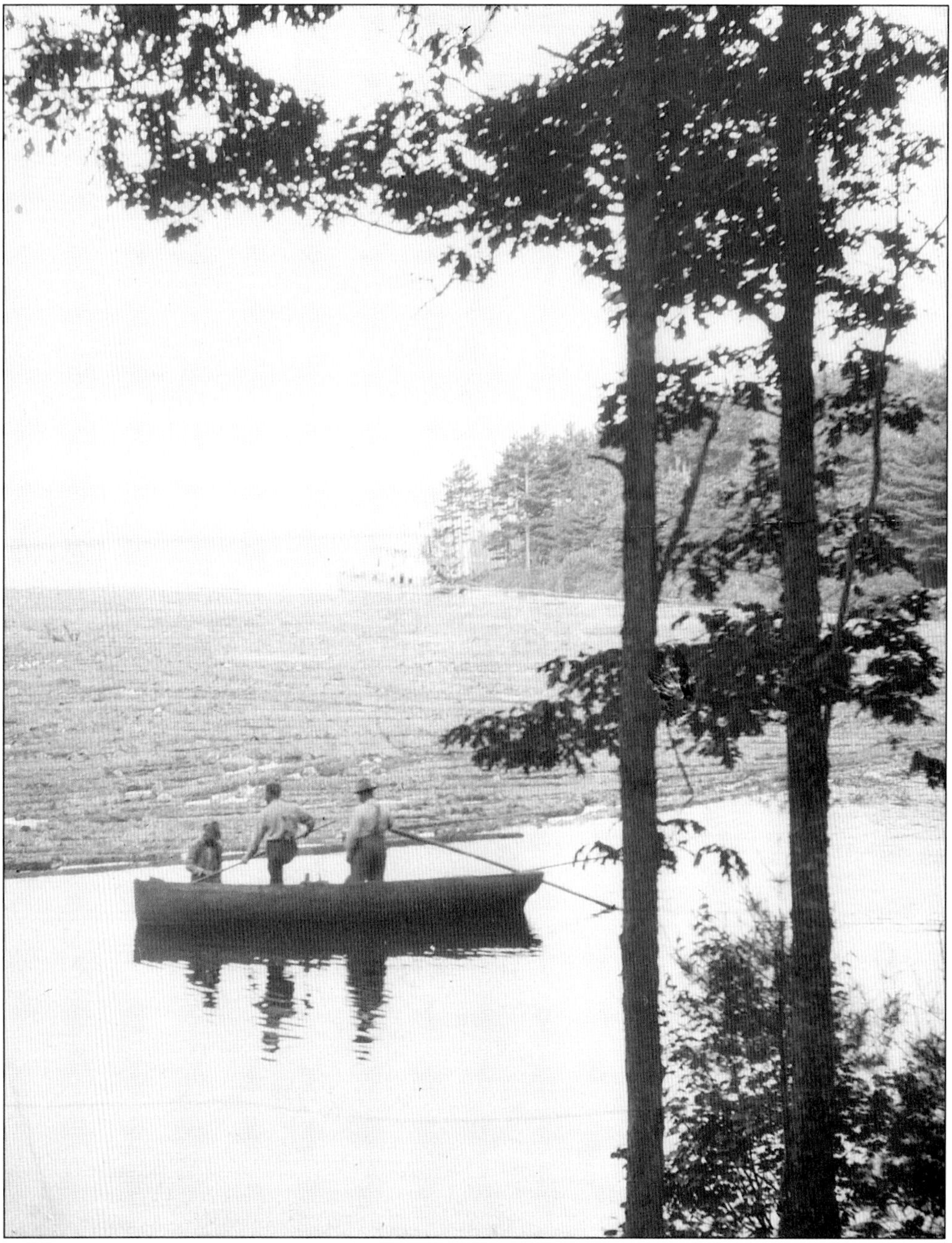

A Boon of Logs, c. 1920. A large boon of logs is about to be towed by a Dupont Company boat down Long Lake and Brandy Pond and then driven down the Songo River where they will be towed the length of Sebago Lake.

IMAGES *of America*

THE SEBAGO LAKE AREA

WINDHAM, STANDISH, RAYMOND, CASCO, SEBAGO, AND NAPLES

Diane and Jack Barnes

ARCADIA PUBLISHING

ISBN 978-0-7385-4943-9

Published by Arcadia Publishing
Charleston, South Carolina

Printed in the United States of America

Library of Congress Catalog Card Number: 2006932345

For all general information contact Arcadia Publishing at:
Telephone 843-853-2070
Fax 843-853-0044
E-mail sales@arcadiapublishing.com
For customer service and orders:
Toll-Free 1-888-313-2665

Visit us on the Internet at www.arcadiapublishing.com

The creation of this book was greatly enhanced by my own personal recollections of people and events while growing up at Long Beach in East Sebago within sound and sight of Sebago Lake. I have treasured memories of all six towns that comprise this work.

Jack C. Barnes

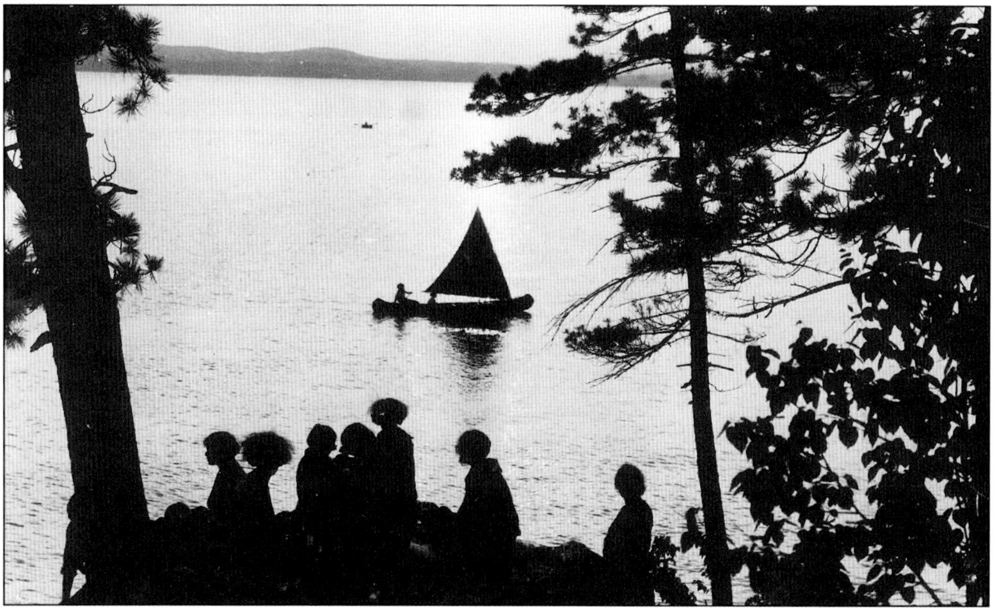

The View Never Changes, c. 1924. A quiet late afternoon sail on Sebago Lake at the Luther Gulick Camps on the Raymond Cape.

Contents

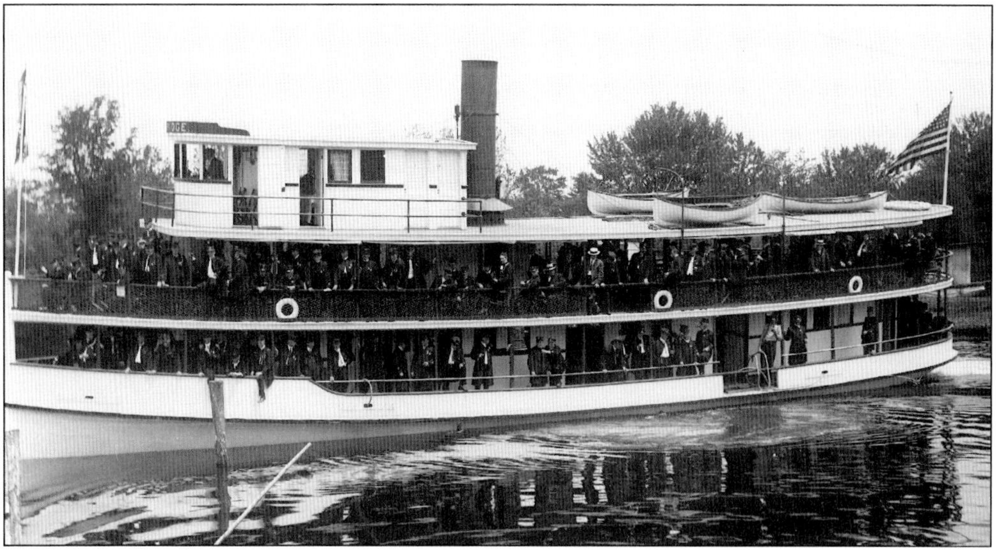

Introduction

Central to this work is beautiful Sebago Lake and the streams, lakes, and ponds that either feed into it or are located within the towns of Windham, Standish, Raymond, Casco, Sebago, and Naples—the towns that surround the second largest lake in Maine and the third in New England. This imposing glacial body of water, located solely within Cumberland County in southwestern Maine, is 8 miles wide at its broadest expanse in the Big Bay, 11 miles long, and 46 miles in circumference. (Distances may vary somewhat according to the source used.) Despite the rapid development that has taken place along its shores and on Frye (Frye's) Island since World War II, its crystal waters have remained basically unpolluted. The purity of its waters is due largely to its extraordinary depth. The deepest area thus fathomed, located almost in the middle of the Big Bay between Raymond Cape and the West Shore, is 316 feet—49 feet lower than Portland.

Long before the first European settler glimpsed the sparkling waters of the lower part of Sebago, this great expanse of fresh water and its tributaries served as a vital artery for the Native Americans on their annual treks from Canada to the Atlantic Coast. It also provided them with a bountiful supply of fish, and they hunted and trapped along its shores for meat and furs. Appropriately, Sebago is an Indian name given to it by the Rockameecook branch of the Sokokis or Pequawket tribe meaning "great stretch of water."

Other Indian place names and legendary figures abound, such as Waldola, Naragora, Minnehaha, and her father—Chief Worrambus or Polin. Mortally wounded in his unsuccessful attempt to capture a blockhouse guarding the community of Gorham in May 1756, the dying chief was conveyed in a canoe up Sebago and the Songo to the confluence of the Songo and Crooked Rivers; and on the bank of the Songo near the present locks, his body was buried under a large beech tree. John Greenleaf Whittier immortalized this legendary event in the poem *Funeral Tree of the Sokokis*: "O, long may sunset's light be shed/As now upon that beech's head,/— A green memorial of the dead!"

It was a human tragedy that the lifestyles of the Native Americans and the European settlers were so diametrically opposed to each other nearly from the very beginning. The indigenous tribes depended upon hunting and gathering and a minimum of horticulture for their livelihood. The settlers wanted to clear and farm the land. The bloody conflicts here in New England that ensued, beginning with the King Philips War in 1675, were inevitable. King Philip was ultimately captured and killed; and many of his people, including his wife and son, were deported to the West Indies. The war set Maine back fifty years.

Realizing they could not drive the British settlers from their lands, the Indians turned to the French for help. The series of so-called French and Indian Wars again proved devastating to Maine, and merely the most intrepid settlers dared venture far from the security of a few coastal settlements guarded by blockhouses. The conflicts did not terminate until the British captured Quebec and the Treaty of Paris was signed in 1763. In the Sebago Lake area only Windham (New Marblehead) and Standish (Pearsontown) were settled before this treaty, and both tiny communities were almost constantly threatened until the defeat of Chief Polin in 1756.

Shortly thereafter, in the summer of 1770, Joseph Dingley of Duxbury, Massachusetts, and Dominicus Jordan of Cape Elizabeth set out together for the lower part of Sebago Lake, to lay claim to lots in the area then called Raymond-town, after Captain Raymond of Beverly, Massachusetts. Dingley became the first settler in the area which is now South Casco and Dingley Brook, which runs out of Thomas Pond into Sebago Lake, and the cluster of little islands in Sebago Lake—the Dingley Islands—bear his name. Jordan became the first settler of Raymond in the Jordan's Bay area. In 1790, Joseph Lakin of Groton, Massachusetts, and Jacob Howe chose to settle on hill farms in Sebago, which was a part of the town of Baldwin (Flintstown) at the time. Howe carried mail once a week on horseback from Bridgton to Portland over Indian trails. George Peirce—a noted surveyor who settled in Edes Falls on Crooked River (then a part of Otisfield) in 1774 and built a cabin, a sawmill, and a gristmill—is generally credited with being the first settler in Naples.

Although many such as Joseph Lakin followed the typical pattern of the late eighteenth century and early nineteenth century and began clearing land on the summits of ridges, hills, and mountains to take advantage of a longer growing season, others such as Dingley and Jordan began clearing land down to the shores of Sebago, and as Sheep Island—the largest of the Dingley Islands—implies, some of the islands were cleared for grazing sheep. Obviously no stone walls or fencing were needed.

It was the gristmills, the blacksmith shops, sawmills, and related wood industries that set the settlements and eventually the towns around Sebago Lake in motion. As soon as a plot of land was cleared, corn was planted Indian style between the stumps. And the corn needed to be ground into meal. Primitive log cabins sufficed for a time, but lumber and shingles were necessary for more permanent dwellings. Barrels were in demand to store such basic commodities as flour, vinegar, and cider. Brick yards, lime mills, cloth mills, tanneries, and carriage and sleigh shops also developed to fill the needs of the settlers. Even on the smallest tributaries, dams were constructed to create power to turn the water wheels of one or more mills.

Although the early settlers struggled to coax enough from the newly cleared land—much of it sandy or hardscrabble—to feed their families and have something left over to barter for essentials, and the mill operators basically geared their production to meeting local demands, it was not long before the farms and the mills were producing a surplus. Portland was a ready market and goods could be shipped by water to Boston and beyond. Long Lake, Brandy Pond, and the Songo linked settlers from Harrison, Otisfield, Bridgton, and Naples to Sebago Lake; but Portland was 17 or more miles from the lower end of Sebago, and the Presumpscot River was not navigable out of Sebago Lake except for sluicing logs during high water down to Saccarappa (Westbrook).

The completion of the Eire Canal in 1825 ignited the canal craze throughout the newly formed nation, facilitating the growth of nationalism that had emerged as a result of the War of 1812. And fortunately for the Sebago Lake region, the Cumberland & Oxford Canal was constructed in 1830, linking all six towns plus others with Portland and spurring the development of both agriculture and industry.

But the canal era here in Maine as elsewhere in the nation was destined to be short lived. Within twelve years of the opening of the Cumberland & Oxford Canal, rails were laid connecting Portland with Portsmouth, and in 1870 the Portland & Ogdensburg Railroad, paralleling the canal, bonded Sebago Lake with Portland. Two years later the canal closed. Freight traffic on the lake system continued, however, until 1923.

Sebago Lake's famous landlocked salmon attracted fishermen to the area even before Maine became a state in 1820. They boarded wherever they could, often in farmhouses, until eventually inns and hostelries were built to accommodate a growing tourist trade. Before the railroad, sightseers made excursions to Sebago Lake on stage coaches that ran daily from Portland. By 1850, when the Atlantic and St. Lawrence (Grand Trunk) Railroad was completed between Portland and South Paris, the more indefatigable tourists had the option of taking the train out of Portland to this Oxford County terminal and then traveling by stage coach to Harrison. From Harrison they could travel by water down Long Lake, Brandy Pond, the Songo River, Sebago Lake, and return to Portland via the stage leaving Standish.

One of the most momentous events in the history of the Sebago Lake region was the introduction of the steamboat. The first passenger steamer, however, was the ill-omened *Fawn*, which operated briefly beginning in the summer of 1847. Poorly designed and constructed, it was auctioned off in 1855. Mary Emerson, the sister of Ralph Waldo Emerson, was a frequent passenger on the *Fawn*. The real era of the steamboat, however, began in 1869; and steamboats made regular runs during the summer between Sebago Lake Station and Harrison until 1933.

The coming of the railroad sparked the vacation era in all the towns surrounding Sebago Lake. Farms and taverns converted to guest houses, and it would not be long before hay fields were transformed into golf courses. By the 1880s a number of hotels were built in the area.

It was not until the turn of the century that summer people began building cottages around the shores of Sebago Lake, and few cottages dotted its coast line before the late 1920s, when the automobile age was rapidly gaining momentum.

The automobile age ushered in a new phenomena—tourism. Vacationers often came for the entire season and remained in one place—an inn, hotel, or summer cottage. Tourists came for a night or two and moved on. Thus overnight cabins became popular, and hotels and inns began closing by the 1930s. With few exceptions, those that survived until a decade or two after World War II, along with the overnight cabins, fell victim to the motel era. It is interesting that inns are once again in vogue and many old houses, some of which once served as hostelries and summer boarding houses, have become popular as bed and breakfast places. The pendulum swings.

We the authors welcome you to a world of ineffable beauty—the Sebago Lake region.

Acknowledgments

We should like to express our deep appreciation to the Windham Historical Society, the Standish Historical Society, the Casco Public Library, the Raymond-Casco Historical Society, the Sebago Historical Society, and the Naples Historical Society, for their willingness to avail their fine collections of photographs, memorabilia, and research material. We should also like to thank the many individuals who willingly shared their knowledge, personal photographs, and other materials. We are especially grateful to Ernest Knight, Edith Bell, Betty Barto, Lois Varney, Susannah Swihart, Wilma Irish, Mary Watson, Stewart Ross, Ann Burns, Leona Greene, Raymond Anderson, Alfred Jordan, Cindy Choate, Franklin and Helen Irish, Laurence and Vera Fitch, Sandy Strand, Louise Van Winkle, Ronald K. Hall, June Gray, Patricia White, Ruth Chaplin, Aubrey and Edna Kenney, Myrlice Waite, Marion Dumbrocyo, Sidney Gordon, and Richard Fraser.

One

Windham

First Settled: 1737
Incorporated: 1762
Population: 15,000
Area: 48 square miles
Principle Settlements: South Windham,
North Windham, Windham Center,
Foster's Corner, Newhall, Windham Hill

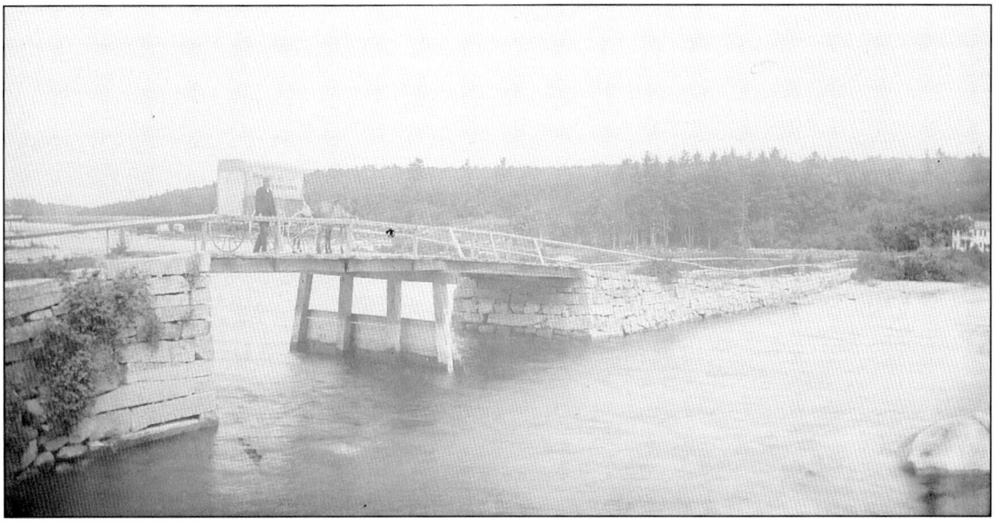

White's Bridge, c. 1895. Sometime between 1737 and 1738 Thomas Chute poled his way up the Presumpscot River and laid claim to a parcel of land near the river just a few miles south of here, where Sebago Lake narrows to form the Basin and empties into the Presumpscot River, the earliest artery between the lake and Falmouth (Portland). When Chute—a tailor and merchant—returned to dig his cellar, build a crude log cabin, and clear 7 acres of land, he became the first settler of Windham (then called New Marblehead) and therefore the first settler in the entire region sharing a shoreline with Sebago Lake.

This early bridge spanning the split-stone causeway separating the Sebago Lake Basin (in the foreground) from Jordan's Bay is a part of the White's (Whites) Bridge Road connecting Standish with North Windham. Sumner Shaw, an itinerant peddler of meats and provisions, pauses on his way to North Windham and perhaps up to Raymond and Casco to enjoy the view of the Basin.

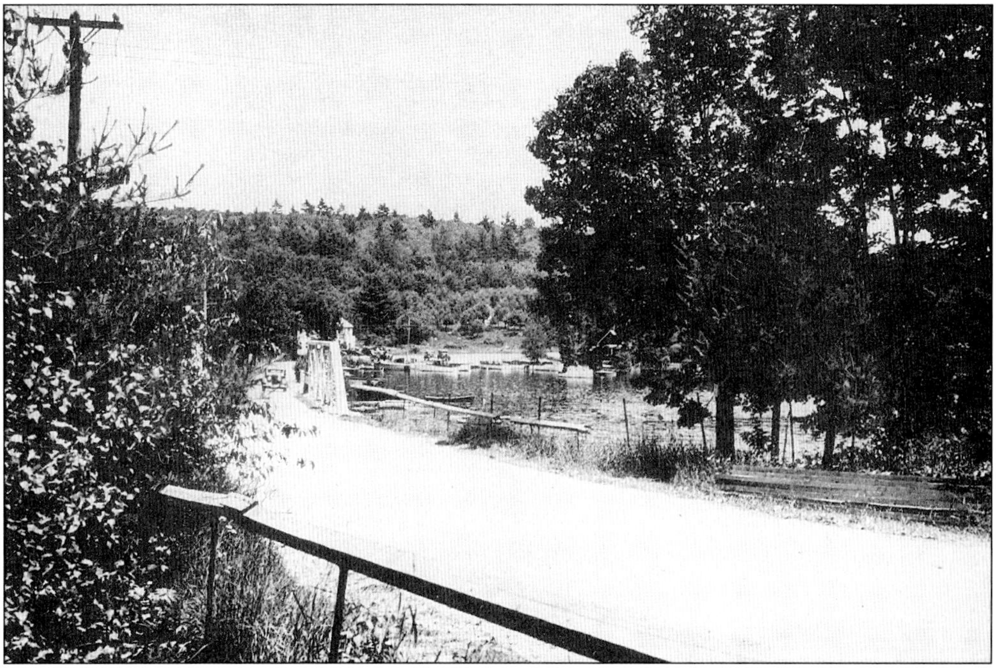

White's Bridge, c. 1930. Sometime in the late 1920s the old wooden bridge at White's Bridge was replaced by a steel bridge, which in turn was replaced by the present bridge shortly after World War II. This scene was taken from the Standish side of the Basin. The old Kennard Homestead, visible on the Windham side, was demolished in more recent times.

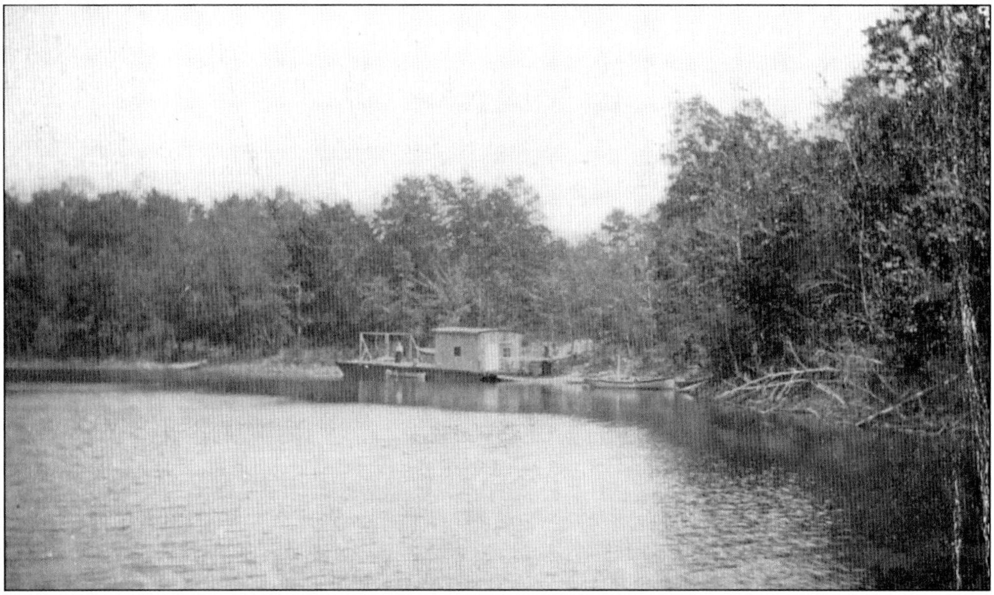

Boat Landing, Little Sebago Lake, c. 1930s. Windham proudly lays claim to 25 miles of lake frontage on eight different bodies of water, which includes most of scenic Little Sebago, a few miles east of Sebago Lake. The present outlet was created in May 1861 when a catastrophic cloudburst known as Pope's Freshet washed out a dam on Pleasant River, lowering the level of the lake by several feet.

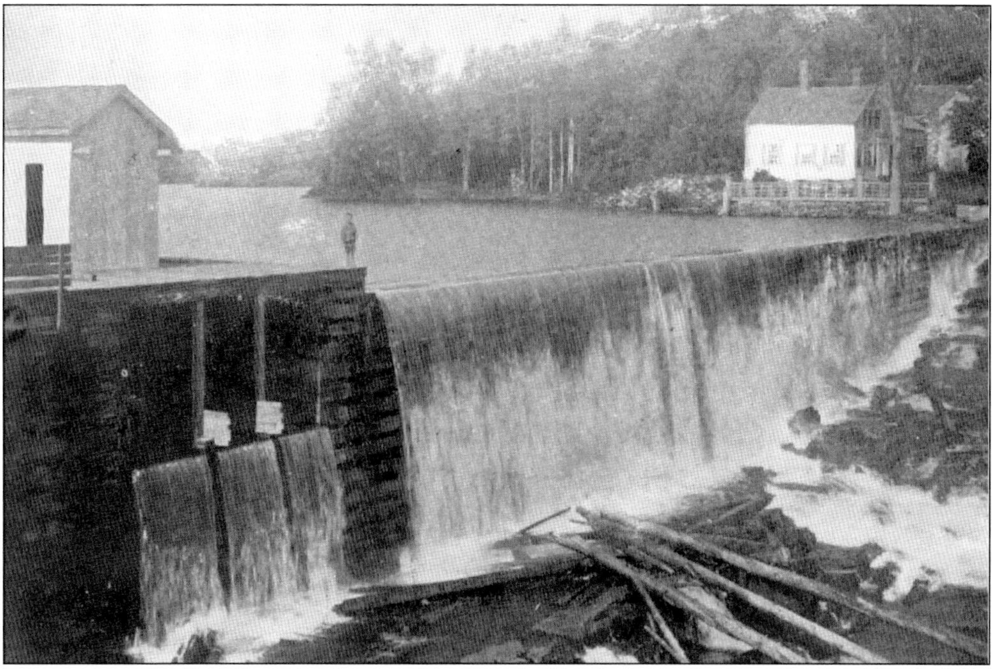

Great Falls on the Presumpscot. Great Falls was just one of a series of falls between the Sebago Lake Basin and Portland Harbor that provided the essential hydraulic power for operating the many mills constructed on both sides of the river. Here, where the river separates North Gorham from Windham, there were several sawmills as well as the Keyes Indurated Fibre Company—an early form of plastic industry that manufactured buckets and pans produced from paper infused with varnish.

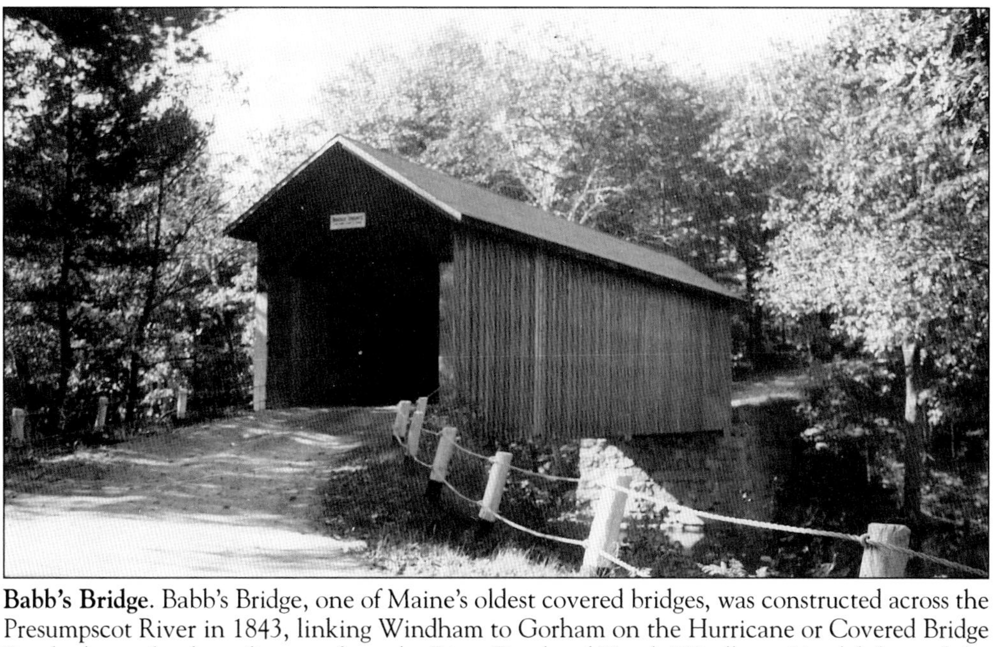

Babb's Bridge. Babb's Bridge, one of Maine's oldest covered bridges, was constructed across the Presumpscot River in 1843, linking Windham to Gorham on the Hurricane or Covered Bridge Road—located a short distance from the River Road and North Windham. Vandals burned the bridge on May 6, 1973. It has been replaced by an exact replica.

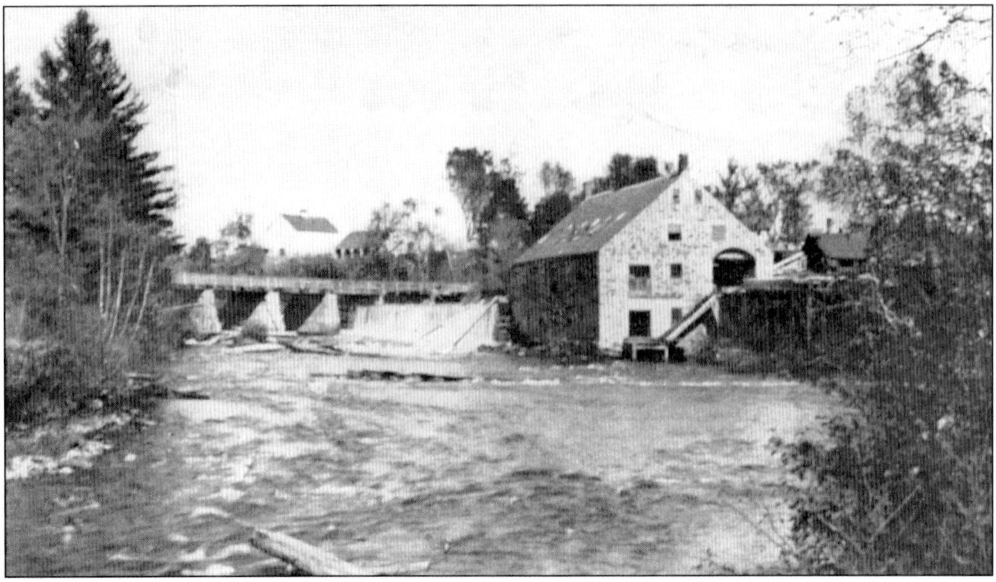

The Old Stone Mill at Newhall. The Old Stone Mill, located at Gambo Falls on the Presumpscot River, was reputed to have been constructed around 1800. It became a part of the Oriental Powder Mills, referred to locally as the "Gambo Powder Mills," and served as a carpenter shop and foundry. It was the first mill to make gun powder in Maine (c. 1824), the largest mill of its type in the state and probably at one time the fourth largest in the United States, and it operated the longest of any of the powder mills in Maine (eighty years).

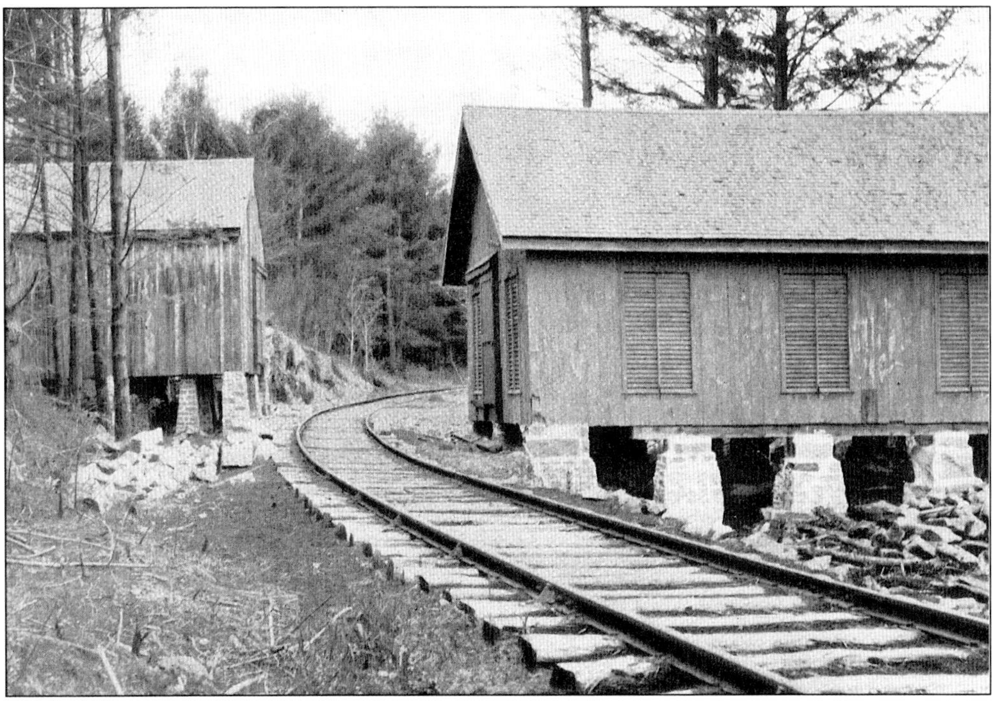

The Oriental Powder Mills. This photograph of a storehouse on each side of a spur of the Portland & Ogdensburg Railroad was taken sometime after 1872, when the Powder Mills sold the railroad a right of way.

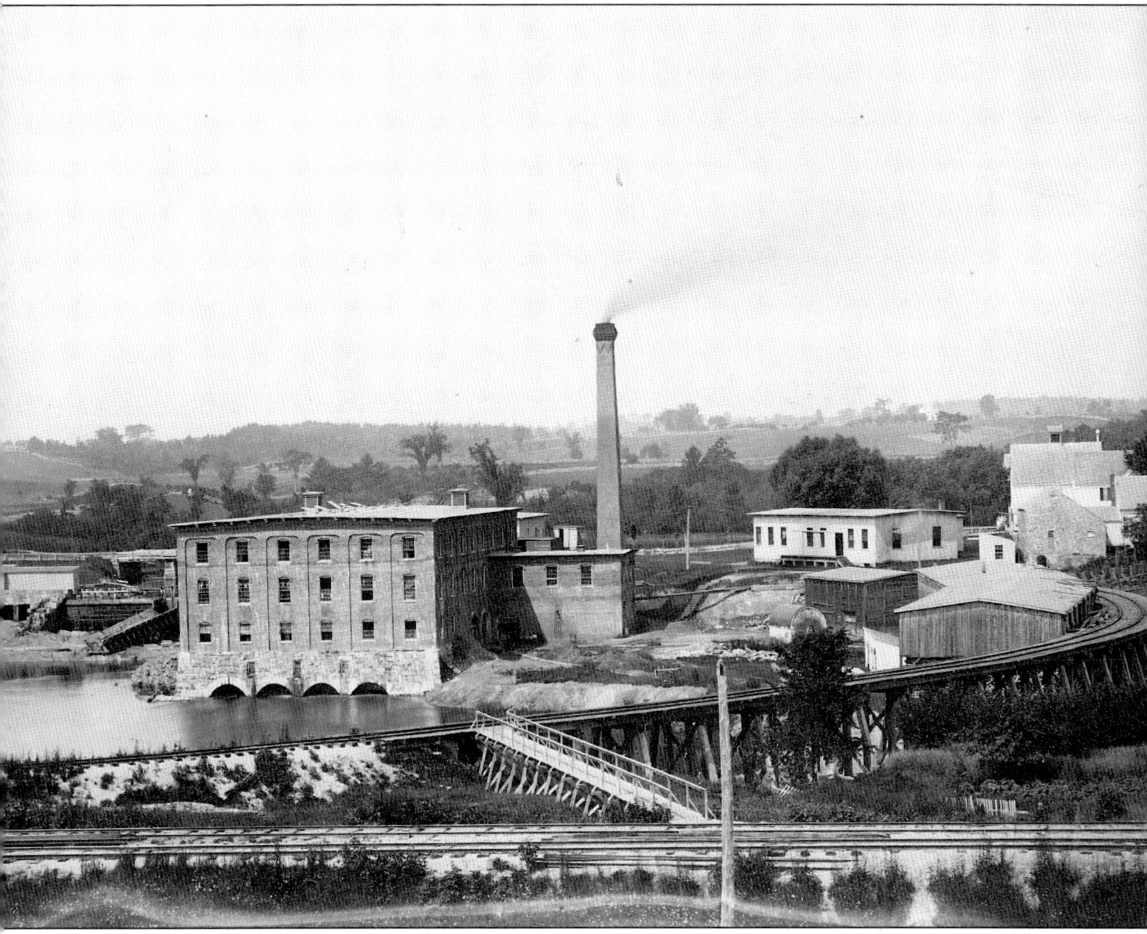

The Androscoggin Pulp Mill, c. 1900. The Androscoggin Pulp Mill was the most recent of a number of industries located at this site on the Presumpscot River at Little Falls in South Windham. The first was a sawmill, the second oldest in Windham, built sometime prior to 1756 by Major William Knight, who claimed to be the first settler on the Windham side of Little Falls. After Knight sold the mill and moved to Naples, two buildings were eventually constructed to accommodate the needs of the local farmers. One was a gristmill operated for many years by William Johnson. The other building served as a wool carding mill operated first by Leonard Bacon and later by Lathrop Crockett.

In 1875 C.A. Brown and Company purchased water rights to both sides of the Presumpscot here at the falls, constructed the large brick factory shown here, and manufactured "wood board" for a few years before selling out to the Androscoggin Pulp Company. The Pulp Company proceeded to expand rapidly by erecting an additional large cement-and-iron structure, equipping it with the latest machinery, and by building a number of large residences for their employees. Fire damaged much of the plant in 1954, and it was abandoned after an even more destructive fire in 1970.

One of the key factors in the industrial growth of South Windham was the Portland & Ogdensburg Railroad, which by 1888 had been taken over by the Maine Central Railroad, and was thereafter referred to as the Mountain Division.

The well-manicured fields and the neatly maintained farm buildings in the background are a reminder that agriculture was a mainstay to the area at the turn of the century, and would remain so for several decades to come.

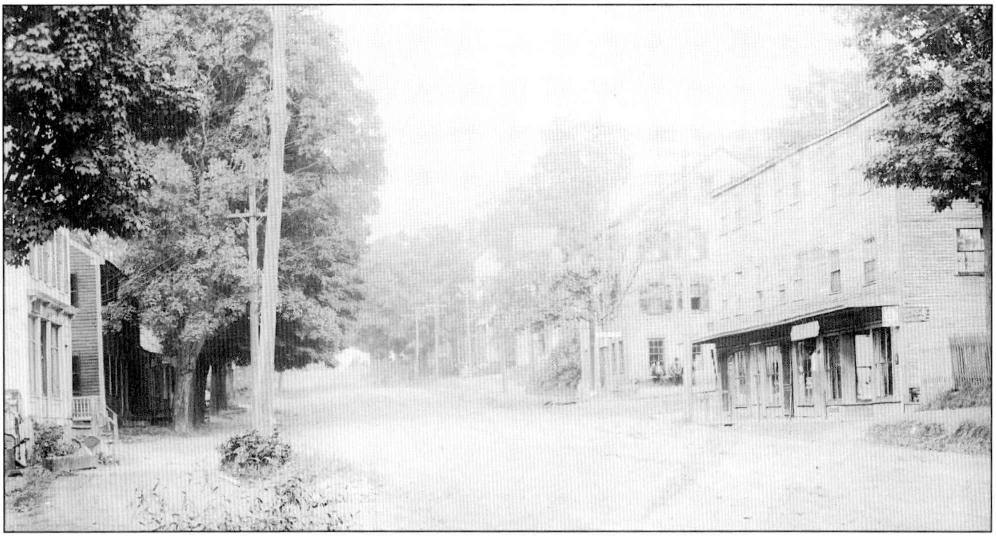

Main Street, South Windham, c. 1895. The "Old Tavern," viewed here on the right at the corner of Main and Depot Streets, was first constructed as a tavern or public house in 1832. It later was converted into a tenement house, and in more recent years the ground floor was operated as Pattsy's Pizza. It is now Denise's Variety.

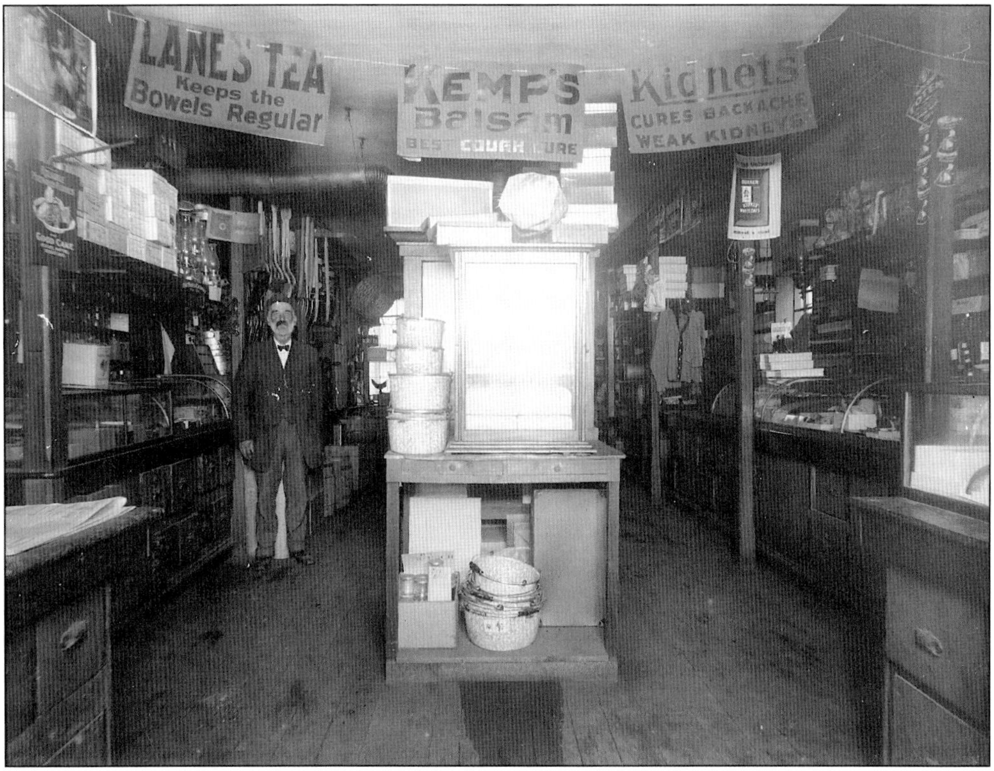

Henry Bickford and Store, c. 1890. Henry Bickford poses here in his general store which he built on Cross Street (Depot) in 1869. The prominent display of advertisements of various remedies delineates the popularity of pattern medicines before and after the turn of the century. Bickford's son William continued to operate the store well into the twentieth century.

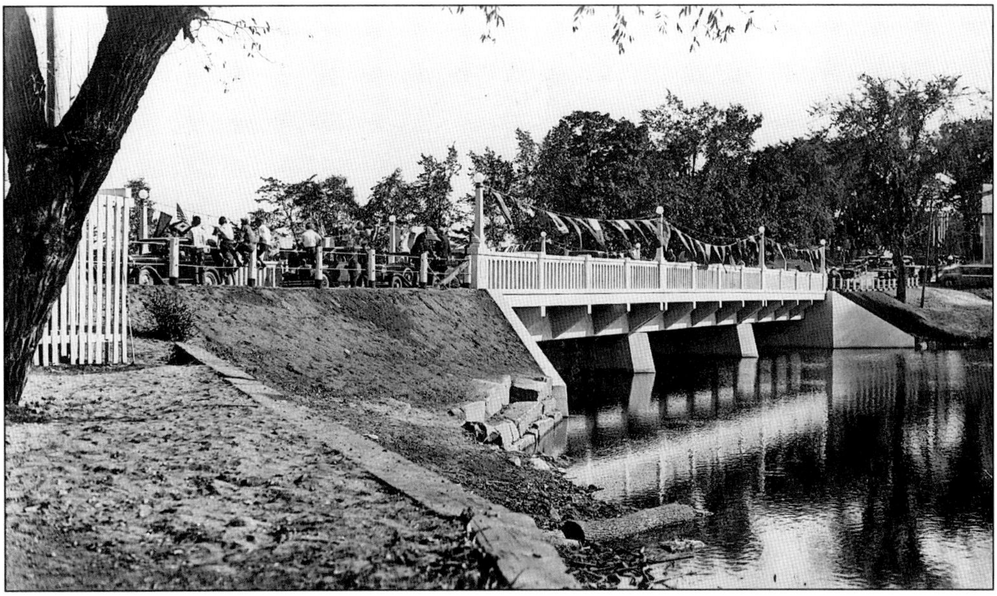

The Dedication of South Windham Bridge, 1931. Banners flutter in the breeze from the new cement bridge spanning the Presumpscot River between South Windham and Gorham. The bumper-to-bumper parade of cars was part of a joint celebration of the two towns, sponsored by the South Windham Community Club and Fire Department, of the grand opening of the new structure in September 1931. The previous bridge was a narrow wooden structure.

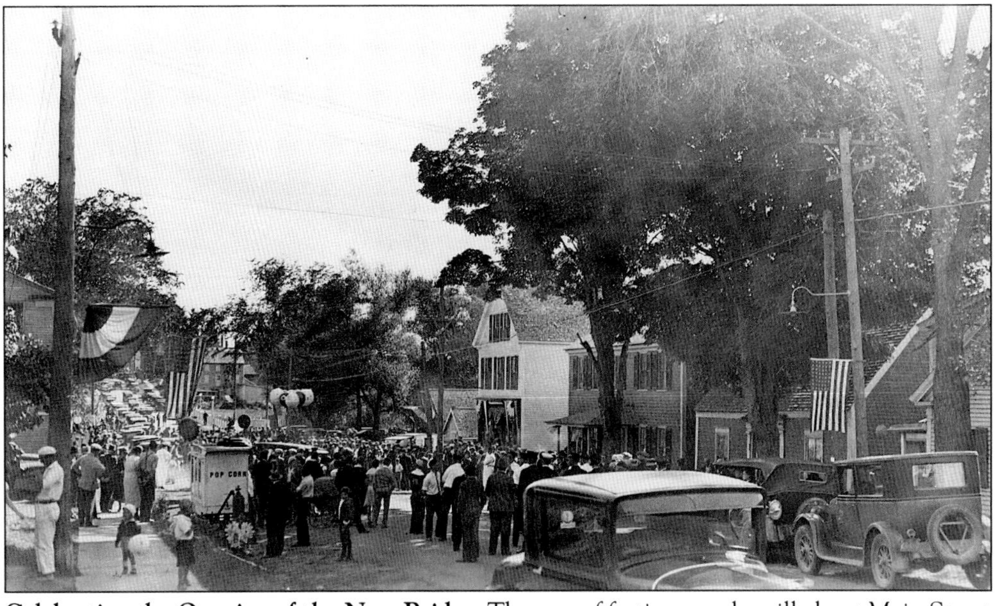

Celebrating the Opening of the New Bridge. Throngs of festive people mill about Main Street in South Windham during the celebration which featured such activities as a baseball game between the Windham and Westbrook Fire Departments, a parade of fire departments from a number of Maine towns, music by the Gorham Band, and a dance in the evening. The long lines of automobiles testify to how rapidly they had gained popularity.

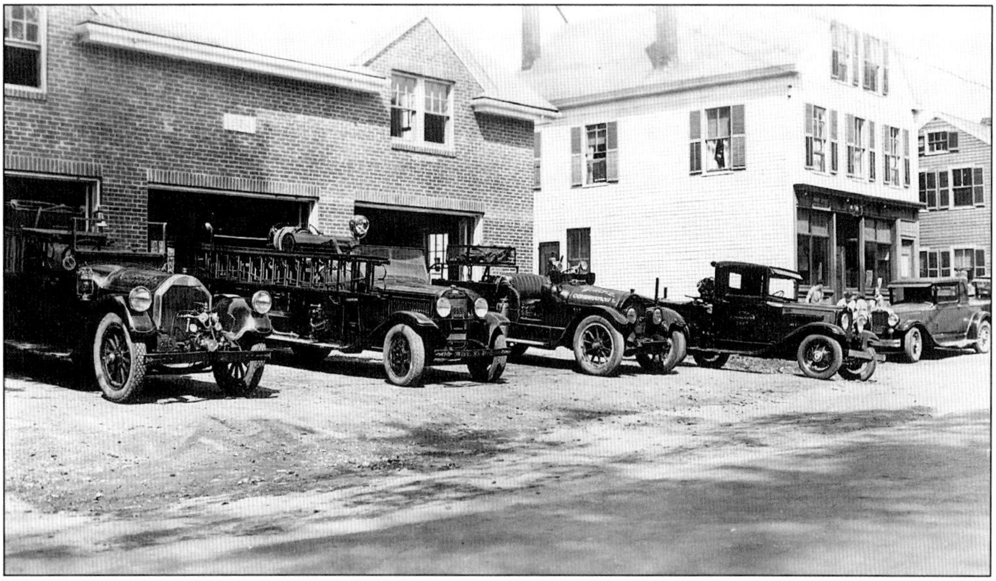

The South Windham Fire Station, c. 1938. The South Windham Fire Department displays its fire engines and other vehicles in front of the new brick station, built in 1937 by the WPA. Unfortunately the building proved to be poorly constructed and had to be replaced two decades later. The oldest fire truck, a c. 1917 Pierce Arrow, is to the left.

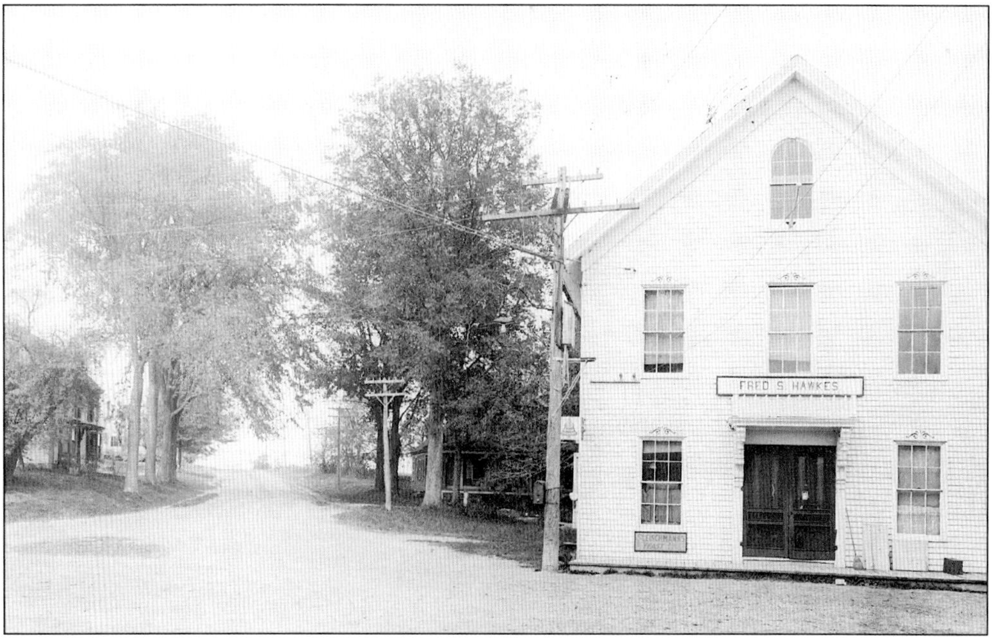

Windham Center, c. 1910. Elm-shaded Windham Center at the cross roads was a hub of activity and remains the civic center of Windham today. Hawkes Store, which is now known as Corsetti's, was a typical general store serving the needs of the village and the outlying rural population engaged primarily in agriculture. The road going north (Route 202) leads to Foster's Corner.

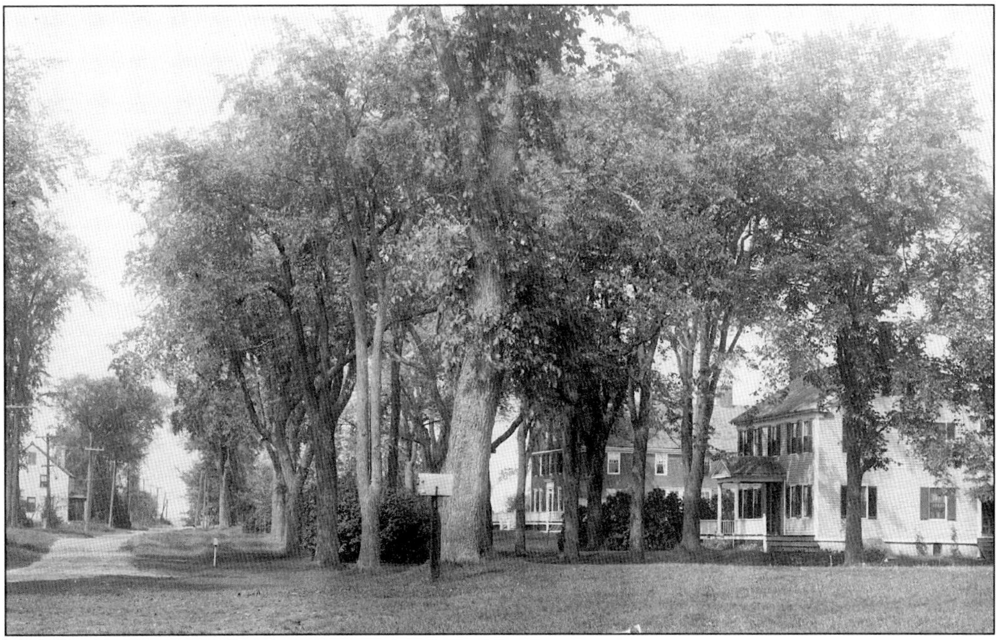

Windham Hill, c. 1910. Long before the turn of the century, Windham Hill had become what it is today, a quiet residential area. But before the Cumberland & Oxford Canal diverted most of the traffic, farmers and traders all the way from northern Vermont and New Hampshire—their pungs (in winter) and wagons (as soon as the muddy roads were passable) laden with produce and handcrafted goods—trundled through Windham Hill on the way to Portland. Briefly, Windham Hill was a bustling community.

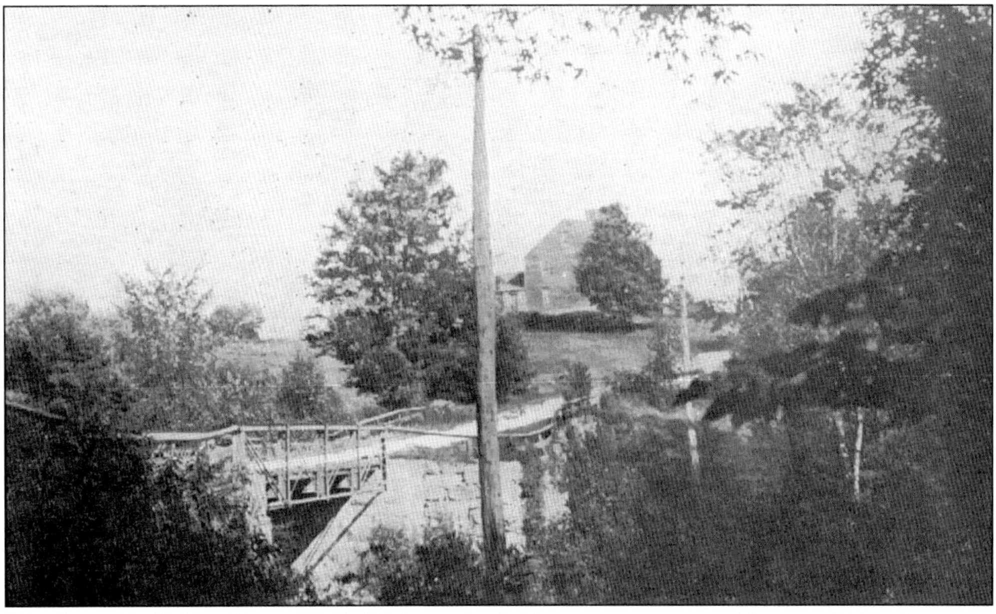

"Anderson's Bridge," c. 1900. This rustic bridge once spanned Pleasant River between Windham Hill and Windham Center. The large house (still standing) on the hill was built in 1792 by Major Edward Anderson, who had a ditch dug across a ridge separating Little Sebago from the valley to provide more water for his sawmill.

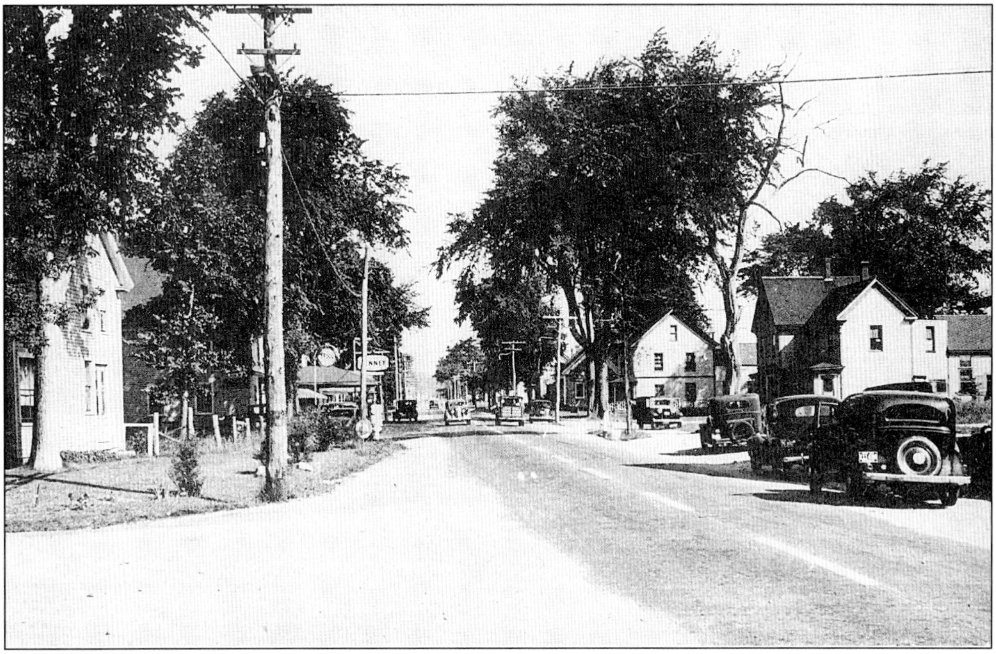

North Windham, c. 1937. North Windham in the 1930s was still largely residential and would remain that way until two decades or so after World War II, despite its favorable location on the Roosevelt Trail (Route 302).

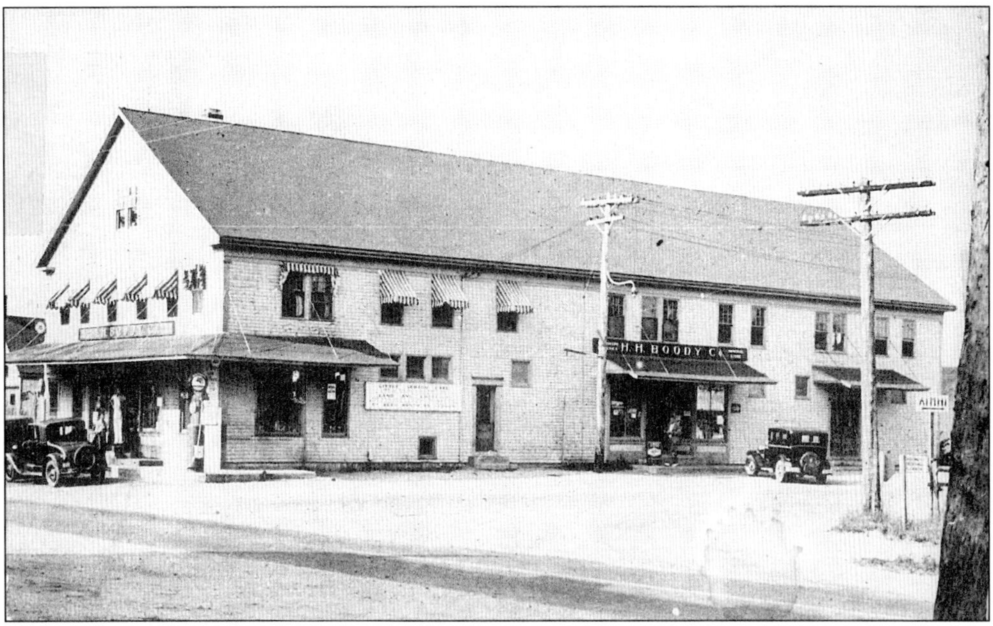

Boody's Store in North Windham, c. 1929. For those who were unfamiliar with North Windham a few decades ago, it may be difficult to conceive that Boody's Store, located on the corner of Routes 302 and 35, was the entire shopping center of North Windham. Boody's sold everything from grain, hardware, and paints to meats, fruits, vegetables, and groceries. It is interesting that, of all the communities surrounding Sebago Lake, only North Windham has been drastically altered in the twentieth century.

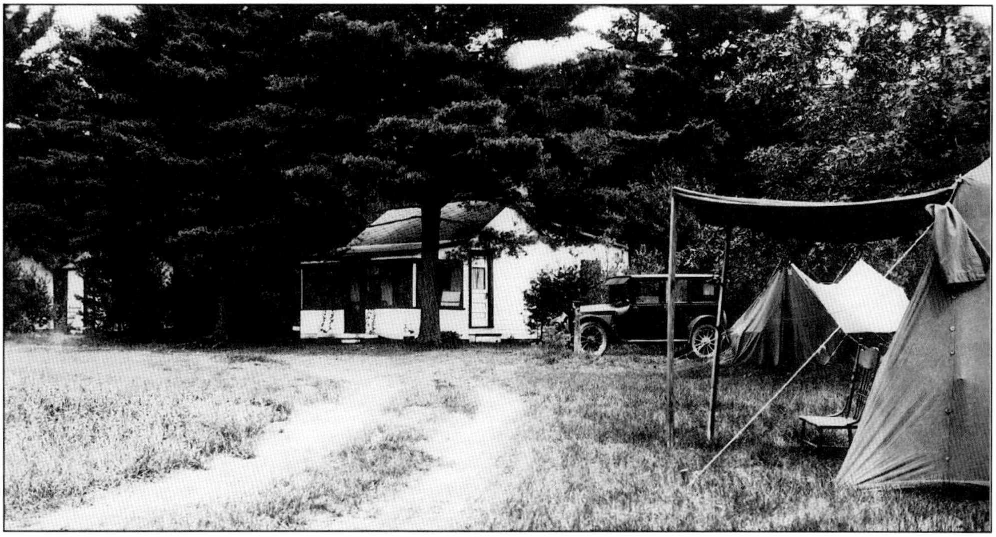

Overnight Cabins, c. 1918. With the ever-growing popularity of the automobile in the 1920s, existing roads were improved and new highways were constructed. Those with mobility were more interested in touring about rather than remaining sedentary at an inn or hotel for the entirety of their vacation. Overnight cabins, such as this cluster of cabins nestled under an umbrella of white pines (probably along the Roosevelt Highway/Route 302), became commonplace. Camp grounds for tenters also became popular at this time.

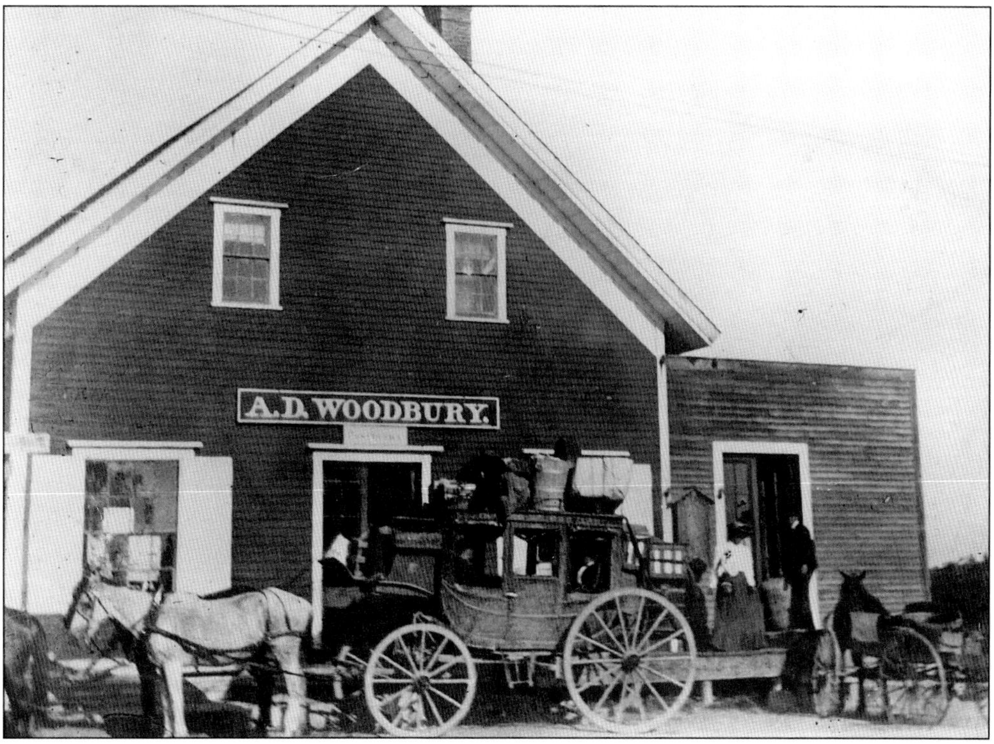

Murch's Stagecoach, c. 1900. There are still a few novagenerians in the Sebago Lake area who recall trundling over rutted roads in stagecoaches such as this one in front of Woodbury's Store (now Bailey's) on Duck Pond Road just off Route 302 in Windham.

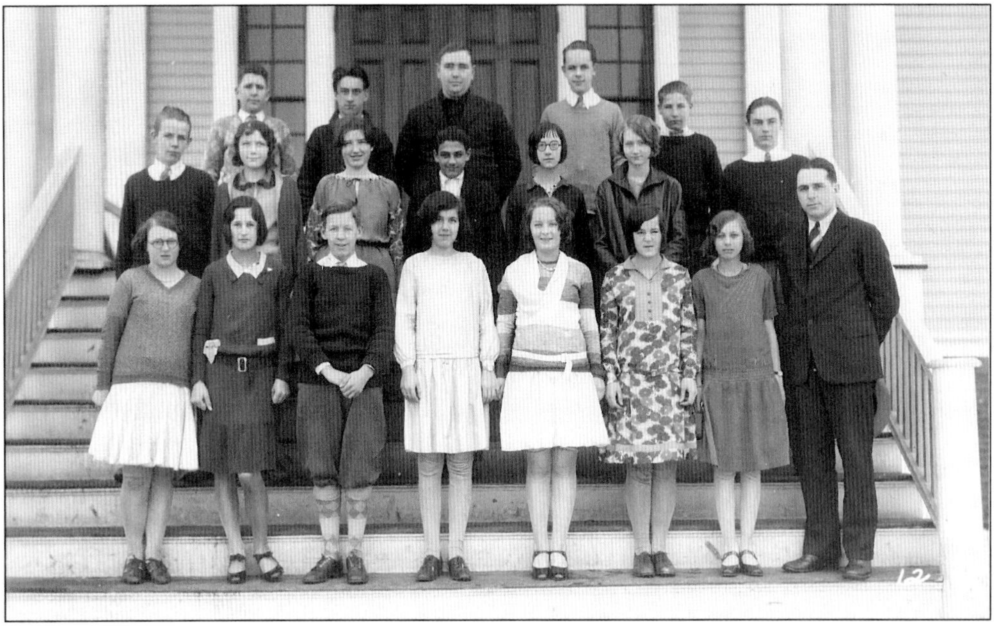

The Windham High School Class of 1932. The class of '32 poses in the fall of '31 in front of the old Windham High School, built in 1910 at Windham Center. Shown here are, from left to right: (first row) Frances Atherton, Marcia Atherton, Stanley Gilman, Ethel Pierce, Addie Lombard, Marriet Atherton, Mona Quint, and John Shaw (teacher advisor); (middle row) Walter Pendexter, Lillian Manchester, Virginia Sylvester, Eugene Pecoraro, Gertrude Skillins, Florence Anthoine, and Cuyler Hawkes; (back row) Elroy Morrell, Theodore Cobb, Alton Young, Robert Toms, and Lawrence Wescott.

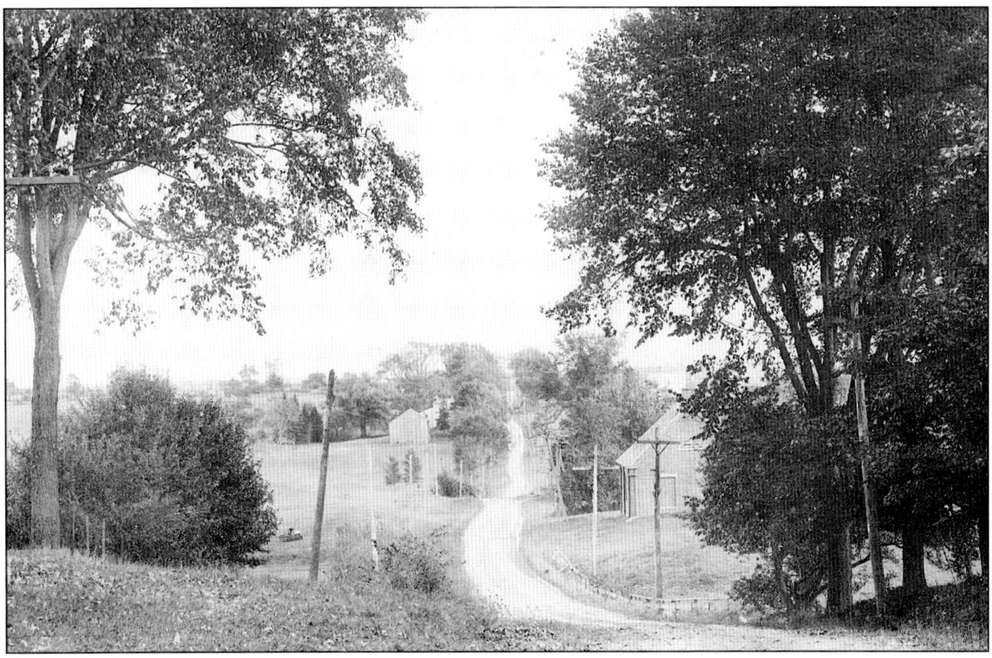

The Old Brick School, c. 1900. For many years this little brick school at the foot of the hill on Center Road provided education to children from the surrounding farms.

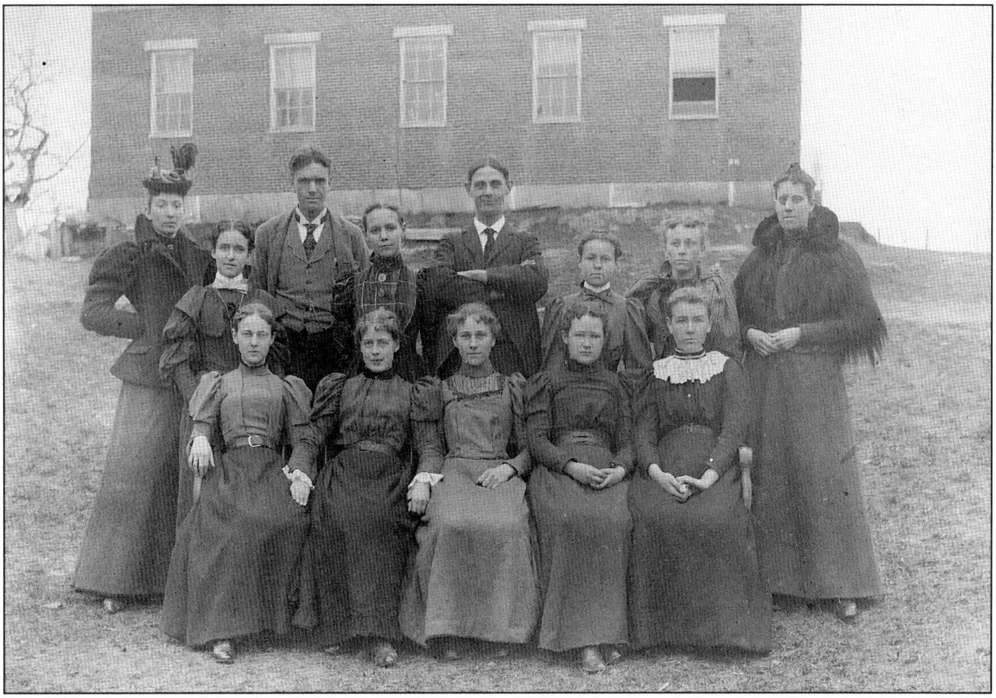

The Class of 1899. The class of 1899 poses in front of the Old Town House School, built in 1833 and later known as the Old Town Hall. It is now owned by the Windham Historical Society. Shown are, from left to right: (front row) Mildred Cobb, Annie Varney, Clara Nash, Annie Anthoin, and Blanch Douglass; (back row) Mildred Varney, Linwood Crockett, Edith Hawks, Albert Haskell, Carrie Lamb, and Miss Harlow.

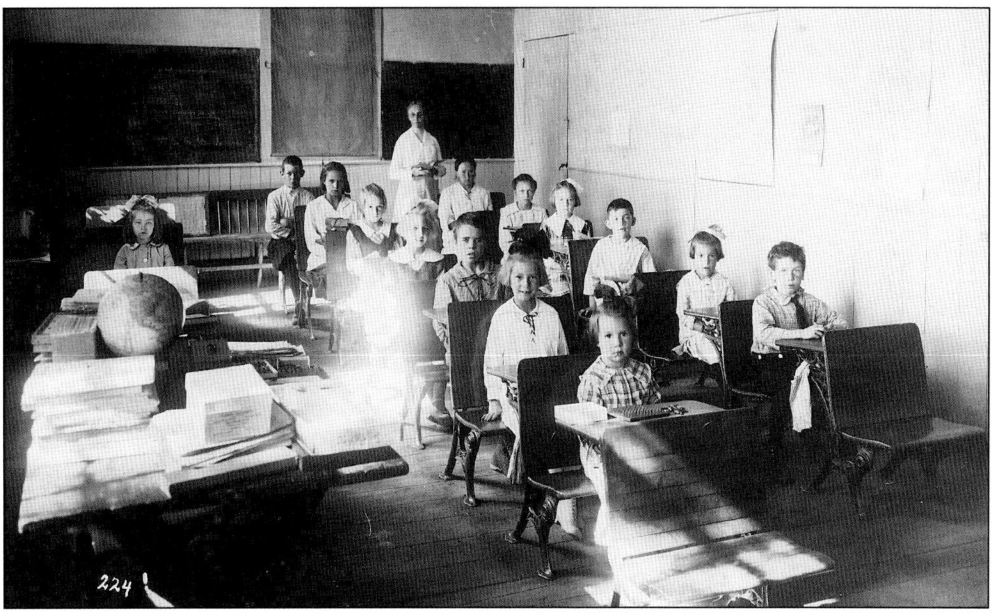

The Old Town House School, 1920. Many of us were lucky enough to receive our early education in classrooms such as this one in the Old Town House School in Windham Center, where several grades sat together in one classroom.

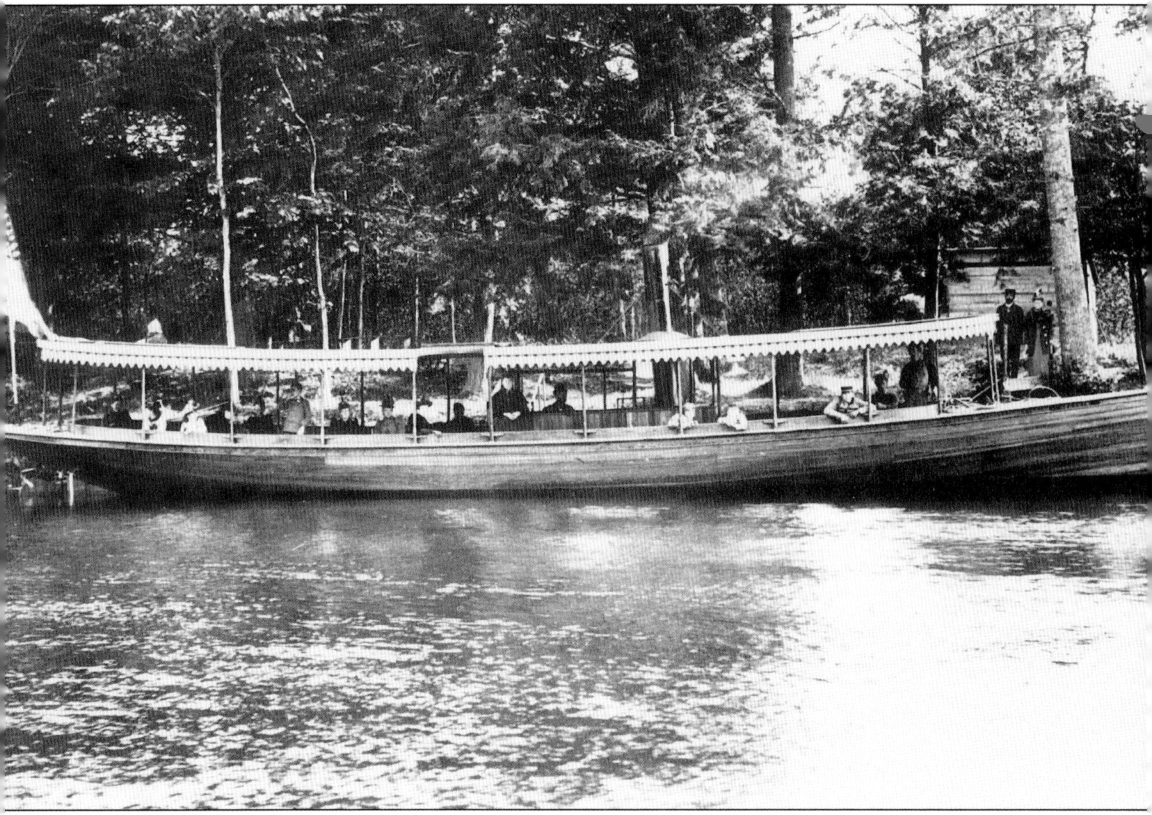

The Steamer *Sokokis,* c. 1895. This suave 60-foot steamer, bearing the name of the legendary Chief Polin's tribe, never sailed on Sebago Lake itself, but for eight years beginning in 1893 it plied up and down the serpentine Presumpscot River, making the 11-mile route from the electric car terminus in Westbrook to Mallison or Horse Beef Falls in South Windham and back to Westbrook. The *Sokokis*, built by Joseph Dow at one of the shipyards in Portland, was a paradigm of the fine craftsmanship practiced by shipwrights here in Maine during the era of wooden boats. As this photograph indicates, it was constructed entirely of beautiful brown cypress wood, which often blended with the color of the waters of the Presumpcot. It was owned by Captain Joseph Haselton and operated by him and his son, Joseph Jr. During the warm months of the year it made three round trips a day. Its total carrying capacity was 125 passengers.

One of the most popular excursions was the moonlight sail to the dance pavilion at the dock in South Windham, shown here. Since there were no lights along the wooded banks of the Presumpscot, Captain Haselton and his son had to navigate this devious, narrow course by the open skyline dimly outlining the river. On foggy nights, this took great skill and familiarity with the river.

By the late 1890s the electric railway was extended from Westbrook to South Windham, thus bringing about the demise of the abbreviated steamboat era on the Presumpscot. On a warm winter day, the *Sokokis* was hauled on skids by four pair of horses and twelve pair of oxen to Stroudwater and then to Portland Harbor, where briefly it conveyed sportsmen to the cod fishing grounds 10 miles out to sea. Eventually it ended up in New Jersey serving as a ferry boat.

The steamboat era on Sebago Lake, however, was far from over, as we shall soon see. And the Presumpscot River, as it had been doing since the town of Windham—as well as Standish, Gorham, Westbrook, and Stroudwater in Portland—was first settled, would continue to generate the power needed to operate the mills along its banks.

Two

Standish

First Settled: 1750
Incorporated: 1785
Population: 7,000
Area: 61.4 square miles
Principal Settlements: Standish Corner,
Steep Falls, Sebago Lake Village, Richville

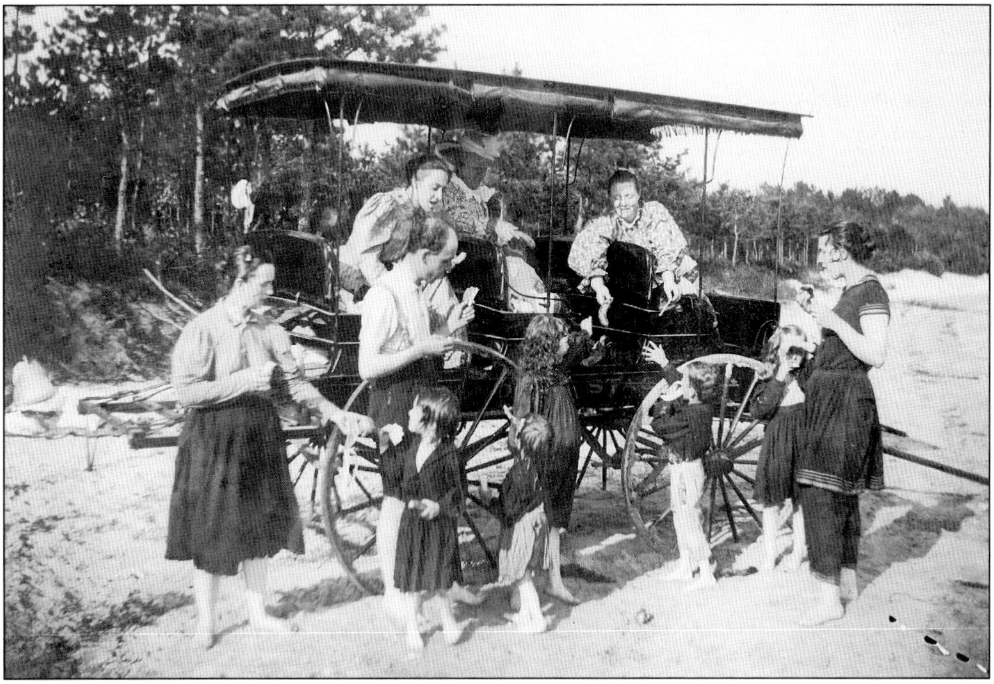

A Picnic at the Beach, c. 1900. Long before the more affluent, mostly from urban areas here in Maine and out of state ("people from away"), began clearing lots along the shores of Sebago, the long stretches of white sandy beaches attracted both locals and vacationers staying at inns and farms. This photograph of a family or group outing was taken on the beach near Sebago Lake Station at the foot of Sebago Lake, known as the Lower Bay—an area made readily accessible from Portland, Boston, and beyond with the construction of the Portland & Ogdensburg Railroad in 1870. Inns and boarding places in the Sebago Lake area provided their guests with transportation to and from the shores of Sebago. Some inns maintained bath houses near the beach where guests could change into swim suits, such as the one the young lady on the far right is wearing.

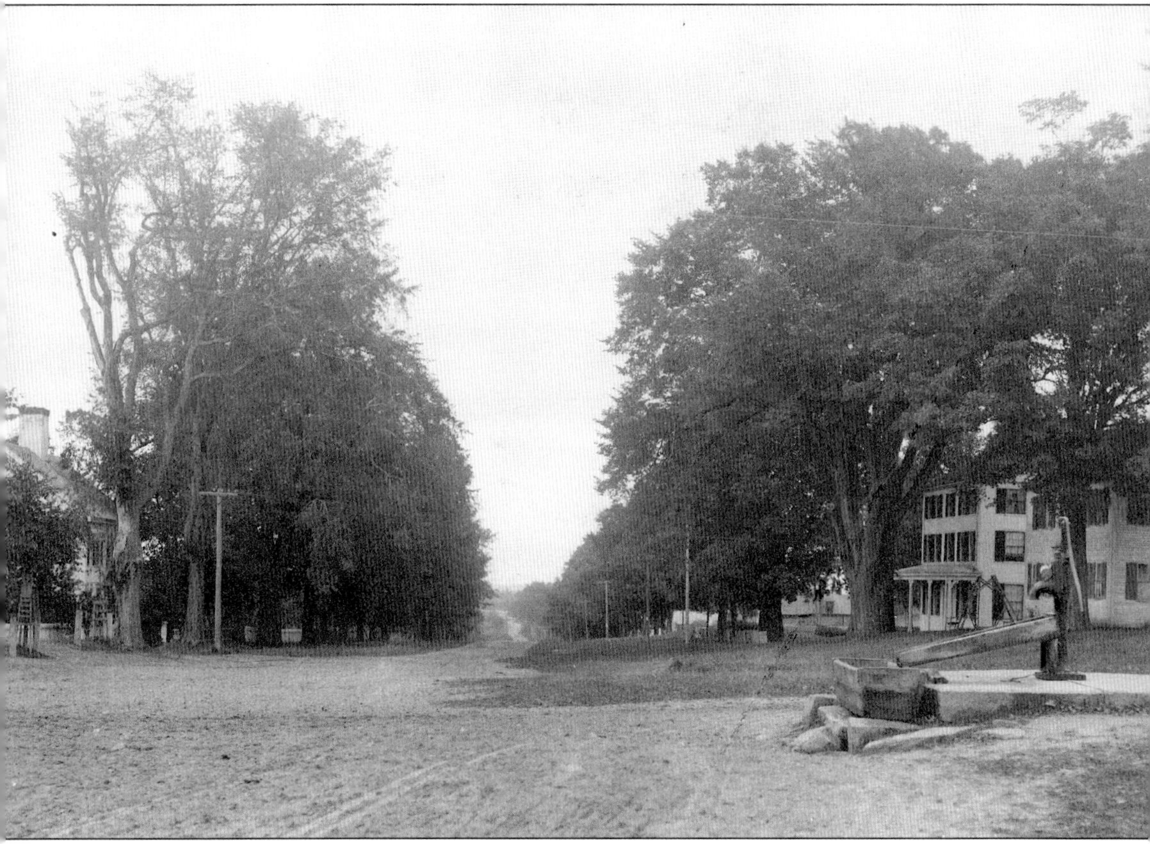

Standish Corner, c. 1890. The town of Standish was originally named Pearsontown after Captain Moses Pearson of Falmouth, a veteran officer during the first siege of Louisburg in King George's War and one of the town's first proprietors. Although Captain Pearson never resided in the town that bore his name, he was a key figure in its early settlement. On November 30, 1785, Pearsontown became Standish, in honor of the famous Captain Myles Standish.

Central to its early settlement was Standish Village or Standish Corner. It grew up where four roads, laid out in 1752, converged—and where a log fort or stockade was constructed as a bastion against impending Indian attacks and as a refuge for the handful of settlers scattered about the area.

Soon after the fall of Quebec to the British, putting an end to the perils of Indian attacks, Standish Village began to flourish. By the early nineteenth century it had become a focal point for stage coaches and freight wagons traversing from Portland to Sebago, Bridgton, Harrison, and Waterford. At its peak there were three tanneries, six stores, three taverns, and a sawmill in the area. But soon after the Portland & Ogdensburg Railroad was constructed, Sebago Lake, Smith Mills, and Steep Falls usurped most of Standish Corner's commercial activities. Gradually it became the relatively quiet and almost somnolent village depicted in this photograph taken before the turn of the century.

Here, at what is today the intersection of Routes 25 and 35, this historic "town pump" (dating to about 1820) provided cool water for thirsty travelers and local teamsters as well as their steeds and oxen. Despite efforts to spare the old town pump, it fell victim to road construction in the early 1950s. More fortunate were some of these stately homes, such as the imposing old Tompson Tavern just beyond the pump on the right—initially built as a home for Reverend John Tompson, Pearsontown's first minister. On the opposite side of the Southeast Road (Route 25), the Parson Merrett Homestead also has stood the ravages of time.

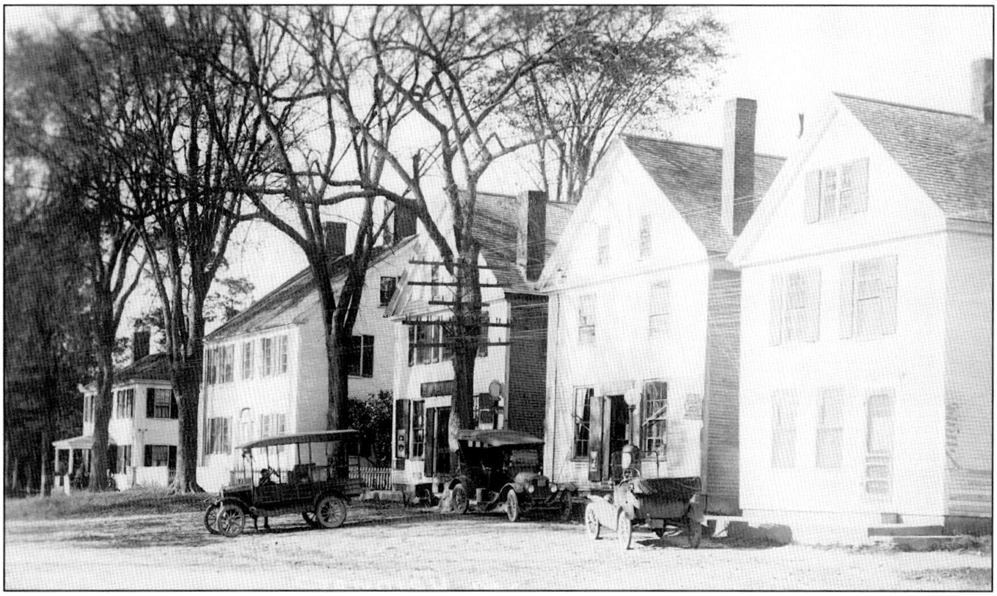

Standish Corner, c. 1920. By the time this photograph was taken, looking north toward the Oak Hill Road (one of the four original roads laid out in 1752), there were only three commercial buildings left at Standish Corner. Prominent in the right-hand corner was the ice cream parlor, followed by the two Doloff stores. The model-T facing Route 25 was the Higgins' stage.

The "Old Red Church." Located at Standish Corner on the Oak Hill Road, the "Old Red Church," or First Parish Meetinghouse, is listed in the National Register of Historic Places. It was opened in 1805 for services about the time a drunken and overzealous local militia, during an annual muster, completely tore down the original meetinghouse, built in 1774. Services are still held here during the summer months. In 1848 the second floor was added and opened as Standish Academy. Unfortunately, three years later the trustees absconded with the school funds and the academy closed. In 1893 the classrooms became the old Standish High School. Today the second floor is the headquarters for the Standish Historical Society.

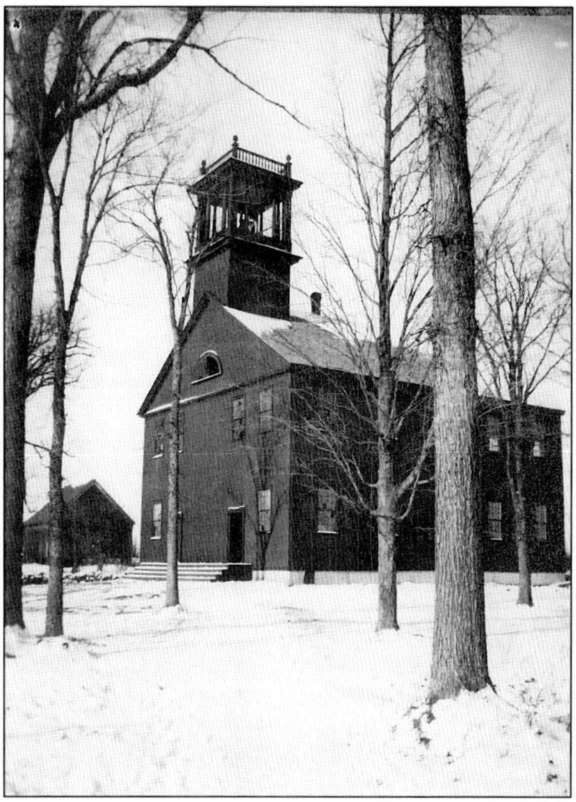

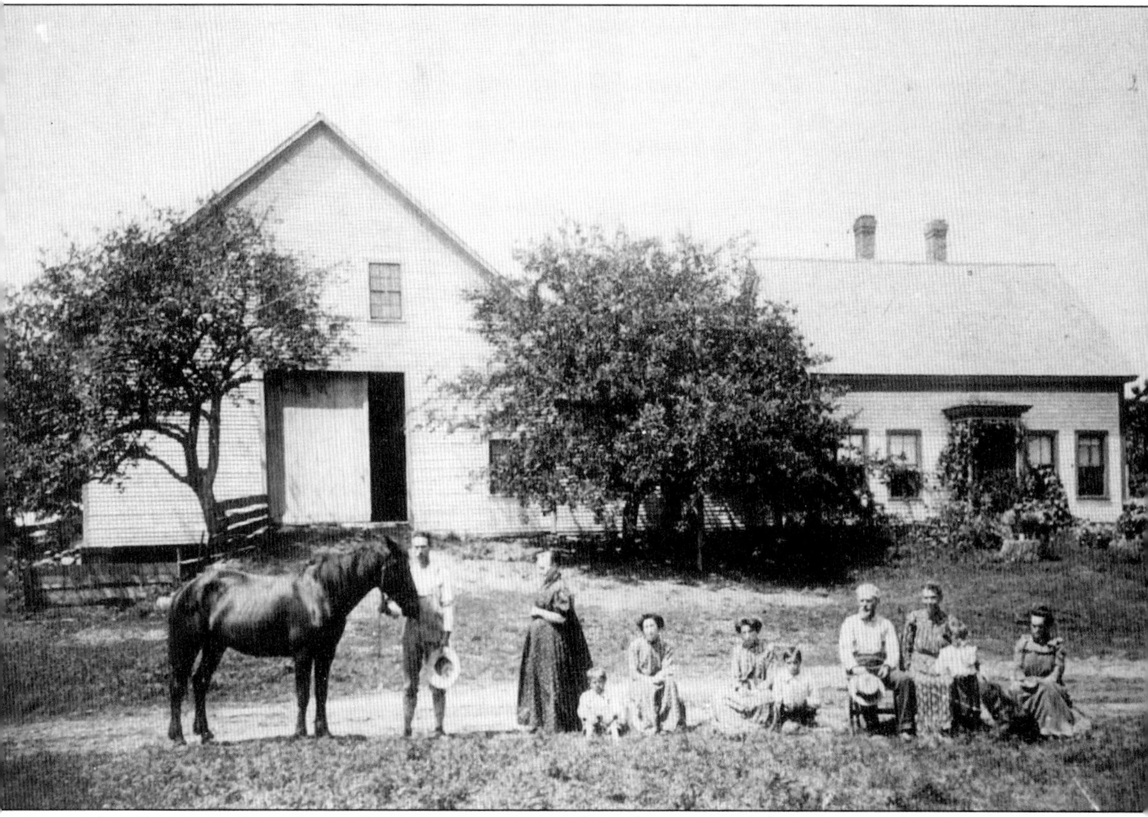

A Waterman Family Gathering, c. 1895. Before the automobile gave people more mobility, when most of the rural population depended upon farming for part or all of their livelihood, families were close-knit. Frequently large extended families shared the same house or lived in adjoining houses on the same property or on farms nearby. Here the Waterman family poses before their typical Maine farm in a section of Standish called Cabbageyard. The young man holding the horse is William Waterman, the son of William and Emily (Moore) Waterman, who are seated over on the right. The elderly lady facing the horse is Elizabeth (Hamblen) Moore, who lived across the road.

One of the most prominent early families in Standish was the Shaw family. The original settler of the town was Ebenezer Shaw from Hampton, New Hampshire. Induced by Moses Pearson, Ebenezer moved his family onto a 200-acre tract of land granted to him by the proprietors of Pearsontown on the Shaw's Mill Road off what is today Route 35 between Standish and Sebago Lake Village. In 1763 he set up and began operating the first sawmill in Pearsontown. Joseph Shaw opened a tavern in 1764, and a Josiah Shaw operated a tavern here during the Revolutionary War. One of the most ingenious Shaws, however, was Thomas Shaw, who erected a wind mill in 1782 that is said to have ground 50 bushel of corn in a day. This was the town's first gristmill. Perhaps the most colorful of the Shaws was Ebenezer's son, Thomas Shaw, who lived near Sebago Lake. He was a prolific writer of rustic verse, particularly lugubrious ballads, and it is said that he rode as far as Augusta peddling his works. The subjects of his verse included catastrophic shipwrecks and the tragic death of Mr. and Mrs. Tarbox on a cold winter's night over on the Raymond Cape. His fame became boundless when sailors discovered and purchased his ballads, which were subsequently sung by seamen in taverns and waterfronts around the world. A sizeable Shaw family cemetery is located on the Shaw's Mill Road just over the town line in Gorham.

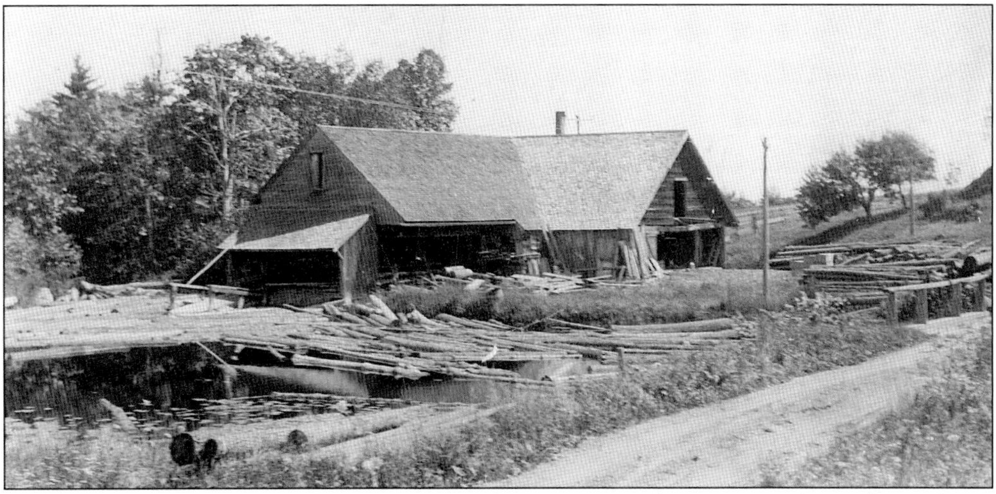

Shaw's Mill. It is said that it took Ebenezer Shaw just nine days to erect this mill on Shaw's Mill Road and begin sawing the logs into lumber used to build the first house in Pearsontown in 1763.

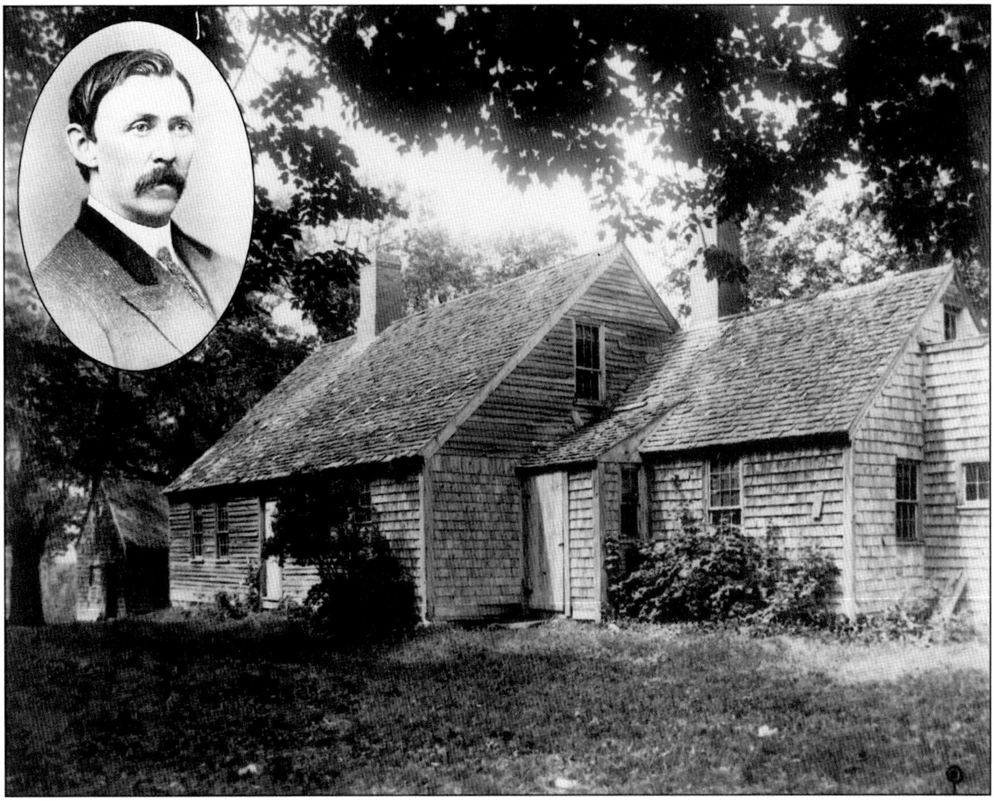

The Thomas Shaw House, 1914. This weathered farmhouse was the home of Tom Shaw, the legendary bard, as well as Thomas C. Shaw (shown *c.* 1895 in the insert). It was on the site of the Arthur Wescott residence. Sometime after this photograph was taken, it was meticulously disassembled, and its lovely wide board paneling was sold and used in building a house in North Conway, New Hampshire.

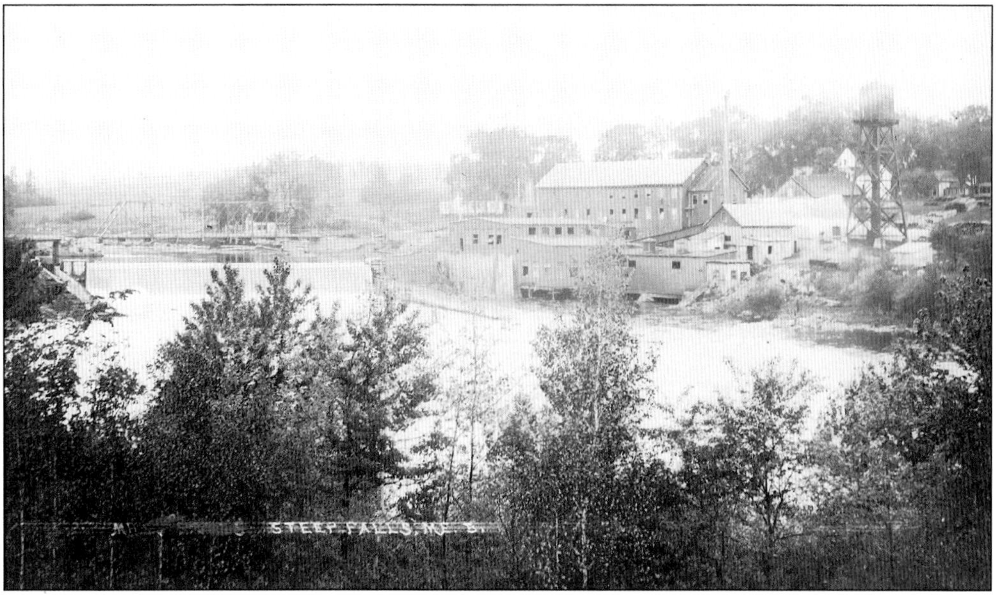

The Androscoggin Pulp Mill at Steep Falls. Two factors played a key role in the development of Steep Falls as a significant industrial and commercial center in the area. The earlier influence, as its name suggests, was the Saco River and the falls that generated the power to operate this industrial plant. Built around 1892 by the Boston Excelsior Company, it was later known as the Damon Pulp and Paper Company, a branch of the Androscoggin Pulp and Paper Company. A devastating fire destroyed it in the 1930s.

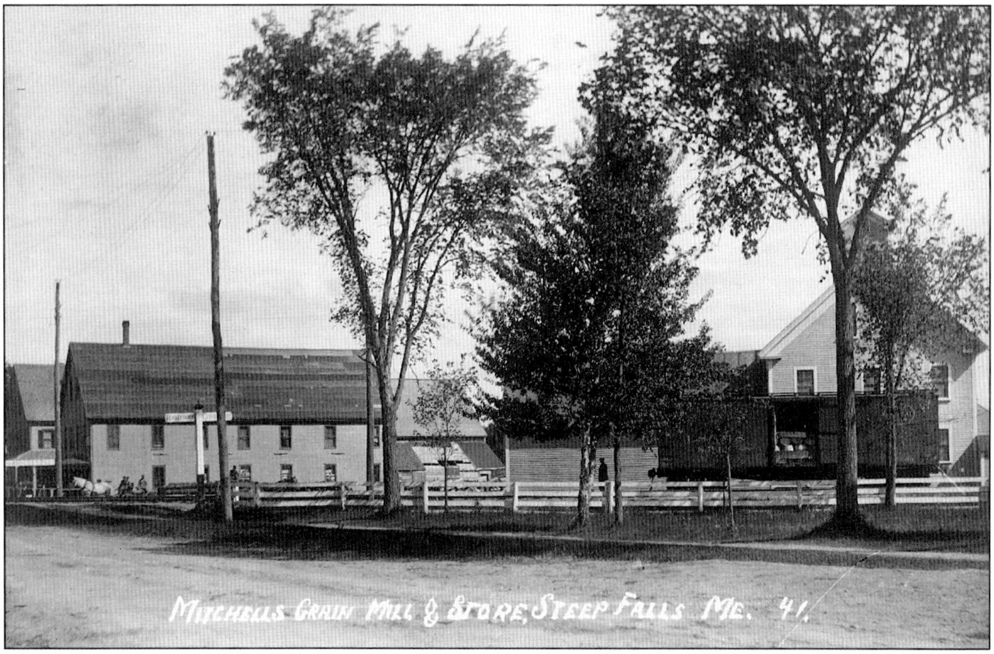

Mitchell's Grain & Feed Store, c. 1925. The second influence was the construction of the railroad through Steep Falls (the Mountain Division of the Maine Central) in 1870. Steep Falls continued to be a major grain and feed entrepot until the rapid decline of the dairy and poultry industries in the area in the 1980s. It also meant the end of Steep Fall's railroad days.

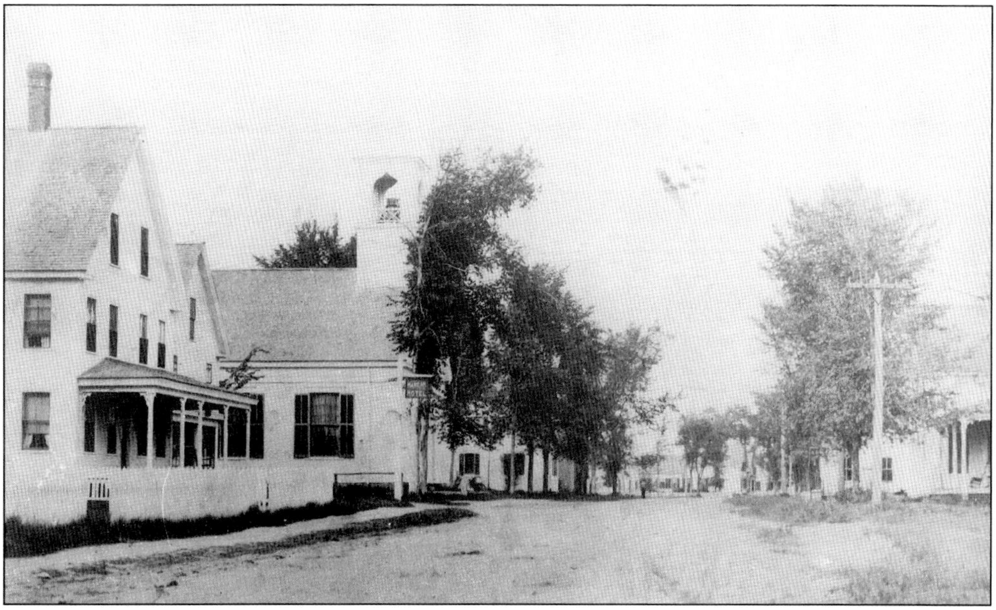

A Street View of Steep Falls, c. 1900. This view, looking down toward the Saco River on the road to Limington, shows a portion of Steep Falls. Prominent on the left is the old Marean Hotel, with Marean's Store next to it. Both burned the night Franklin D. Roosevelt was first elected President. The fire alarm was mistaken for an act of celebration. A stable was maintained behind the hotel. Beyond the hotel and store is the First Baptist Church.

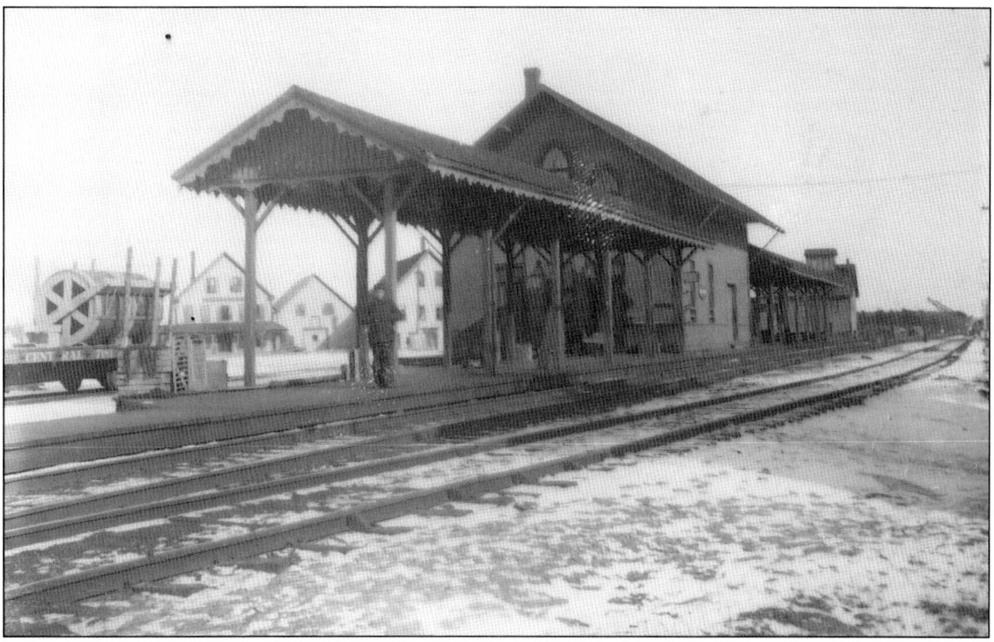

The Steep Falls Railroad Station, c. 1900. This rather large railroad station and freight shed with spurs running on both sides is indicative of the importance of Steep Falls as a rail center serving several towns on both sides of the Saco River, including Sebago and Naples. The snow roller visible to the left on the flat car was just one of many made by Charles Chase of Limington and hauled here to be shipped by rail.

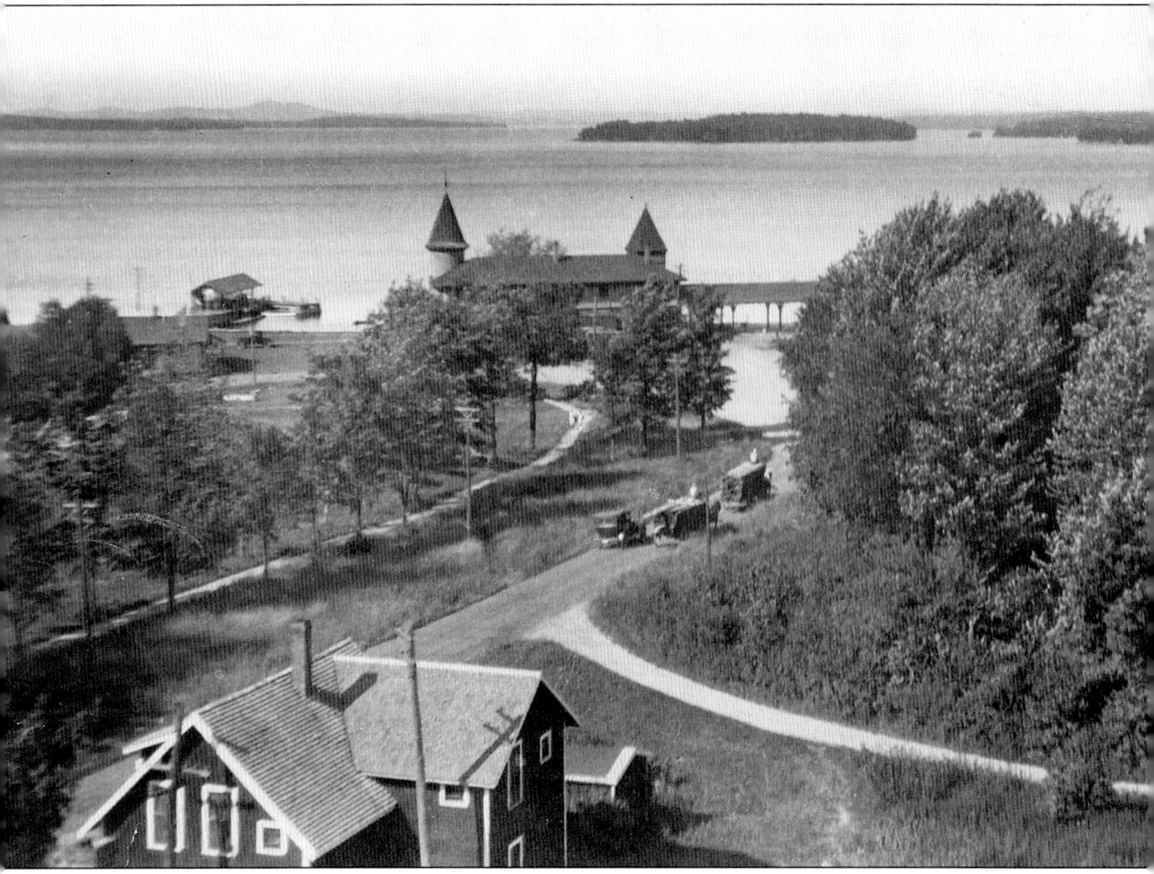

Sebago Lake Village and Station, c. 1920. This panorama shows the shores of Sebago Lake in 1870 at the Lower Bay. Soon after the rails of the Portland & Ogdensburg Railroad were laid, Sebago Lake Village and Station would be destined to perform a vital role in the development of the entire area surrounding the "Queen of Inland Waters"—or the "Switzerland of America," as the lake region was frequently alluded to by early promoters and vacationers alike. For more than sixty years Sebago Lake Station played a pivotal role in a thriving tourist industry centering upon steamboat passenger service and scenic sightseeing tours from Sebago Lake Station to the beautiful Bay of Naples via the serpentine Songo River and up Long Lake to Harrison.

With the advent of the railroad and the arrival of the steamboat, many large farmhouses were renovated to cater to the increasing number of vacationers, and hotels (including some very imposing ones such as the Bay of Naples Hotel) were constructed. The railroad made Sebago Lake Village readily accessible to vacationers from all over the country and even travelers from abroad. Imposing, sturdy docks and piers were constructed along the shore in front of the railroad station to accommodate the ever-increasing number of steamers and private boats, as well as boats carrying freight. And for those who chose not to venture beyond Sebago Lake Station, recreational facilities were made readily available.

Except for the ice industry, Sebago Lake developed primarily because of the vacation and tourist trade. And even though, lamentably, both the steamboat and railroad eras ineluctably fell victims to the automobile and the trucking industry, and there is nothing at the station but rusting rails, the village where Routes 114 and 35 converge still remains a relatively bustling center serving as a convenient stopping place for a steady stream of traffic headed in all four directions.

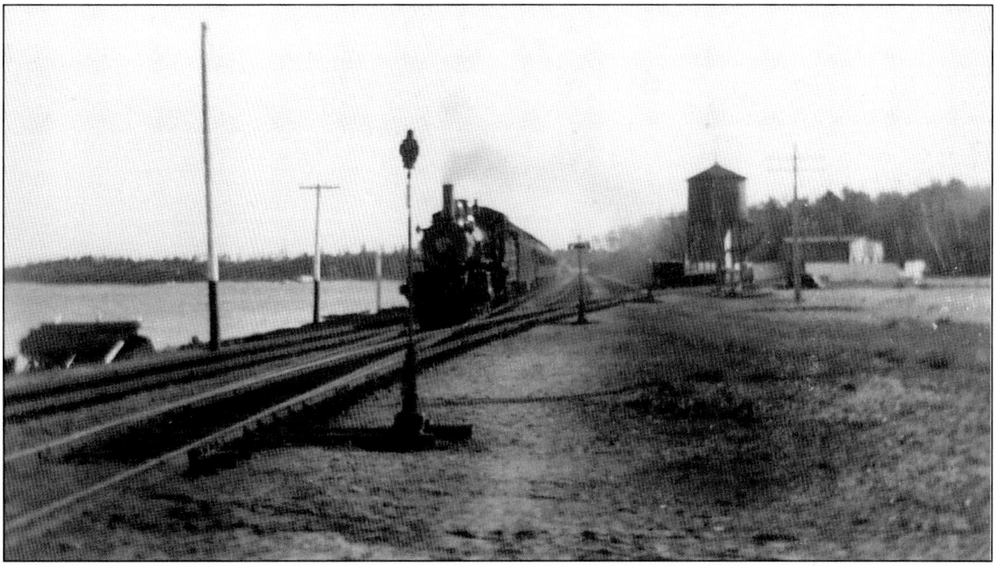

Sebago Lake Station, c. 1925. A passenger train out of Portland is about to pull in at Sebago Lake Station.

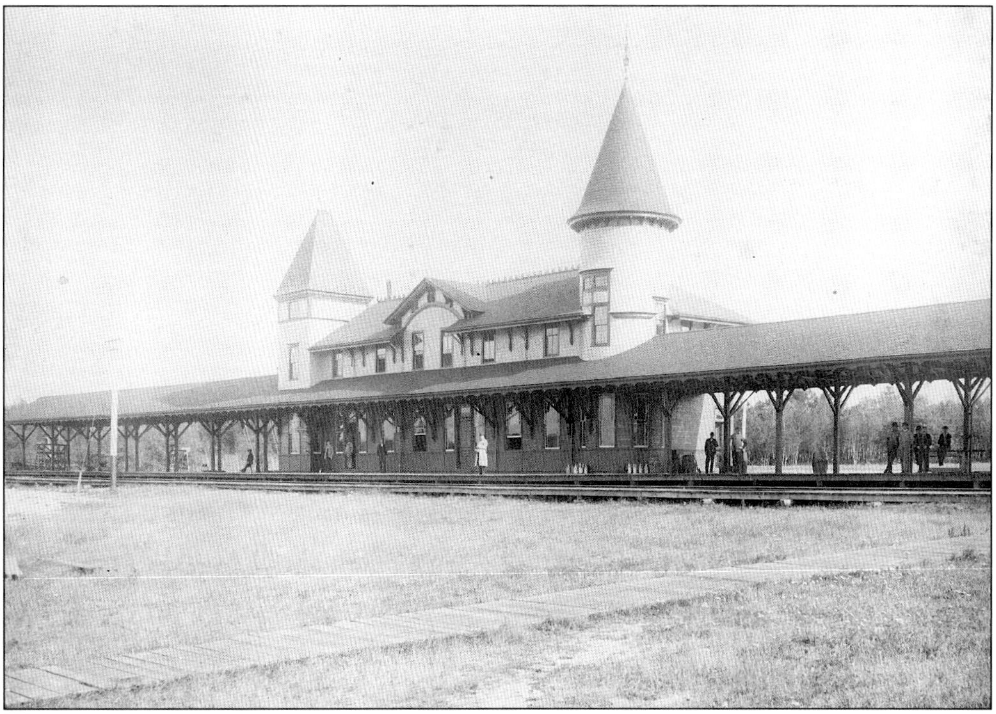

Sebago Lake Station, c. 1920. Sebago Lake Station with its double towers was one of the largest and most impressive stations on what had become the Mountain Division of the Maine Central Railroad—a clear indication of the importance of Sebago Lake as a mecca for sportsmen, excursionists, and vacationers. But with the ever-growing popularity of the automobile and essentially the end of the steamboat era in 1932, this significant landmark was torn down in 1934; subsequently, a part of the freight building was converted to a passenger station until passenger service was discontinued around 1950.

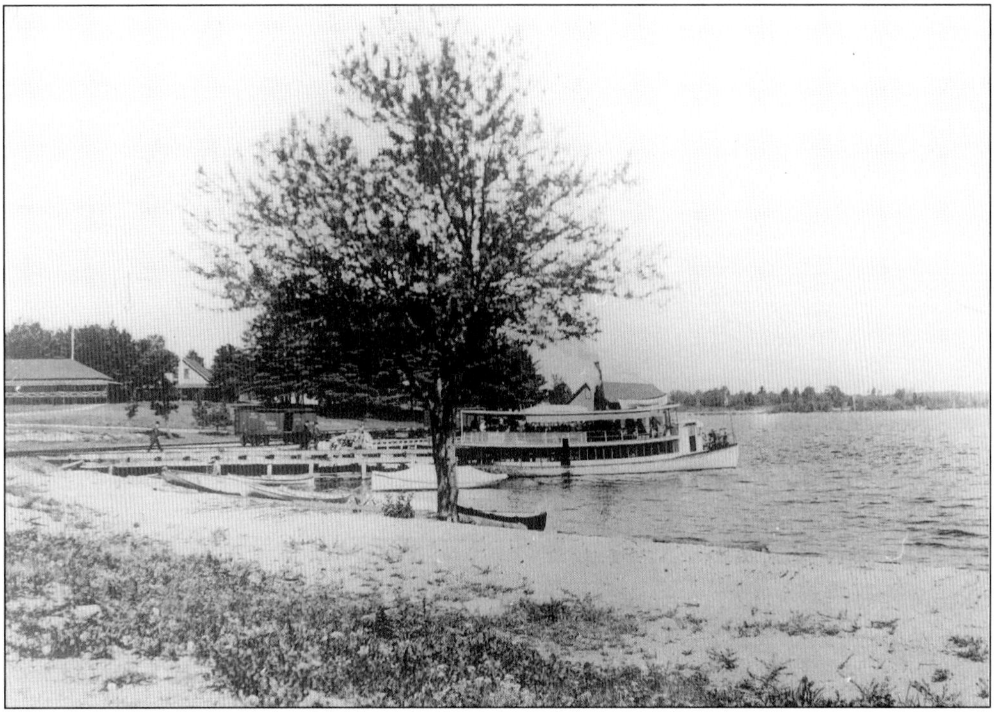

Sebago Lake Station, c. 1920. This photograph says much about the importance of Sebago Lake Station as a center for both recreation and excursions up the lake and beyond. Excursionists could virtually step off the train onto the wharf and board a Songo River Line steamer. Others could spend the day salmon fishing, rent a boat or canoe for fishing or a private outing on the lake, picnic, engage in various sports such as bowling and baseball, or enjoy an evening of dancing at the railroad-owned pavilion visible in the left-hand corner. The building to the right of the pavilion was the concession building where lunches were served.

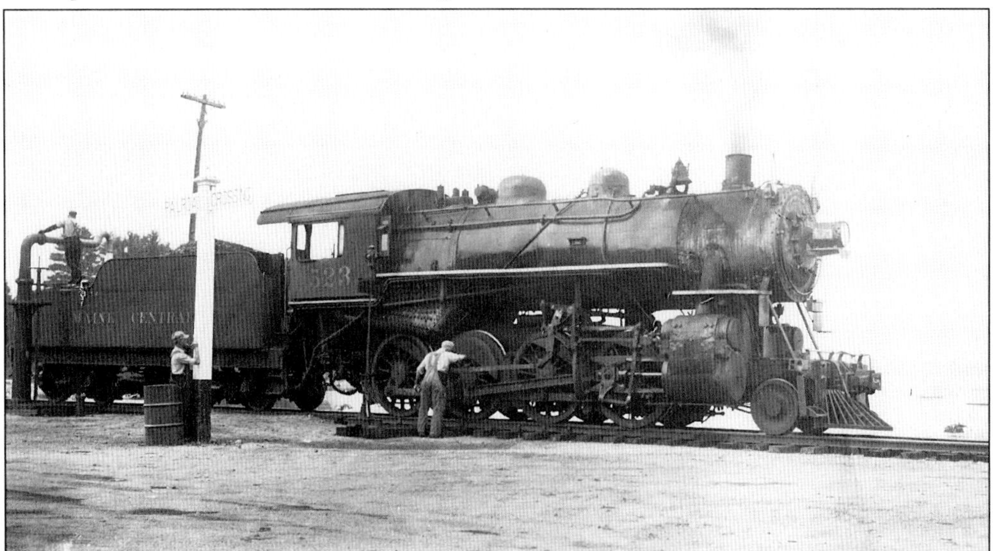

Sebago Lake Station, 1939. Engine 523, built in Schenectedy, New York, in 1913, pauses at Sebago Lake Station to take on water and to be serviced before continuing on to Portland.

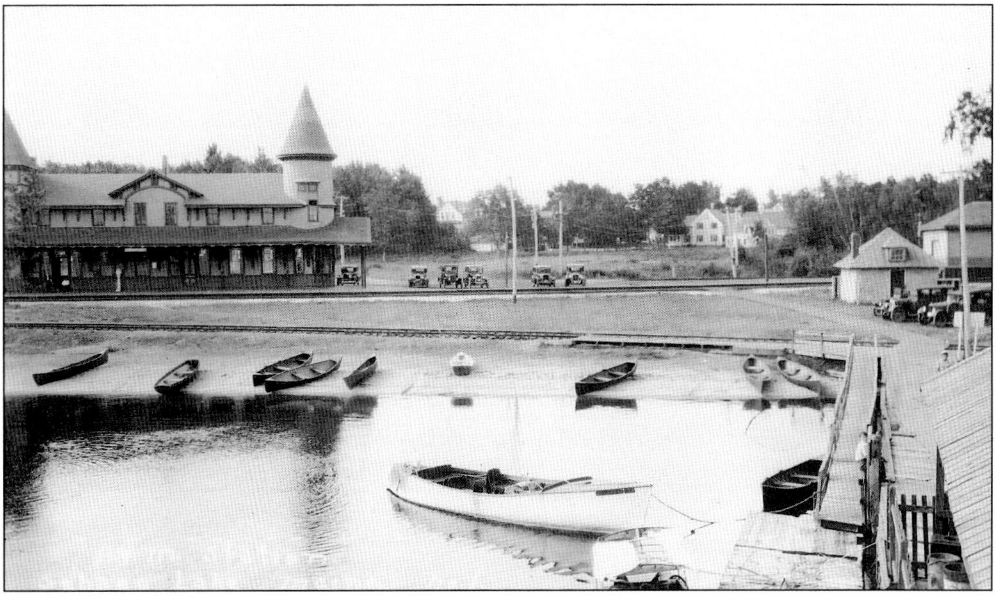

Sebago Lake Station, c. 1930. This is a view of the steamboat pier and waterfront at Sebago Lake Station. Sebago Lake Village is visible in the background. The spur in the foreground enabled groups of excursionists to step off reserved passenger cars onto the steamboat pier. The inboard motorboat was very likely privately owned, but most or all of the canoes and rowboats pulled up on the beach were probably rentals.

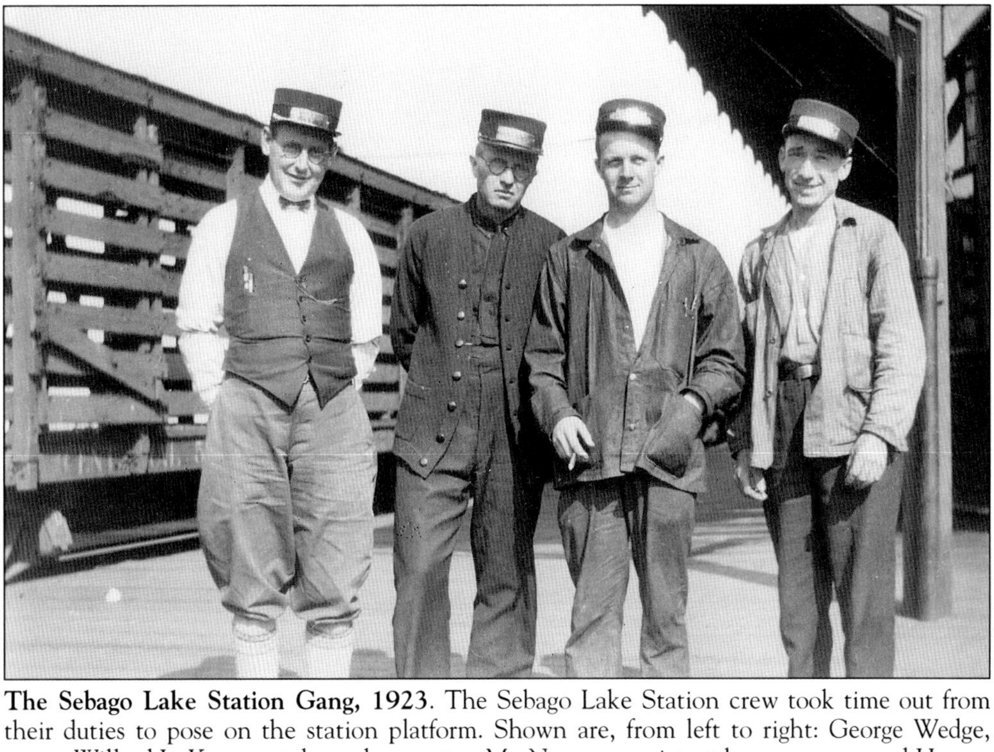

The Sebago Lake Station Gang, 1923. The Sebago Lake Station crew took time out from their duties to pose on the station platform. Shown are, from left to right: George Wedge, agent; Willard L. Kenney, telegraph operator; Mr. Noonan, assistant baggage man; and Horace Ettinger, baggage man.

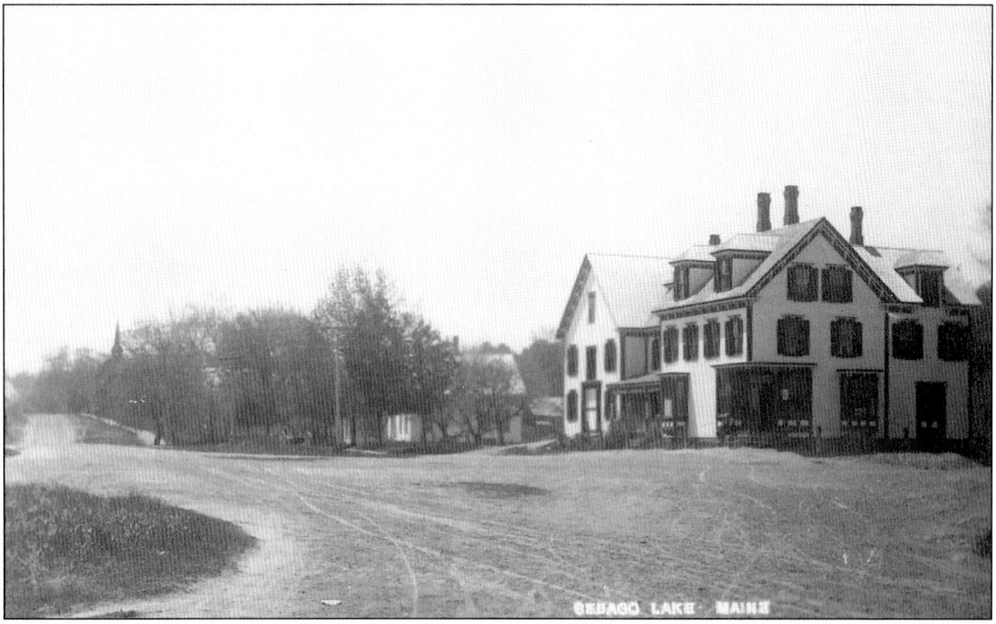

Sebago Lake Village, c. 1910. This is a partial view of Sebago Lake Village and the road leading up the hill (Route 35) to Standish Corner. Prominent in the photograph is the store, then owned by Joe Webster. The steeple of what was then the Sebago Lake Congregational Church is visible up the hill and to the right.

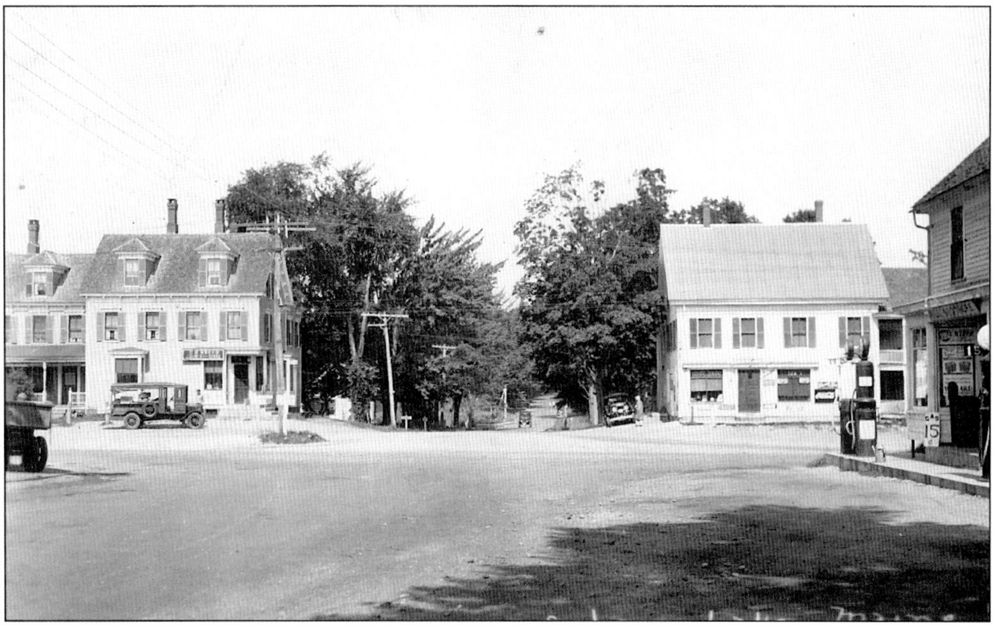

Sebago Lake Village, c. 1920. Except for the gasoline pumps, which were removed perhaps sixty years ago, little else has been drastically altered in this scene at Sebago Lake Village where Routes 114 and 35 converge. At the time this photograph was taken the store to the left was operated by Clinton Weeks. The store on the opposite side was a grocery and hardware store owned by Lem Rich. Sam Hill was the proprietor of the hardware store with the gasoline pumps out front.

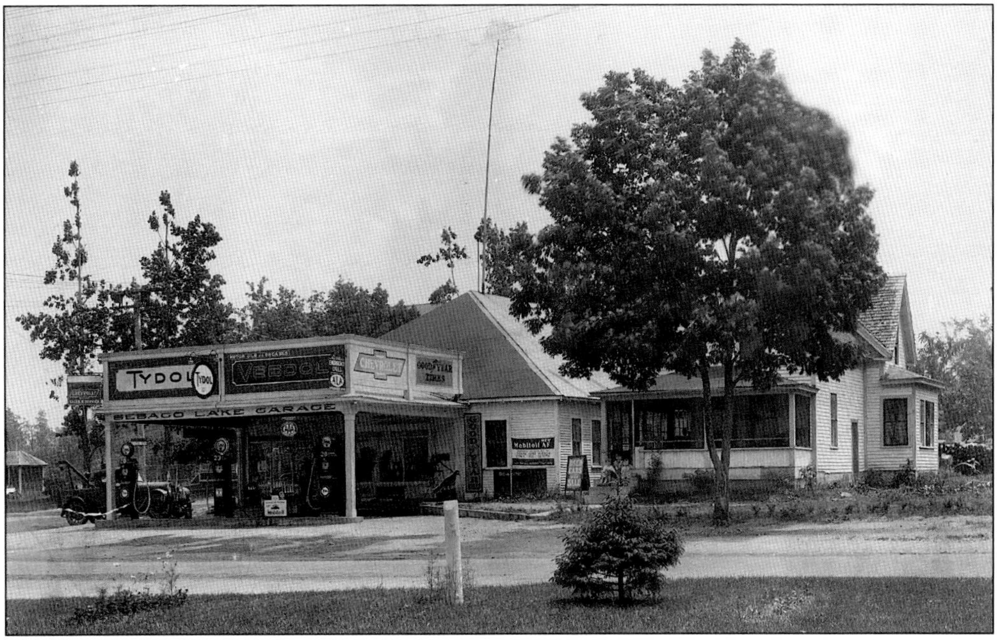

Sebago Lake Garage, early 1930s. In 1920 Victor Woodbrey purchased Peterson's Garage on the corner of Routes 114 and 35 and changed the name to Sebago Lake Garage. Nine years later he obtained the Chevrolet franchise. He and the business soon gained a reputation for integrity and good service, and as the popularity of the Chevrolet increased, so did the volume of business here at the garage. After Victor's death in 1949, the business was passed on to two of his sons—Herbert and Cecil—who, along with their brother Leonard, can be seen sitting on the steps of the family home. By 1950 Herbert had become the sole owner, and in 1969 he opened a much larger garage and show room on Route 114 on the site of the old Sebago Lake House. In 1984 the entire business was moved to North Windham. Today, Herbert's two sons, Mitch and Brad, operate the business.

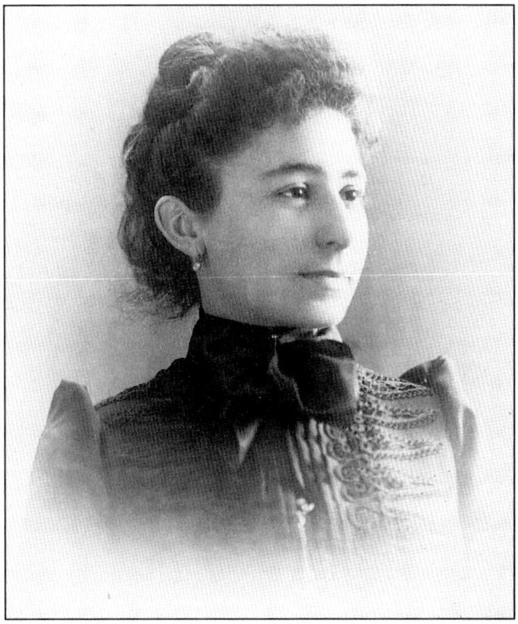

Lena Shaw, c. 1895. Lena Shaw, who was married to Chester Shaw, a captain of one of the Songo River Line steamers, lived in the house next to Hill Brothers Hardware. She was a photographer who also printed and developed film for other people.

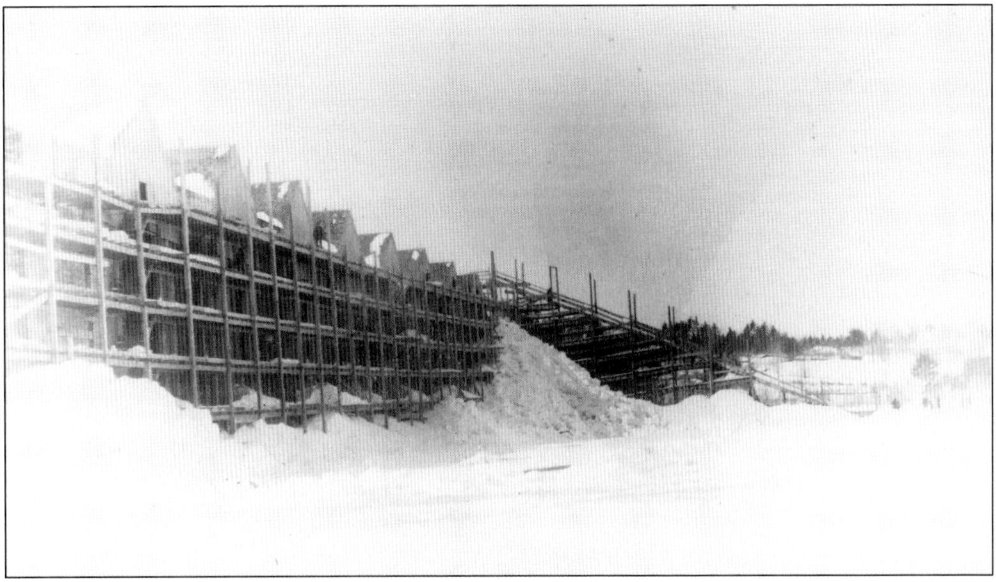

The Portland Sebago Ice Company, c. 1920. This extensive complex of ice houses epitomizes the importance of the ice industry before the refrigerator replaced the icebox. The industry began operating here in 1880 as the Clark & Chaplin Ice Company. Because the Lower Bay freezes over long before the Big Bay, most of the ice cutting on the lake was done at Sebago Lake Station. Often times a dozen boxcars would be loaded daily with "frozen gold" in summer and shipped by rail to Portland, much of it to be loaded onto ships bound for Boston, New York, and even to cities in the south.

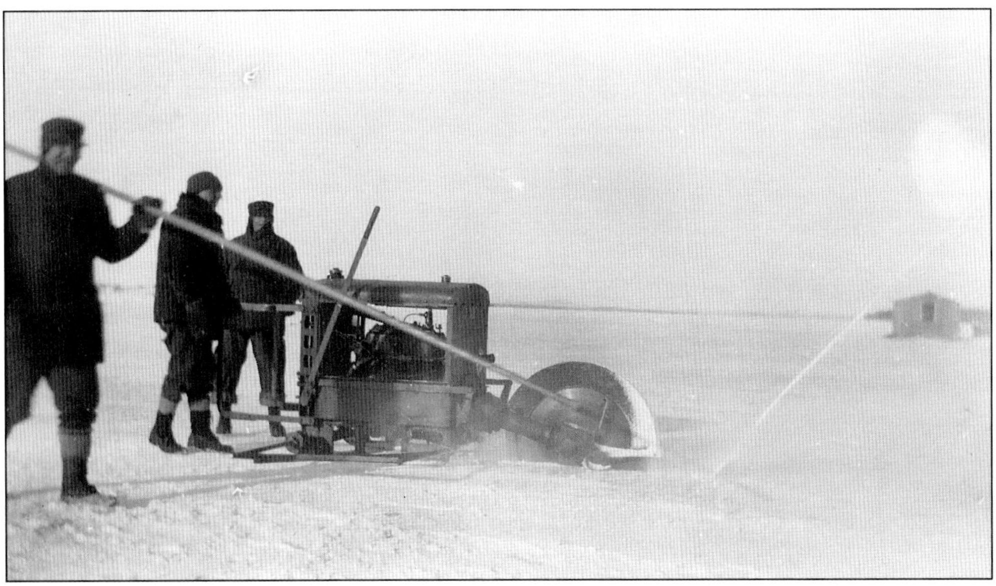

Ice Cutting on the Lower Bay, 1923. This gasoline-powered saw was a great improvement over hand saws, but not until a warm shelter was built to store it at night so that it would start on sub-zero mornings.

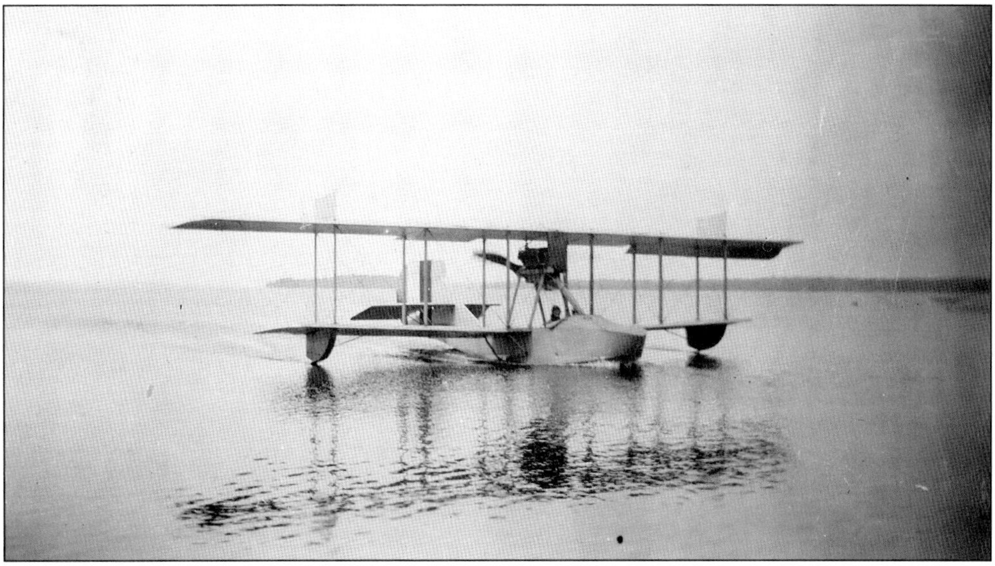

A Hydroplane on the Lower Bay, c. 1922. A familiar sight at Sebago Lake Station in the early 1920s was this hydroplane, piloted by a man from Old Orchard. He has landed at the Lower Bay and is approaching the beach at Sebago Lake Station, hoping to entice the more adventuresome on a flight over a portion of the lake for $5 a person.

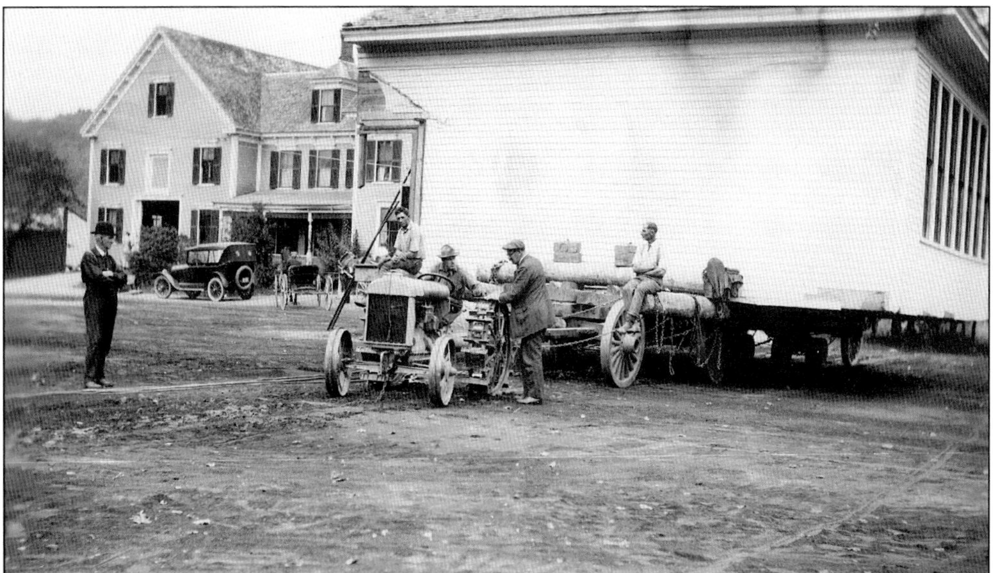

A School on the Move, 1922. When the Portland Water Company purchased the industrial village of Smith's Mills—just a few miles up the lake from Sebago Lake Village—and all the buildings were destined to be razed, the town of Standish moved the Smith's Mills school to School Street in Sebago Lake Village. It is shown here being towed by a Fordson tractor through the Sebago Lake Village square. The driver remains unidentified, but the others are, from left to right: Percy Manchester, Dr. Moulton, John Cole, and Fred Chapman.

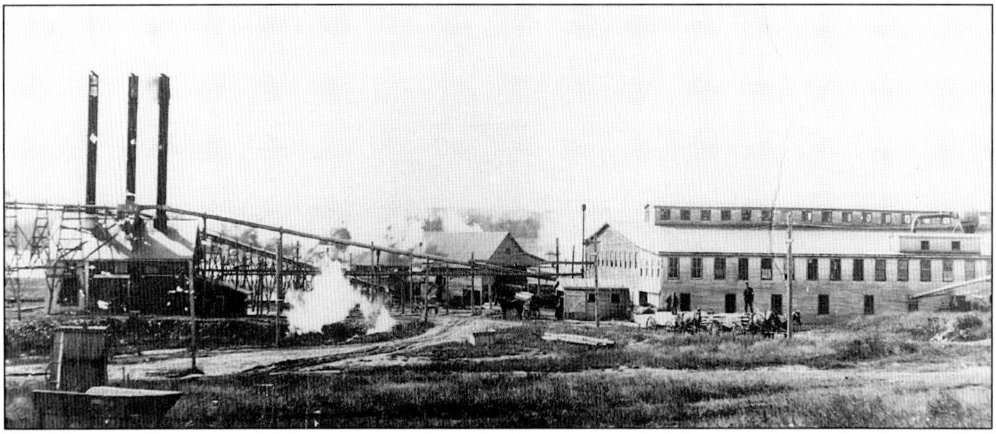

Smith's Mills, c. 1917. In 1907 the E.I. DuPont de Nemours Company purchased a sawmill complex from Benjamin F. Smith, founder of the tiny hamlet of Smith's Mills in 1888, and began manufacturing packing boxes for munitions. With the outbreak of World War I, DuPont rapidly began expanding by rebuilding the original sawmill, introducing band saws, and erecting a second mill with all the latest equipment. During the war it ran night and day, employing over three hundred people with a weekly payroll of $8,000.

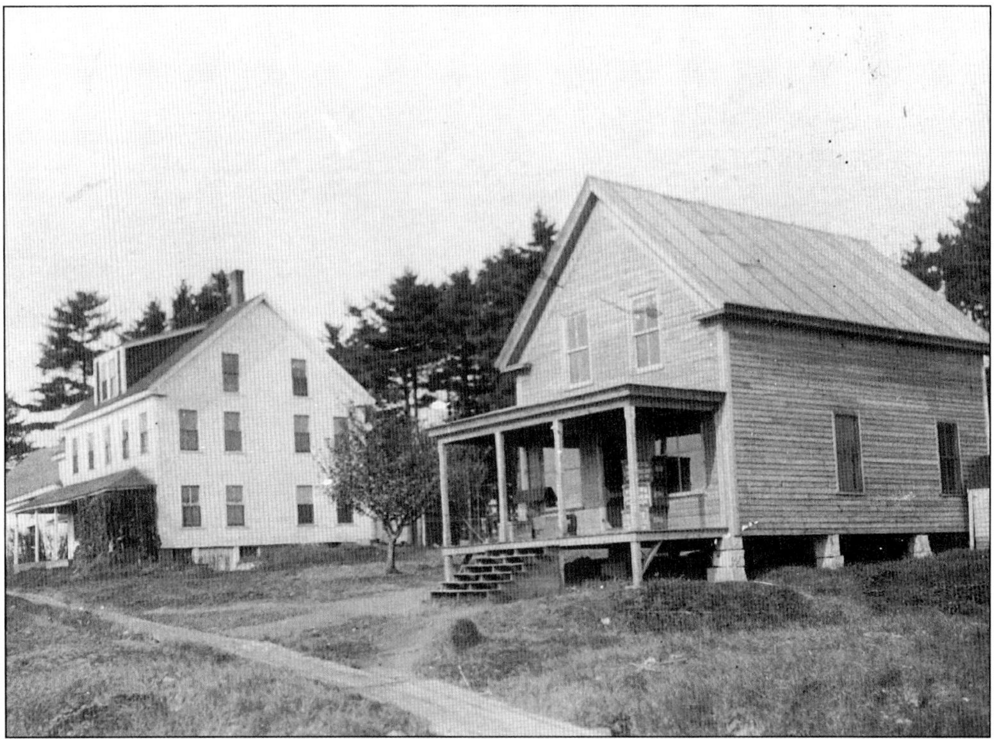

Smith's Mills, 1915. At its zenith Smith's Mills boasted a population of between four and five hundred. Besides the boarding house and the company store shown here, Smith's Mills consisted of a shady main street (every house had electricity, sewage, and running water), school, movie house, chapel, and railroad station.

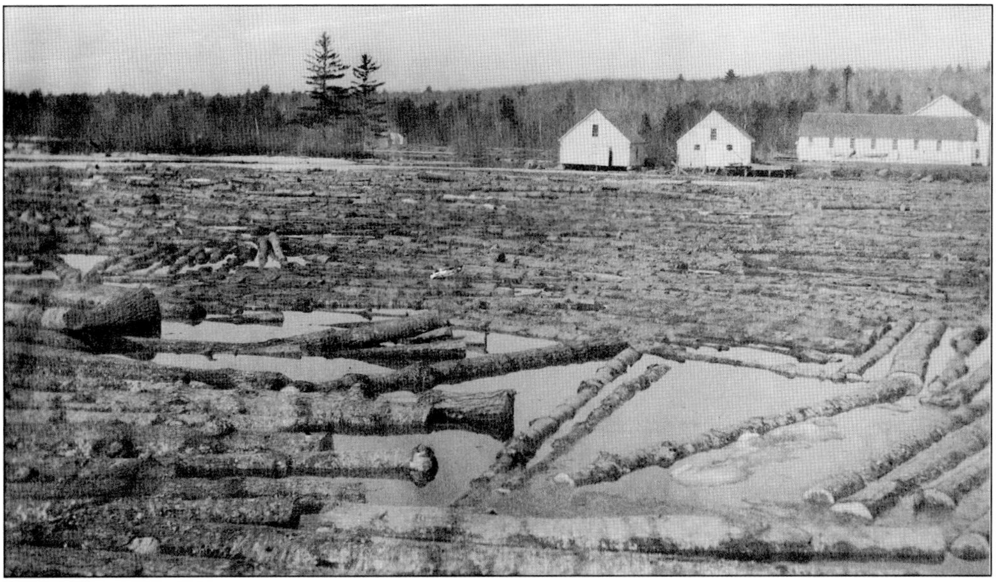

Logs at Smith's Mills, c. 1915. Acres of white pine logs, secured by booms, lay seasoning in the lake to feed the insatiable saws at the DuPont mills, where they were processed into boxes and shipped by rail to the DuPont Powder Mill in Wilmington, Delaware.

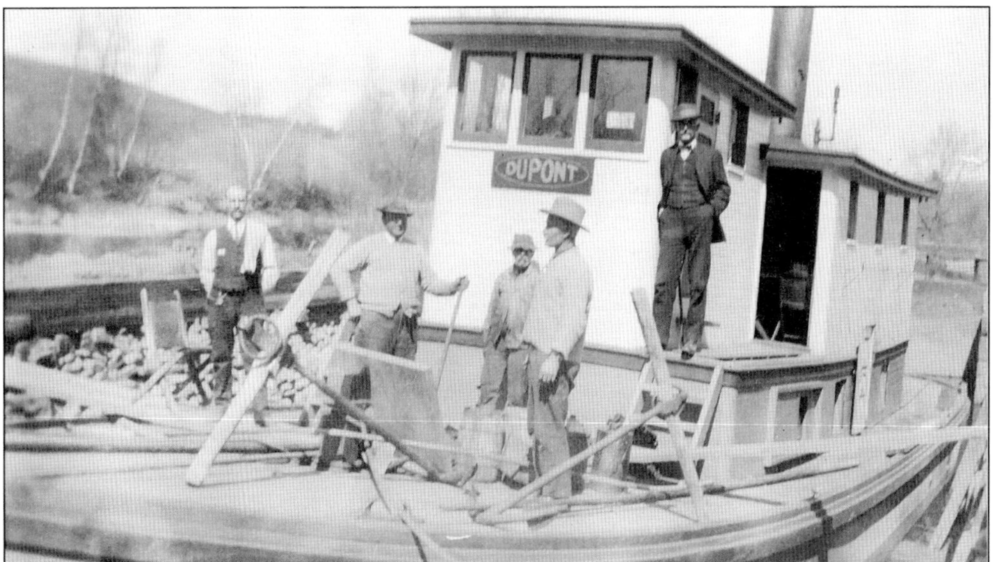

The DuPont Tugboat on Sebago Lake, c. 1918. DuPont maintained its own tugboat for towing huge rafts of logs gathered along the shores of Sebago Lake. The DuPont operation was well within the 2-mile limit controlled by the Portland Water Company; in an effort to keep the water pure within its jurisdiction, the Portland Water Company purchased Smith's Mills in 1922 and closed the mills. Smith's Mills ceased to exist. It was an unique boom town. It was environmental rather than economic reasons that brought about its demise.

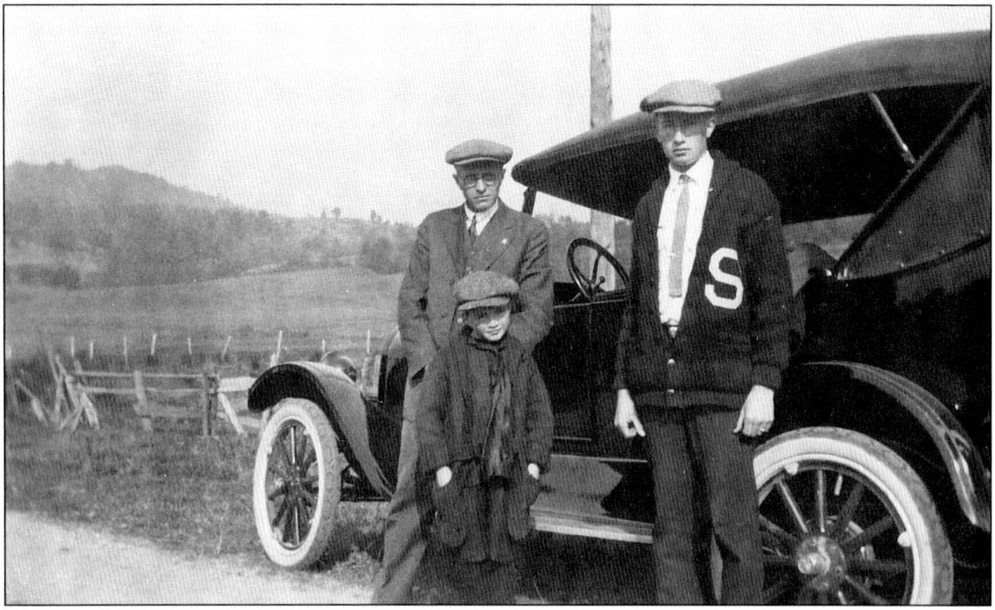

The Kenneys, 1923. Willard Kenney, who was the telegraph operator at the Sebago Lake Railroad Station at this time, poses beside his shiny new Star with his two sons, Donald and Aubrey (wearing his Standish HS baseball sweater). Aubrey, born in 1907, was the postmaster at Sebago Lake Village for many years. He and his wife still live in the village. Donald died at age fourteen of rheumatic fever, a grim reminder that life was still fragile in the 1930s.

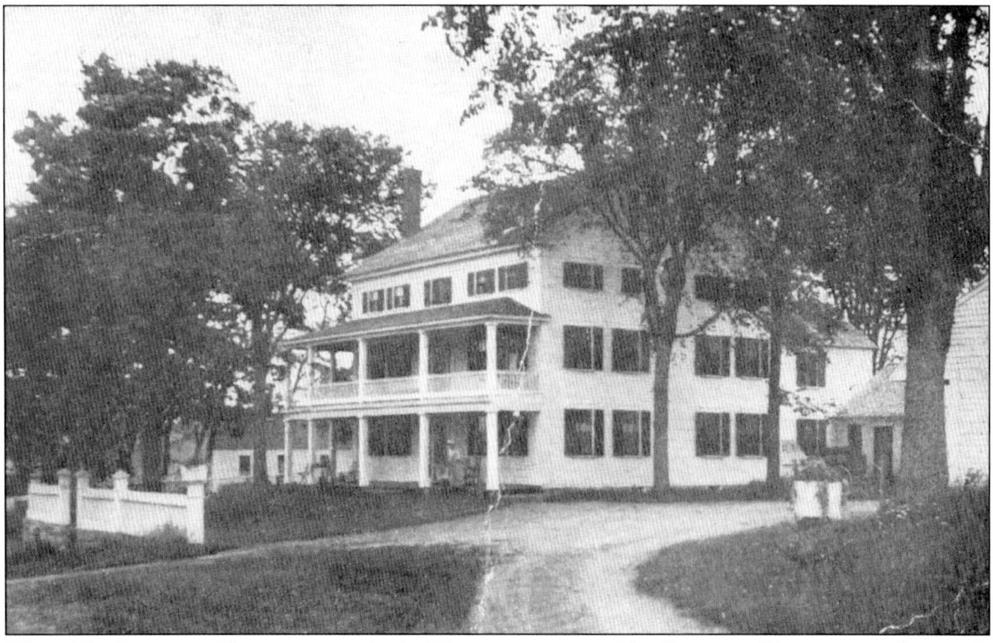

The Chadbourne House, c. 1905. The impressive Chadbourne House, popular with vacationers, was built by one of the region's oldest settlers in 1843 at the foot of Sebago Lake. It was a favorite stopping off place for those either traveling along the bustling highway between Windham and Sebago Lake or, until it closed, the Cumberland & Oxford Canal. It burned on December 1, 1918.

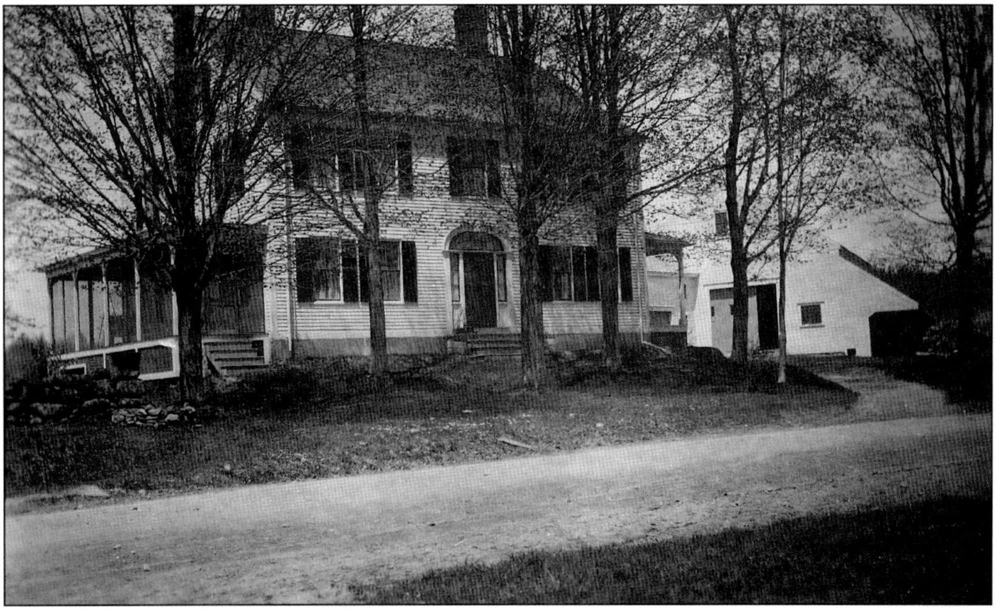

"Squires," c. 1915. "Squires," built in 1808 by Benjamin Mussey, was located between Standish Corner and Sebago Lake Village. For many years it was the residence of Dr. Olin Moulton. Later it was purchased by Walter Greenleaf of Washington, D.C. When the Sylvania plant bought the property, the ell and barn were torn down and the house moved closer to Standish Corner. It is now the home of James and Paula Haddow.

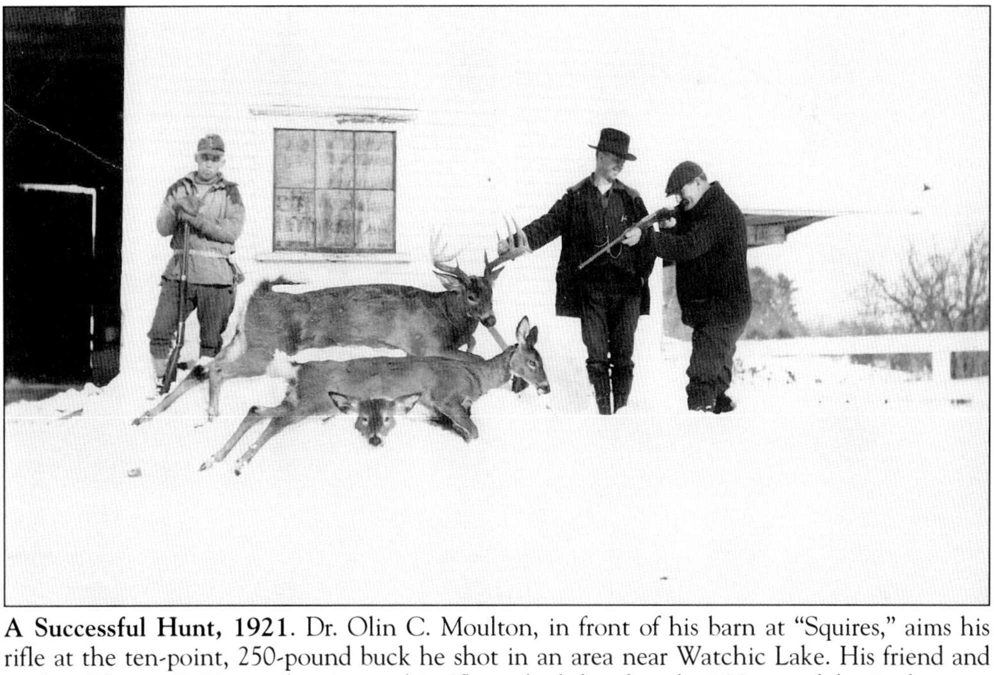

A Successful Hunt, 1921. Dr. Olin C. Moulton, in front of his barn at "Squires," aims his rifle at the ten-point, 250-pound buck he shot in an area near Watchic Lake. His friend and guide—Clayton E. Barnes, leaning on his rifle to the left—shot the 100-pound doe in the same area. The young man holding an antler possibly could have been Dr. Moulton's son Olin, who became a physician in Reno, Nevada.

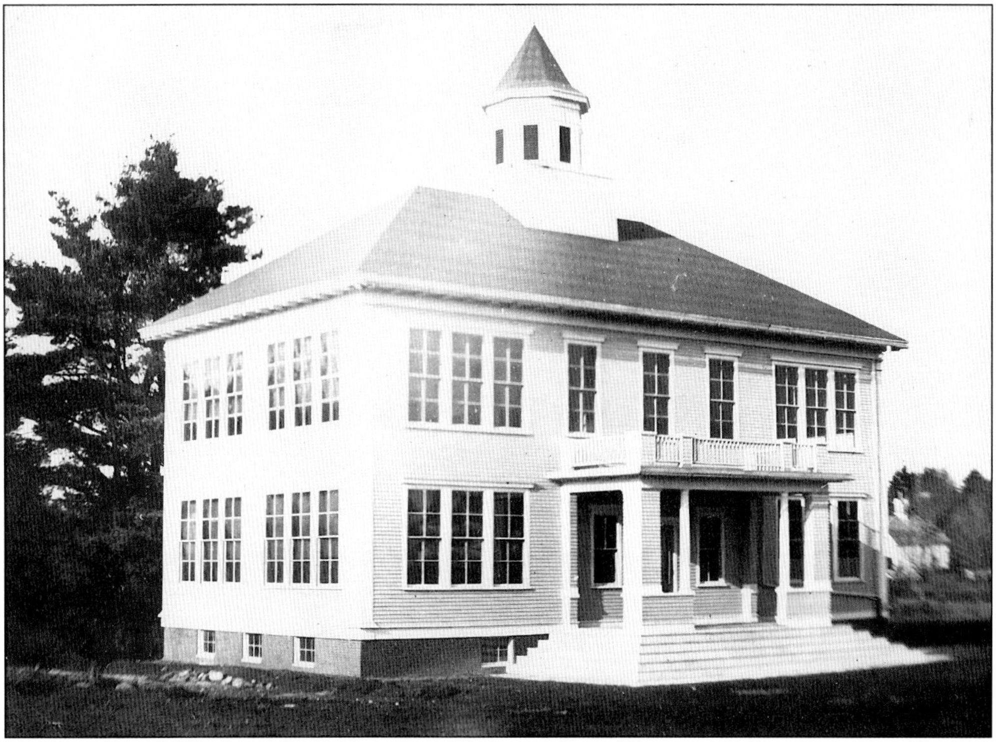

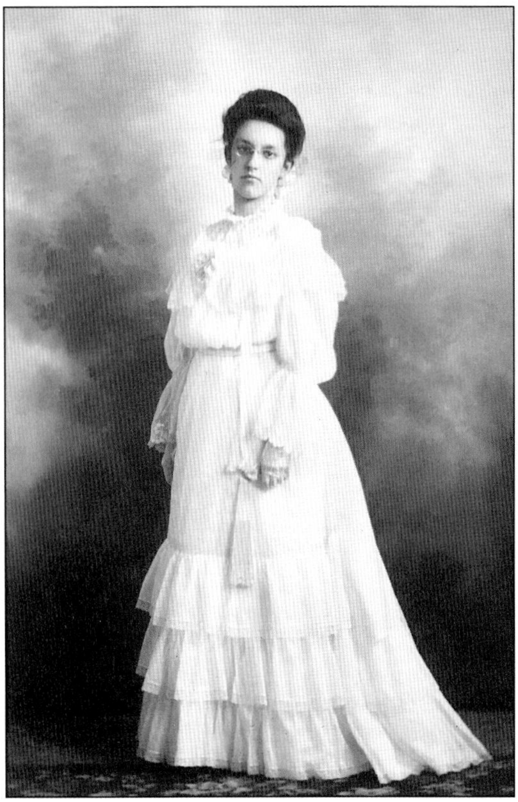

Standish High School, 1918. The new Standish High School, built in 1914 at Sebago Lake Village, was a great improvement over the upstairs of the Old Red Church at Standish Corner. Later an additional wing was added to the left. The high school was closed in 1961 when Standish—along with the neighboring towns of Limington, Buxton, and Hollis—became a part of SAD 6 and Bonny Eagle High School was opened.

Bessie Mae Higgins, 1904. Bessie Mae Higgins, who lived on the Pond Road (off Route 35) on the east side of the Lower Bay, is shown here in her graduation gown. She was in the class of 1904 that graduated from the old Standish High School at the "Old Red Church." Bessie became a teacher.

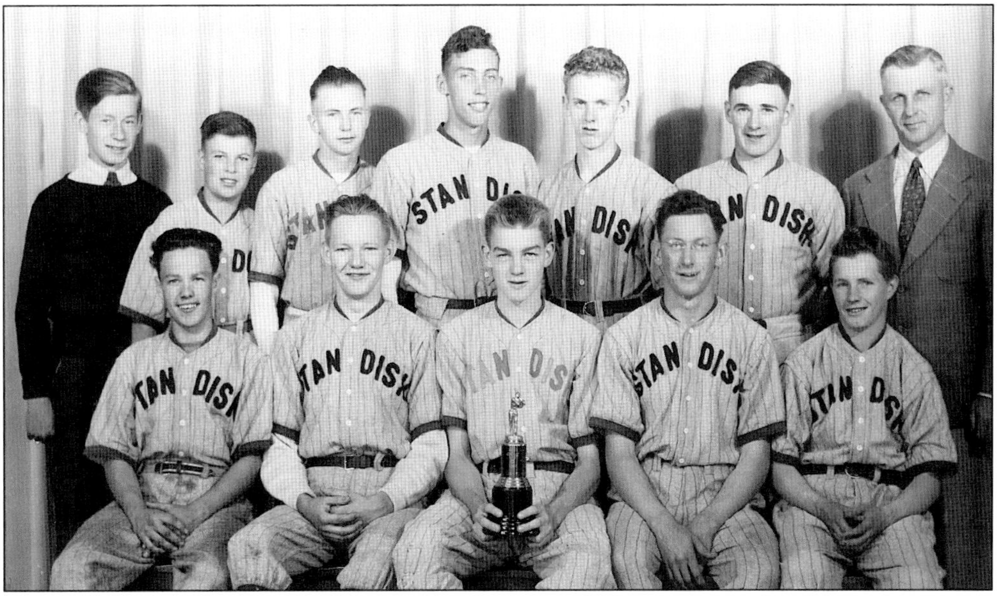

Triple C Champions, 1941. Standish High School baseball teams, under the tutelage of the legendary Rupert J. Johnson, were perennial Triple C champions. Shown are, from left to right: (front row) D. Graffam, J. Lane, W. Moulton, W. Gallant, and E. "Tinker" Day; (back row) O. Thomas (manager), E. Woodbrey, C. Wentworth, W. Dolloff, R. Logan, R. Ettinger, and Coach Johnson. Following his graduation from Bowdoin College in 1924, Rupert Johnson became principal, teacher, and athletic coach at Standish HS. In 1961 he became the athletic director and a math teacher at BEHS until his retirement in 1965.

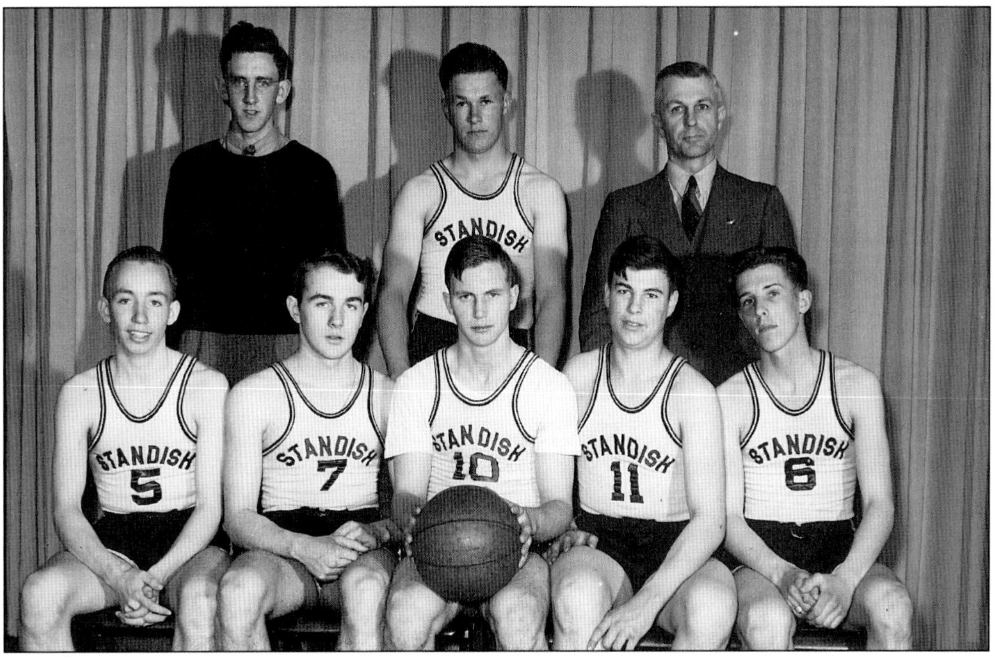

The 1944 Standish HS Basketball Squad. The squad consisted of, from left to right: (front row) J. Barnes, D. Plympton, C. Wentworth, E. Woodbrey, and A. Rines; (back row) P. Walker (manager), G. Warren, and Coach Johnson.

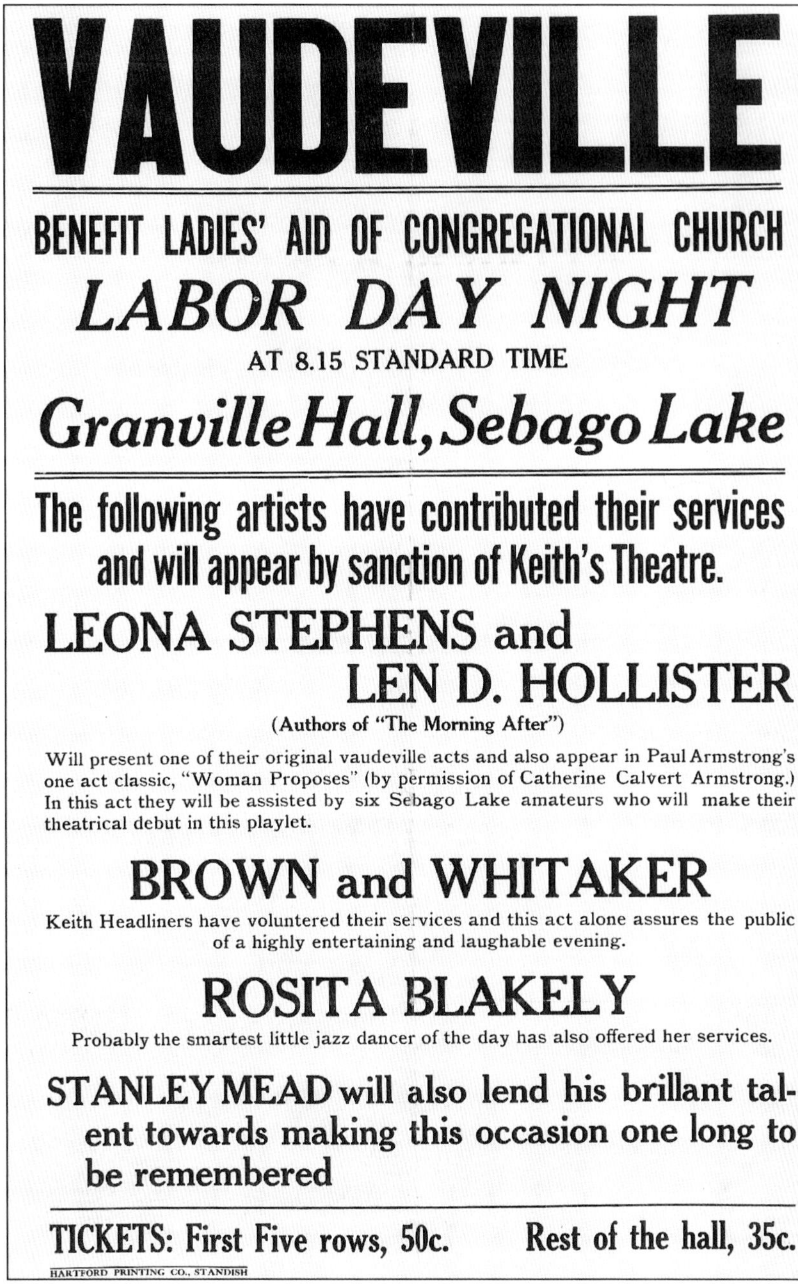

VAUDEVILLE

BENEFIT LADIES' AID OF CONGREGATIONAL CHURCH

LABOR DAY NIGHT

AT 8.15 STANDARD TIME

Granville Hall, Sebago Lake

The following artists have contributed their services and will appear by sanction of Keith's Theatre.

LEONA STEPHENS and LEN D. HOLLISTER

(Authors of "The Morning After")

Will present one of their original vaudeville acts and also appear in Paul Armstrong's one act classic, "Woman Proposes" (by permission of Catherine Calvert Armstrong.) In this act they will be assisted by six Sebago Lake amateurs who will make their theatrical debut in this playlet.

BROWN and WHITAKER

Keith Headliners have volunteered their services and this act alone assures the public of a highly entertaining and laughable evening.

ROSITA BLAKELY

Probably the smartest little jazz dancer of the day has also offered her services.

STANLEY MEAD will also lend his brillant talent towards making this occasion one long to be remembered

TICKETS: First Five rows, 50c. Rest of the hall, 35c.

HARTFORD PRINTING CO., STANDISH

The Vaudeville Comes to Sebago Lake. An exceptionally fine relationship developed between a group of vaudeville stars—who summered over on Raymond Cape and who frequently arrived in their motor launch to purchase supplies at Weeks' store in the village—and local ladies who were members of the Congregational Church. During summers in the early 1920s the vaudeville stars performed shows at Granville Hall to raise money for Ladies' Aid. Separate from the group on Raymond Cape was a colony of thespians—headed by Broadway actress Florence Reed and her husband, Malcolm Williams—who in the 1920s purchased Indian Island and built cottages out there. Their happy retreat, however, was shortly thereafter taken over by the Portland Water Company and again the island became uninhabited.

Three

Raymondtown: Raymond-Casco

First Settled: 1771
Incorporated: 1803
Population: 4,000
Area: 41 Square miles
Principle Settlements:
Raymond, North Raymond, Raymond Hill, Raymond Cape

First Settled: 1771
Incorporated: 1841
Population: 2,400
Area: 34.5 square miles
Principal Settlements:
Casco Village, South Casco, Webb's Mills

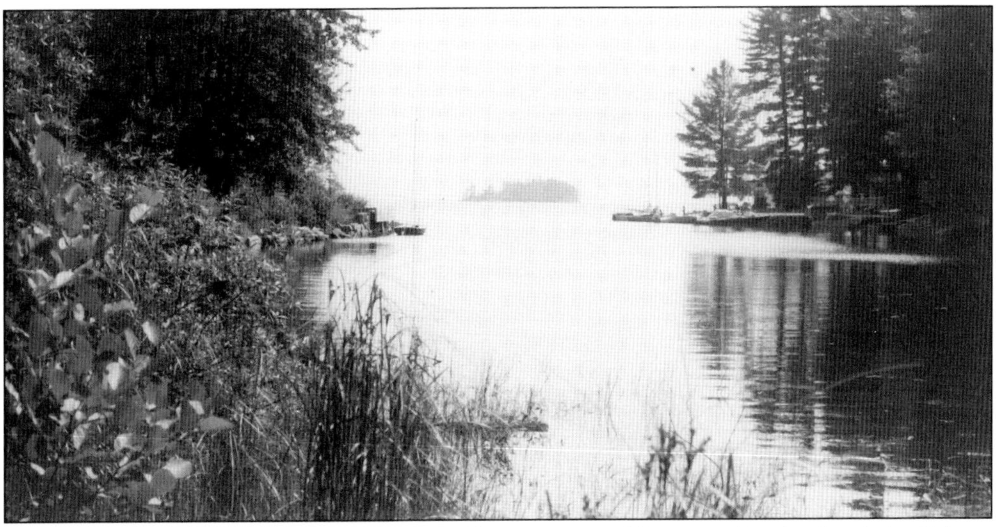

Old Town Landing. In the days when canal boats operated between Portland and the Sebago Lake region—and even after the canal closed, when freight continued to be carried by water on Sebago Lake for another half century—the Old Town Landing was located here in the foreground near the mouth of Dingley Brook, separating the town of Raymond (left) from the town of Casco (right). In late summer and early autumn, when Sebago Lake is usually at its lowest level (the level of the lake was raised in 1880) and the channel up Dingley Brook to the mill sites became too shallow for the freight boats to pass through, it was necessary to load and unload freight here in deeper water. Doctor Island, one of the thirteen Dingley Islands, is visible in the distance.

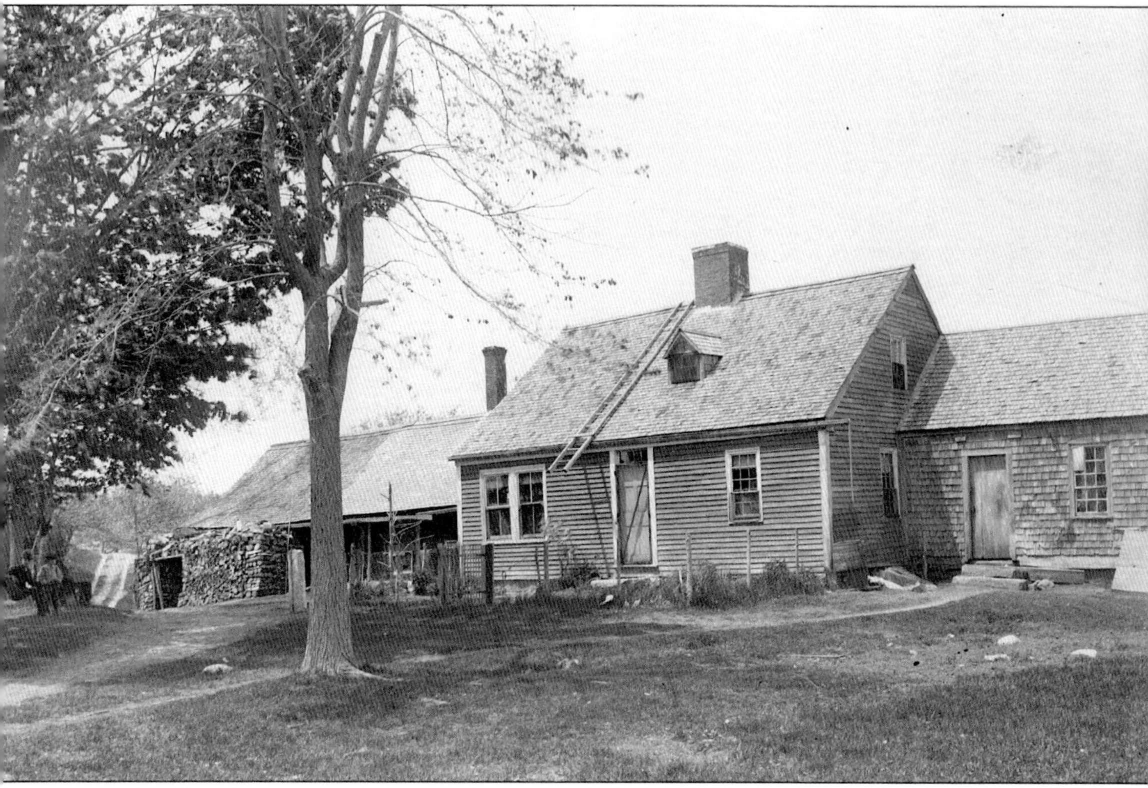

The William Hayden Farmstead, c. 1895. William Hayden cleared the land and built this farm when Maine was still a part of Massachusetts. It was located on the Gore Road in what was called the "Gray Gore." (A gore is a strip land between towns that somehow did not get surveyed and recorded.) The "Gray Gore," like the "Standish Gore," did not become a part of Raymond until 1871.

The original township of Raymondtown on Great Sebago Pond, established in 1767 by the General Court of Massachusetts, consisted of what today is Raymond, Casco, and a portion of Naples. It perpetuates the name of Captain William Raymond, a prominent citizen of Beverly, Massachusetts, who participated in the unsuccessful siege of Quebec in 1690. However, as a result of the Act of 1767, neither Captain Raymond nor any of the original proprietors ever settled in Raymondtown.

In 1769, it was voted to offer an extra 100-acre lot to the first person to settle in the township before December 31, 1770. Consequently, according to one of several versions, Captain Dominicus Jordan of Cape Elizabeth and Captain Joseph Dingley of Duxbury (neither were original proprietors) set out together and arrived at the outlet of Sebago Lake. It seems that Dingley, however, got the jump on Jordan, staked out his claim first, and subsequently built a cabin and a sawmill on the brook that bears his name, in what would eventually become the village of South Casco when Casco (an Indian name meaning "marshland") separated from Raymond in 1841.

Nonplussed, Captain Jordan proceeded to lay claim to an area (which still bears his name) along the beautiful bay on Sebago Lake. He soon constructed a mill, later to be called the Scribner Mill Privilege, on the Jordan River near the outlet to Panther Pond in what still remains today a part of Raymond.

Both men continued to clear land, build roads, and provide work for settlers that followed. With Sebago Lake and the canal linking the area to Portland, farming and especially wood-related industries would become the mainstay of the two towns for over a century.

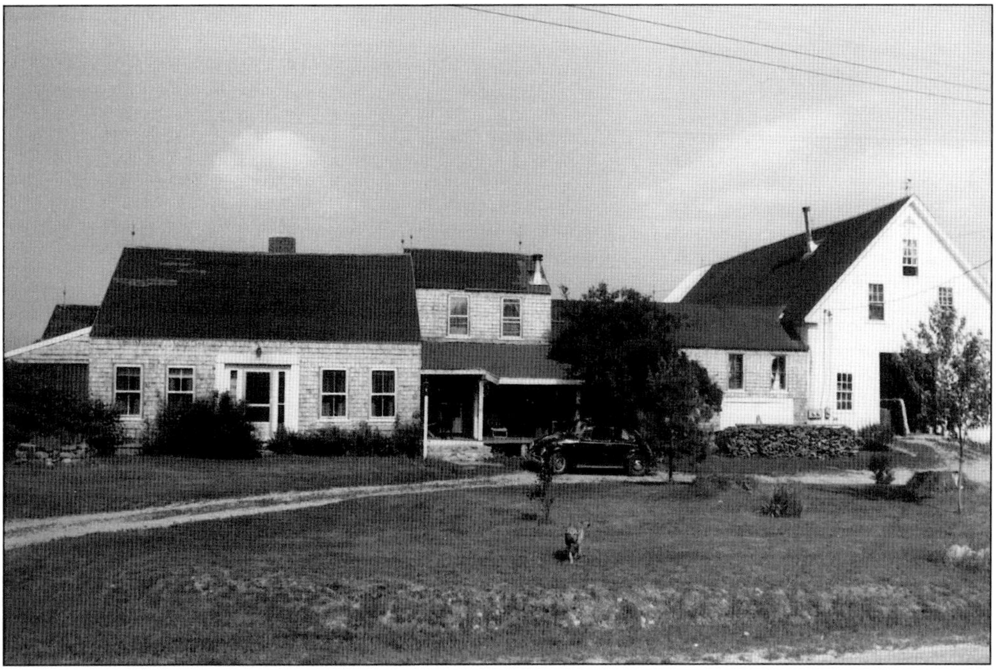

The Captain Joseph Dingley Homestead. Ten years after Captain Joseph Dingley first settled in Raymondtown and built a cabin, a dam, and a sawmill on Dingley Brook, he constructed a two-story homestead near the mill. According to several sources, a fire destroyed a portion of the upper story of the house and the remainder was later remodeled. Captain Dingley died in 1806 and is buried in the family burial ground near the brook. The homestead remained in the family until the 1960s.

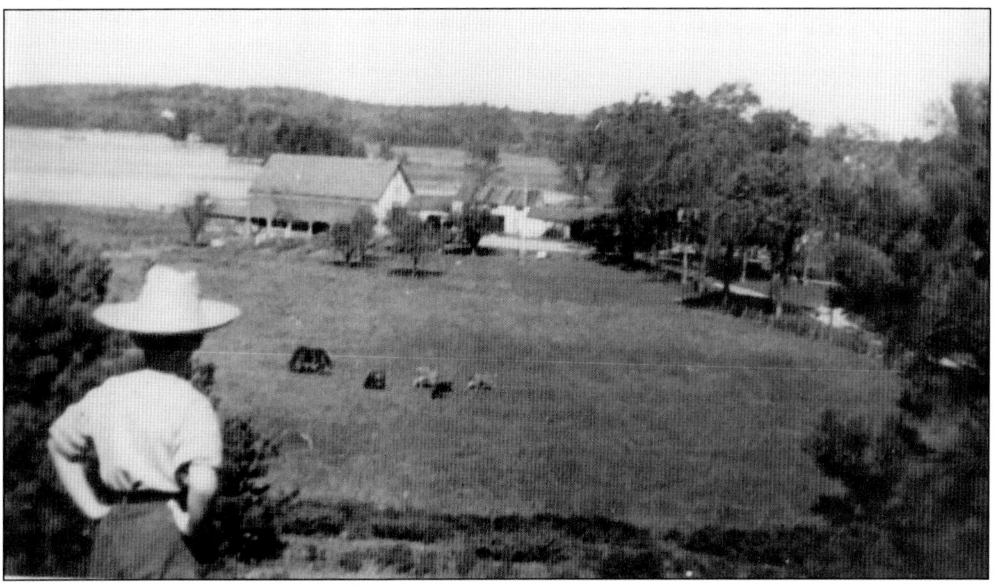

A Pastoral Scene, c. 1905. This peaceful, bucolic view shows a portion of Jordan Bay and what had become in 1900 the Crockett House. The portion of the complex to the right forming an ell to the three-story main house is said to have been the home of Dominicus Jordan, Raymond's first settler.

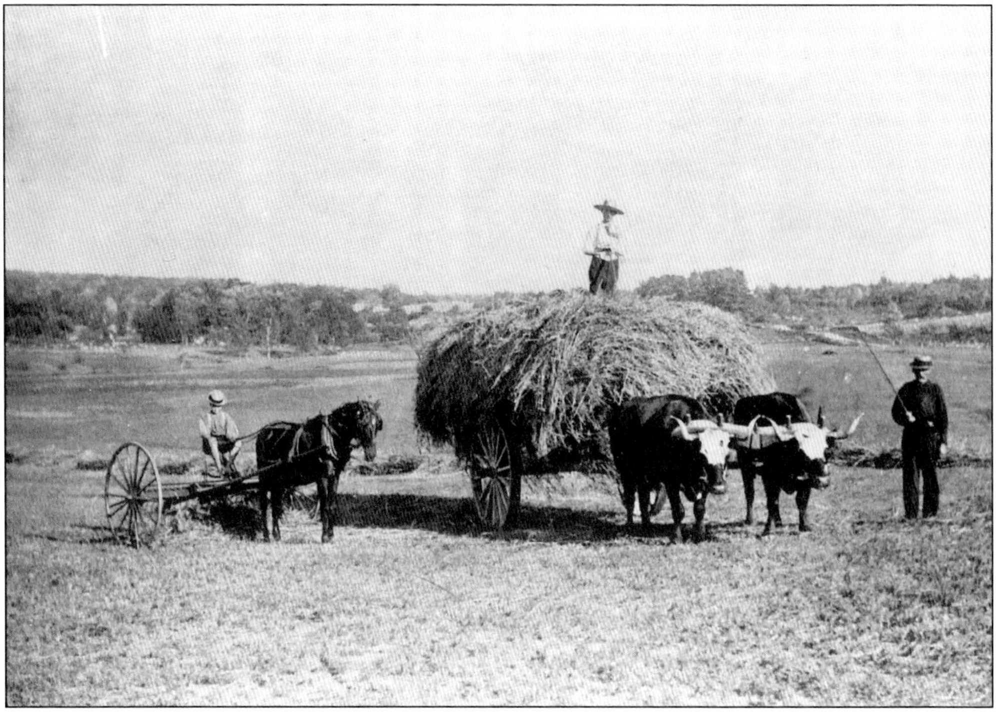

Haying Time, c. 1900. Harvesting the annual hay crop was a vital activity each summer until the farms around the lake began converting to summer boarding houses or sold out to commercial developers. It is unlikely that John Hayden, guiding his team of oxen with a goad, nor Irving Hayden, raking the scatterings with a horse-drawn rake, could have foreseen the day when their manicured hay field would be converted into a golf course.

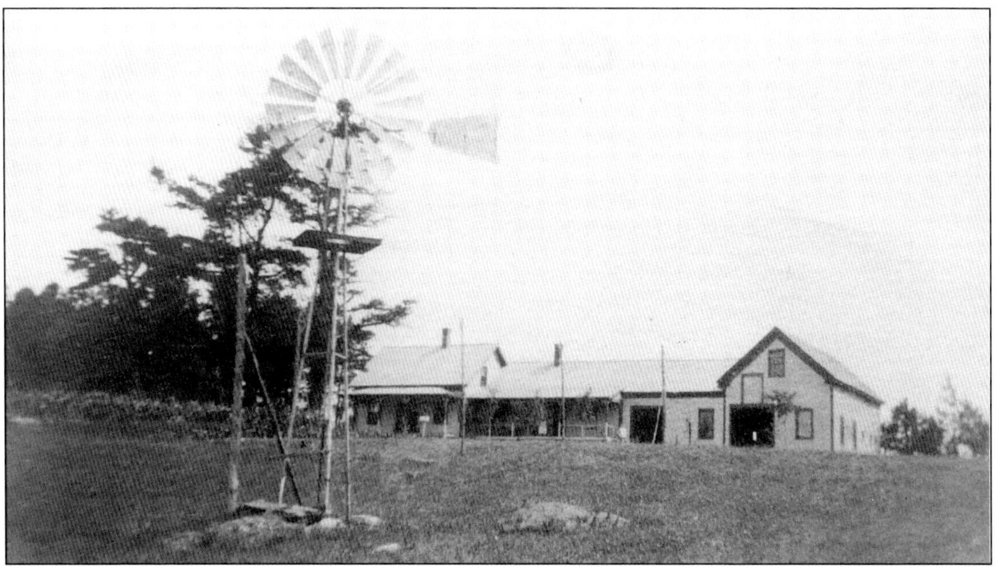

Wind Power, c. 1910. For many years this windmill pumped water into Henry Harmon's house and barn, overlooking Jordan Bay. Under the windmill was a 6-foot well where he kept a goodly supply of frogs, which he sold to fishermen for 5¢ a dozen. Today the farm is the New England Horse Center on Route 302.

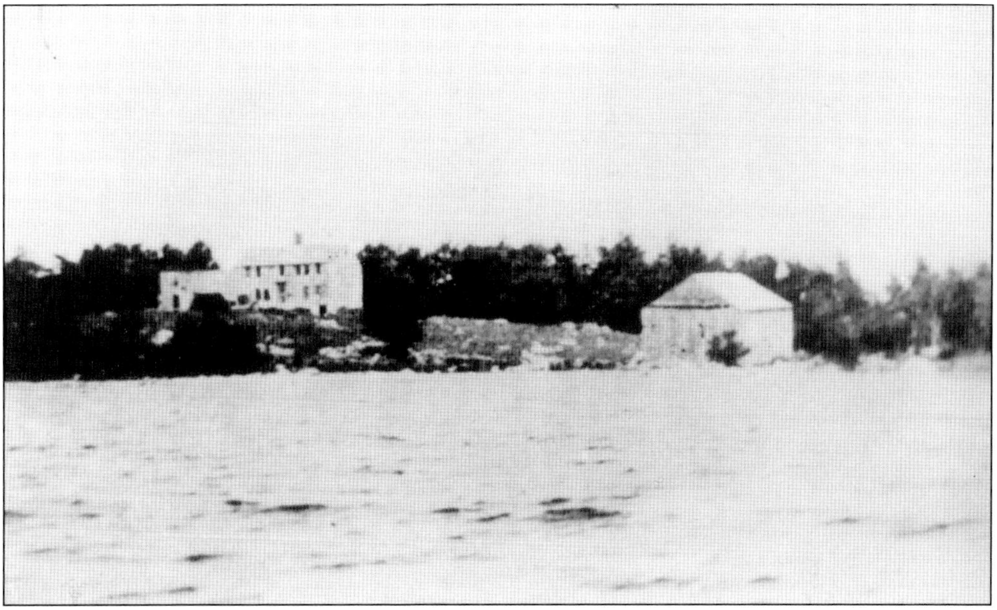

Farming on Frye Island, c. 1885. Although Frye Island is a part of Standish today, it was a part of Raymondtown in the original land grant. This 1,000-acre island, by far Sebago Lake's largest island, once supported several farms—including the Hooper Farm with this magnificent two-story house opposite the present ferry landing. The barn is nearly awash, indicating that this photograph was taken shortly after 1880 when the level of the lake was raised. Soon thereafter farming was discontinued, and a dense growth of forest eventually swallowed up all traces of the abandoned farms. Today roads, cottages, and a golf course have vanquished most of the forest.

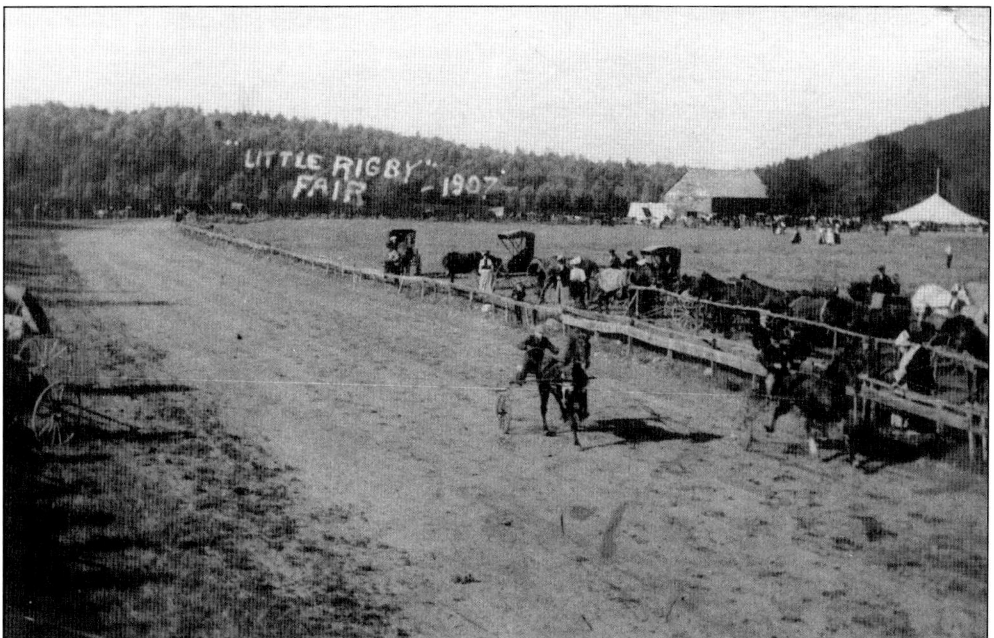

Horse Racing at Little Rigby Fair, 1907. Horse racing was a popular event when the Little Rigby Fair was operating at Pike's Corner near Casco Village.

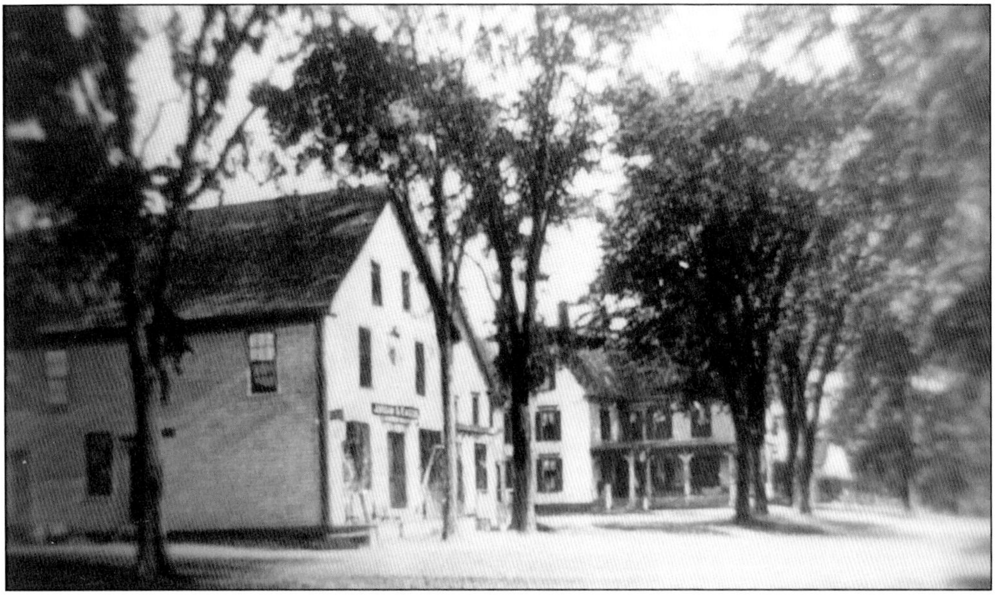

The Jordan & Eager Store, c. 1910. The Jordan & Eager Store, with a post office attached, was located at the corner of Mill and Main Streets in Raymond Village, a village that has been only slightly altered by commercial development. The Knights of Pythias held meetings on the second floor. On Sundays the men in the community would congregate here at the store, where tall tales were spun and ribald jokes told. Like a Middle Eastern coffee house, the women were unwelcome.

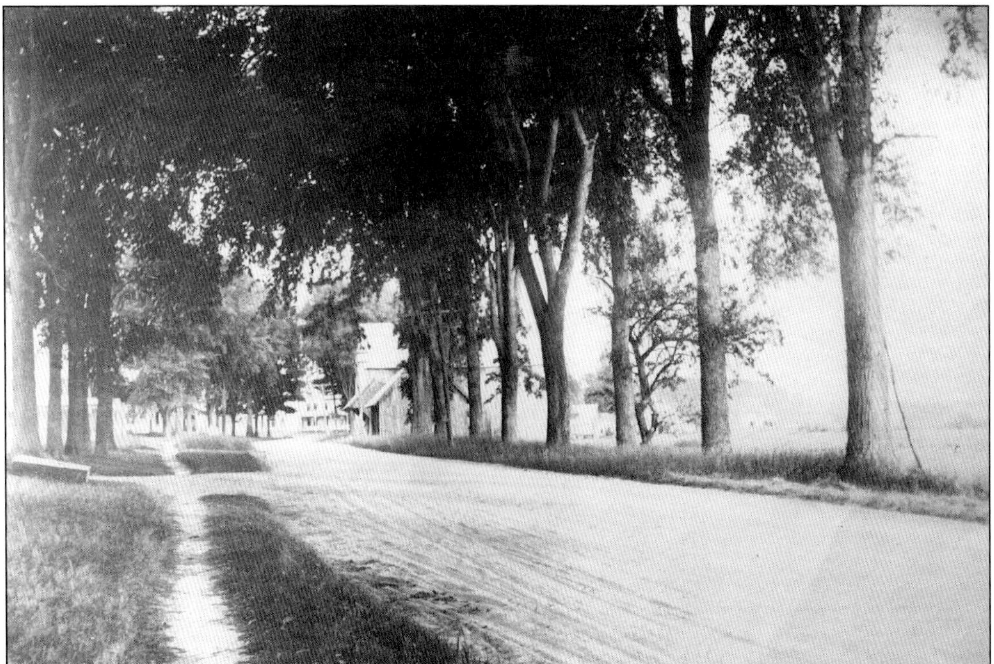

Raymond Village, c. 1920. Like most Maine villages before the arrival of the dreaded Dutch Elm disease, majestic elms lined both sides of Main Street in Raymond. Visible on the right is Eli Longley's barn, where town meetings were held in the early days of Raymondtown.

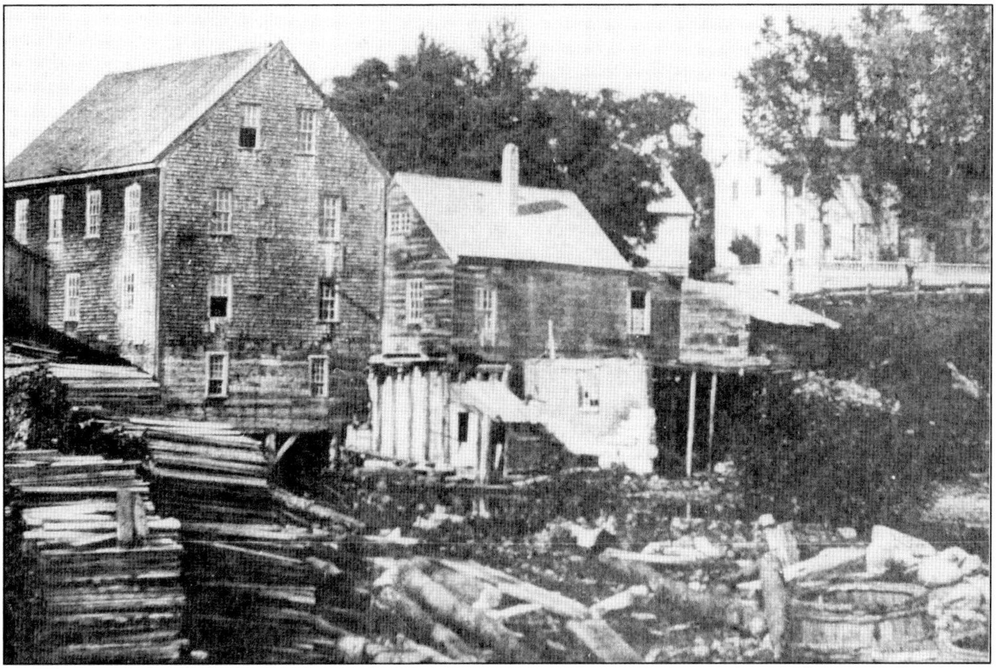

An Industrial Complex, c. 1895. The area below Mill Street in Raymond between Panther Pond and the mouth of the Jordan or Panther River was once a beehive of industrial activity. These buildings served as a gristmill, plaster mill, and a woolen mill. There was also a sawmill at this site and a tannery down at the mouth of the river.

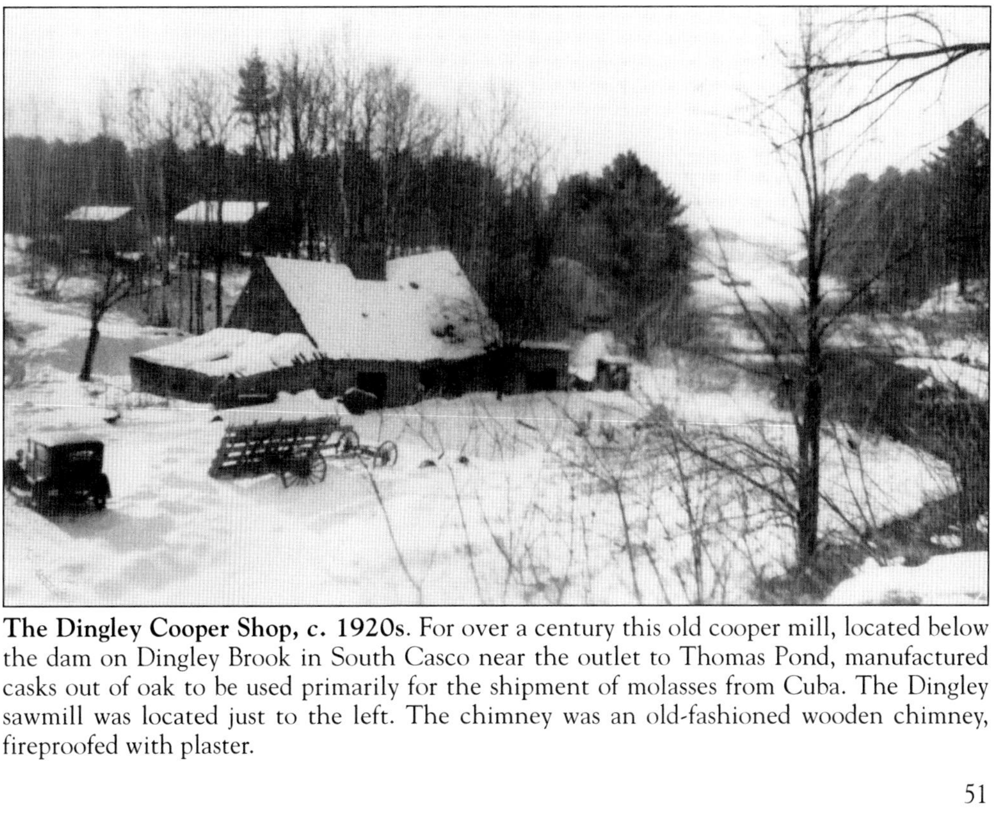

The Dingley Cooper Shop, c. 1920s. For over a century this old cooper mill, located below the dam on Dingley Brook in South Casco near the outlet to Thomas Pond, manufactured casks out of oak to be used primarily for the shipment of molasses from Cuba. The Dingley sawmill was located just to the left. The chimney was an old-fashioned wooden chimney, fireproofed with plaster.

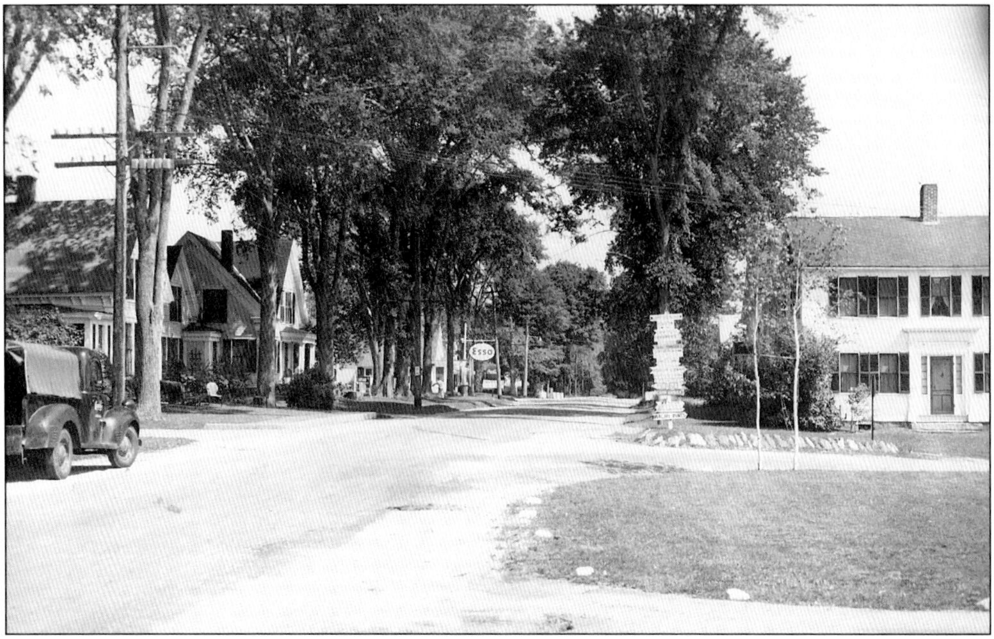

Casco Village, c. 1940. Casco Village has always been an attractive and in many ways a self-sustaining community that has resisted commercial development, even though it is located at the foot of Pleasant Lake and the head of Parker Pond. The village is the civic center of the town of Casco. The road to the right of the Gay House, heading down to the Causeway, is the Mayberry Hill Road, which earlier was called the Post Road.

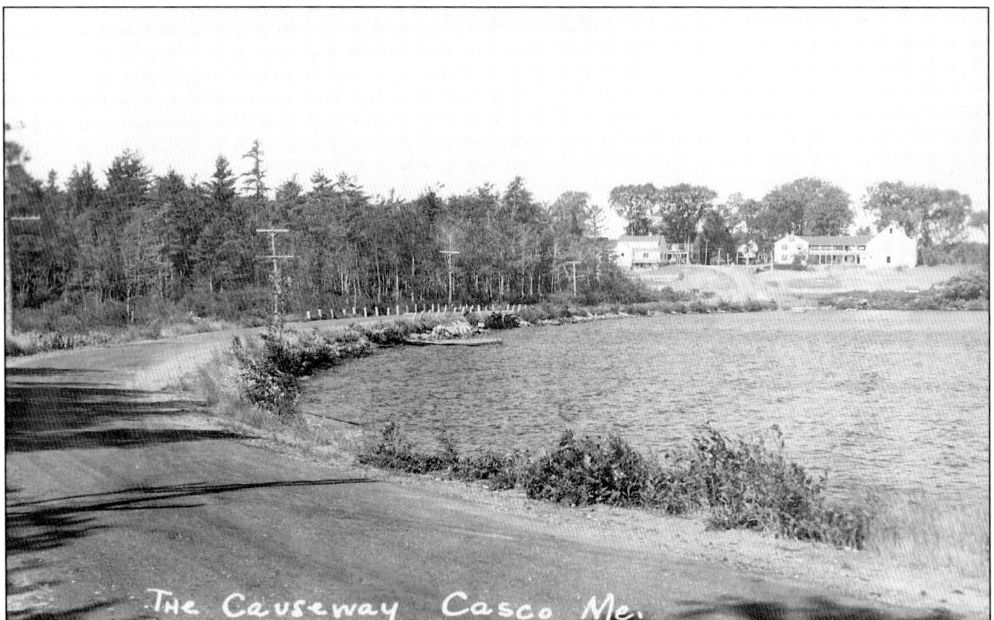

The Causeway, c. 1930. The Causeway, located on the Mayberry Hill Road, separates Pleasant Lake (visible on the right) from Parker Pond (to the left). The large house to the right in Casco Village was built by Colonel Levi Holden and later lived in by the families of Richard Gay and Lyman Holden, who married identical twins—Mary and Martha Brackett.

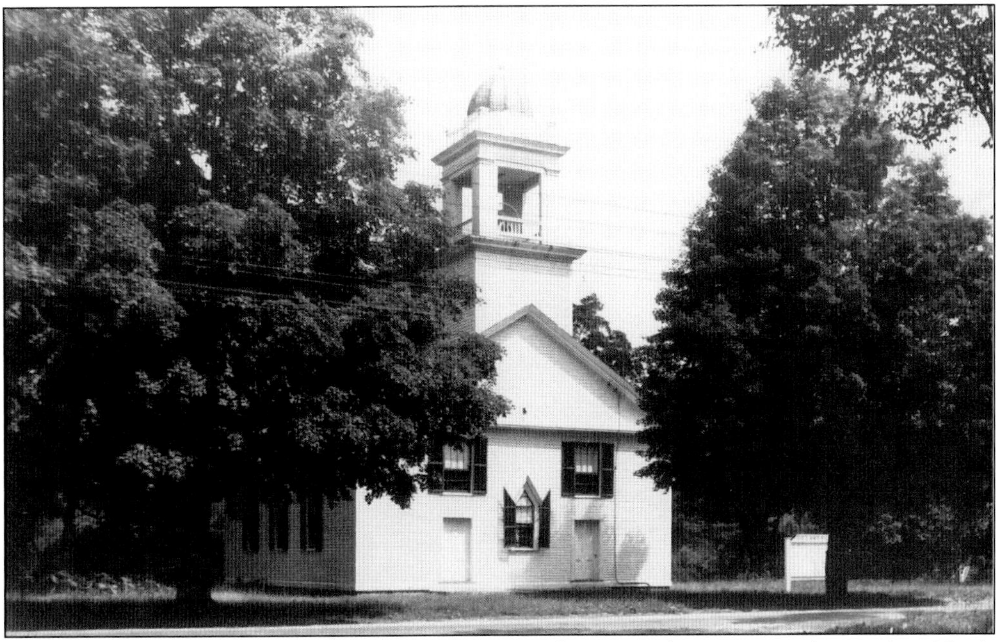

The Casco Village Church, c. 1945. Ever since architect Nathan Nutting designed and built this lovely little church in Casco Village in 1841, the same year Casco became a separate town from Raymond, it has been an important center for social and religious activities in the area. Originally it was called the Union Church, because it was built by the Congregationalists, Free Baptists, and very possibly the Adventists. Four ministers, each of a different denomination, participated in the dedication services.

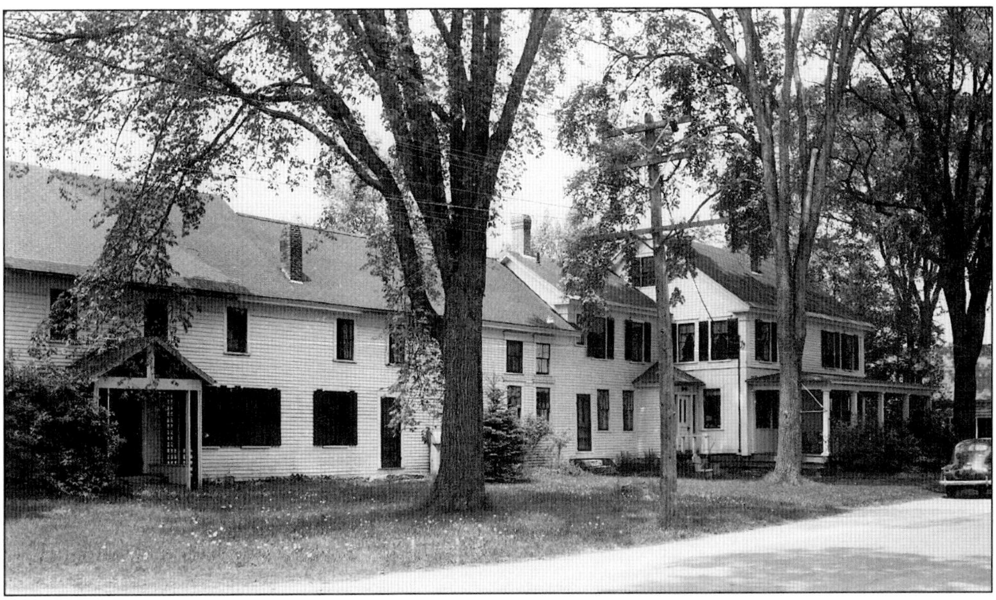

The Casco Inn, c. early 1940s. Once the Mayberry Stock Farm, this familiar landmark in Casco Village near Pleasant Lake was converted to an inn and accommodated vacationers and transients for many years before becoming a residential care facility.

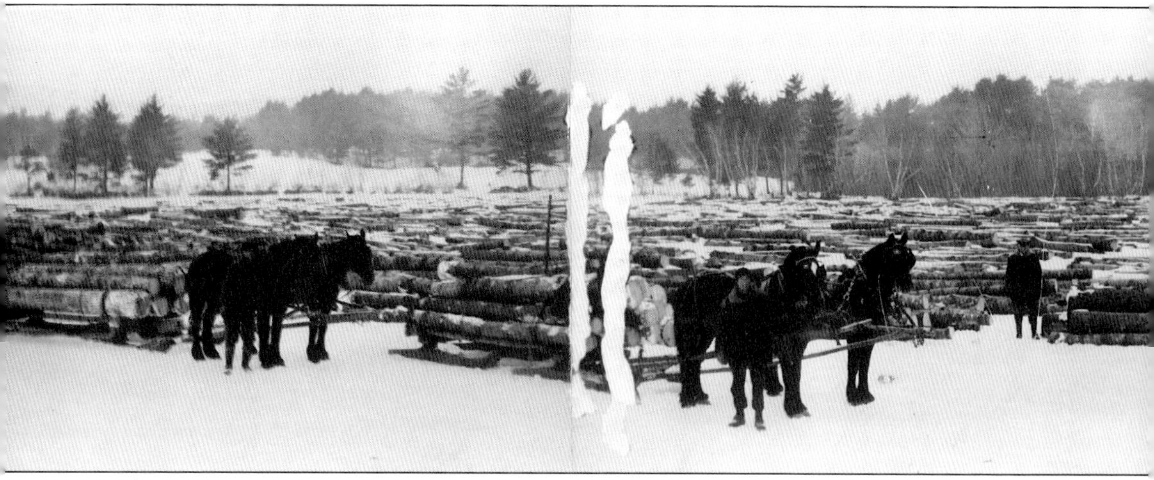

Yarding Logs on Crescent Lake, c. 1925. Until perhaps a little over a half century ago, Crescent Lake bristled with activity from early winter on as teamsters—many of them local farmers—yarded logs out on the thick ice. Usually by late March or early April the ice would have melted; and as soon as Sebago Lake was free of its icy fetters, the logs were sluiced down Tanney River into Panther Pond and then down Panther Run (Jordan River) into Jordan Bay.

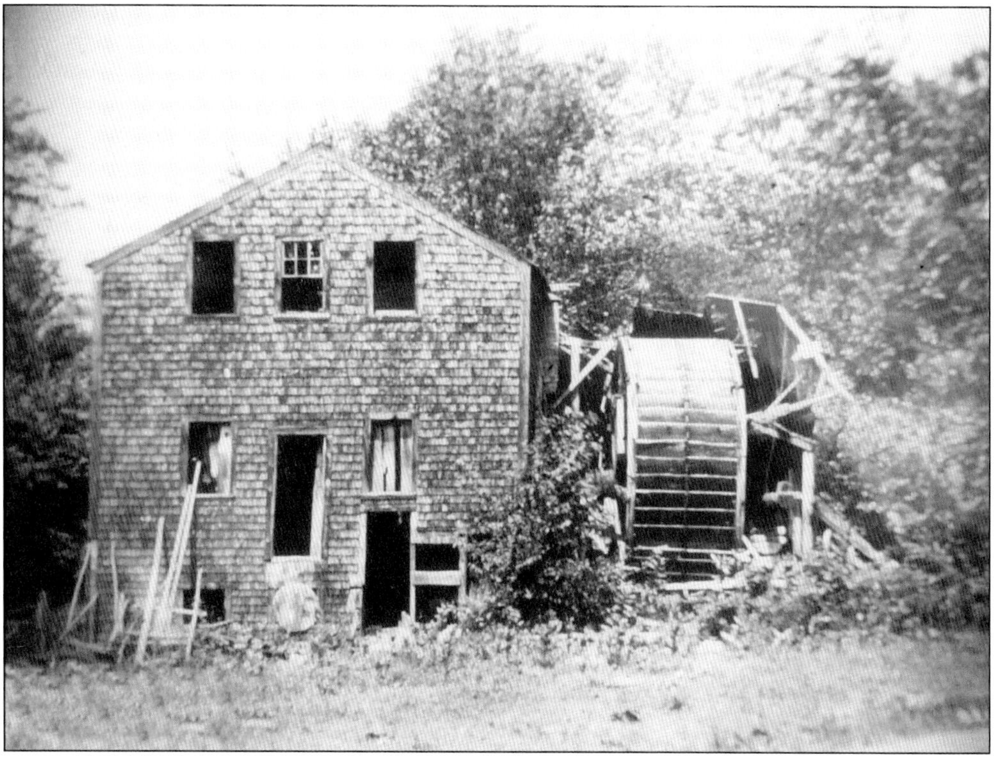

The Hog Meadow Sawmill, c. 1900. The Hog Meadow Sawmill, built in 1856 and featuring an overshot wheel that powered a circular saw, was located at the head of Great Rattlesnake Pond (Crescent Lake) near Webb's Mills in Casco—a wet area once inhabited by an abundance of wild hogs. It was originally built to manufacture shooks, shingles, and axe handles.

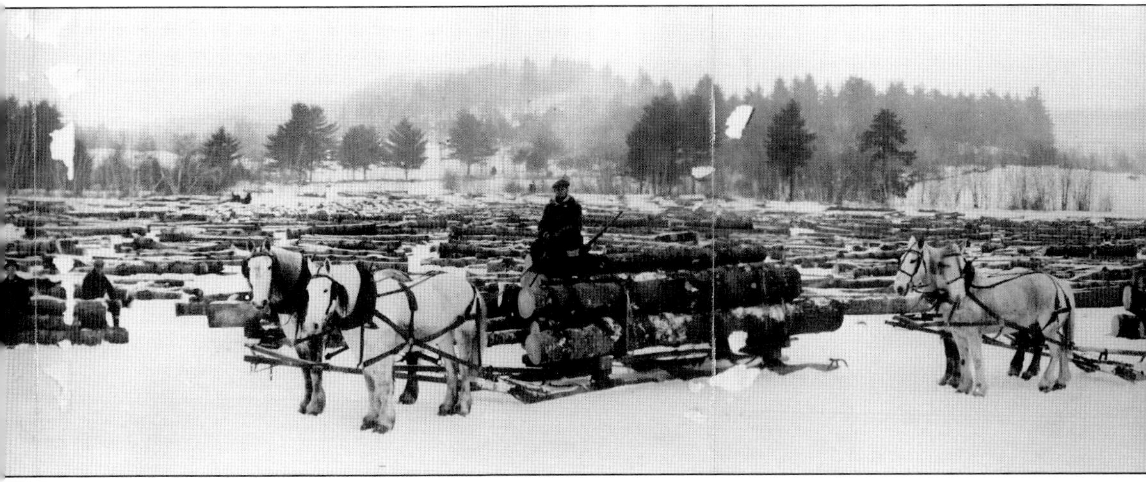

The rafts of logs were then contained by log booms and either moved across Sebago Lake by a capstan-powered headworks, or moved by steamboat to the Sebago Lake Basin at White's Bridge in Windham and then floated down to sawmills along the Presumpscot River. Until the sawmill operated by Plummer & Davis burned in 1890, most of these logs would have gone no further than the dam at Mill Street in Raymond Village.

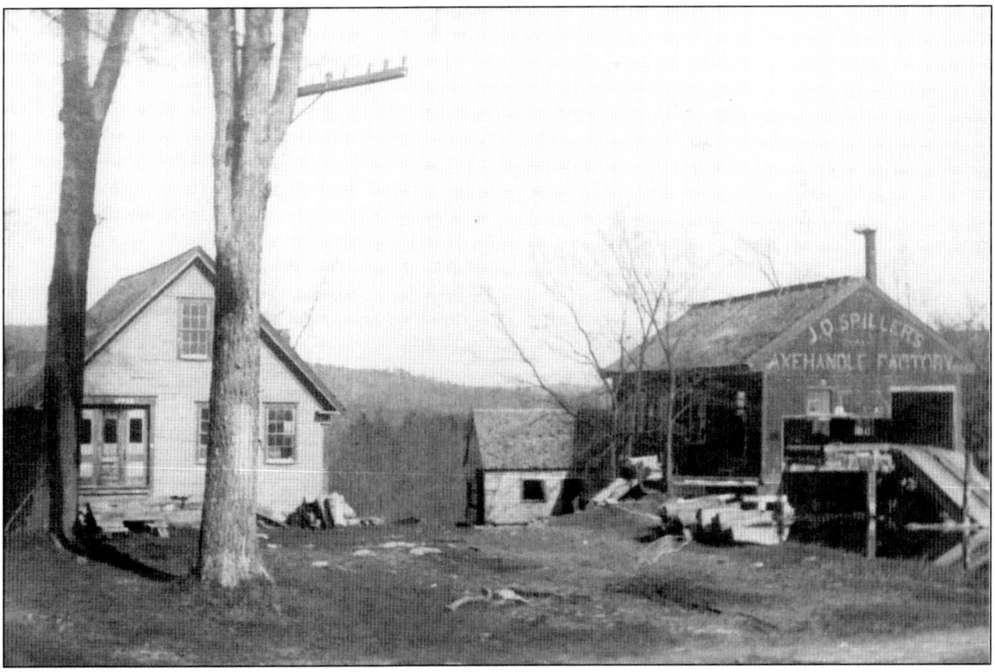

J.D. Spillers Axe Handle Factory, c. 1916. Until the invention of the power saw, the axe was an indispensable tool, especially in rural households and logging operations. Since wooden axe handles were easily broken, establishments such as Spiller's Axe Handle Factory in Webb's Mills (Crescent Lake) once did a thriving business. Logs were rolled up the ramp and sawed into blanks before being shaped into handles.

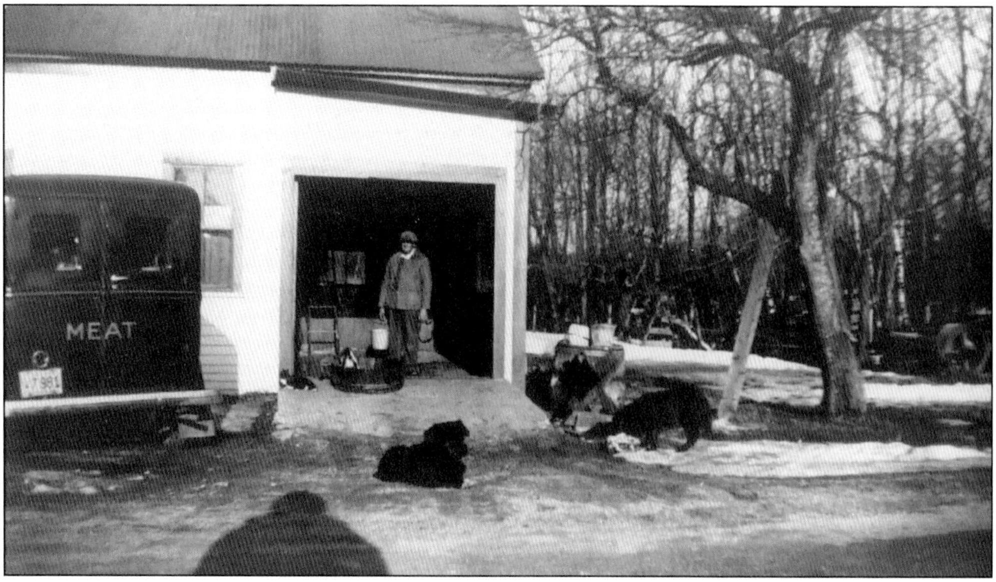

The Local Butcher, c. 1939. Before the days of super markets, it was a common practice for local peddlers such as the meat man to make weekly door-to-door calls and deliveries. Arthur Perris of Pike's Corner in Casco operated his butcher shop at his home and made his deliveries in his panel truck. Earlier, of course, deliveries were made by horse-drawn wagons.

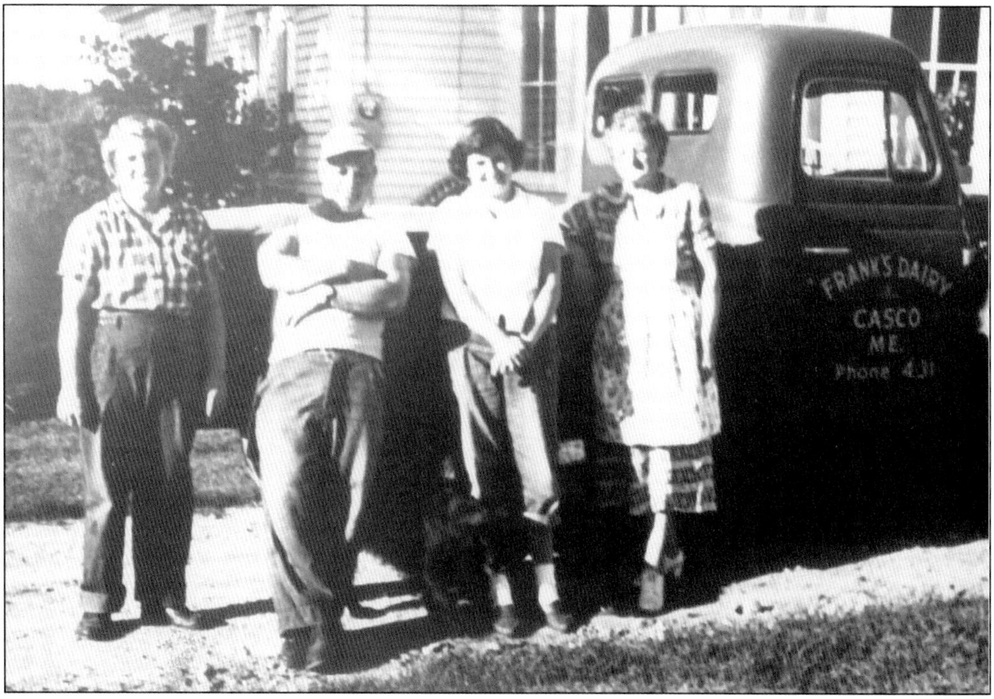

Frank's Dairy, c. 1950. Frank's Dairy over on Quaker Ridge in Casco was typical of the small family-operated dairies throughout the Sebago Lake region that provided local residents with fresh milk, cream, and often butter and eggs on a daily basis. With the arrival of the summer people, business would increase considerably. From left to right are Anita, Richard, Barbara, and Mrs. Frank.

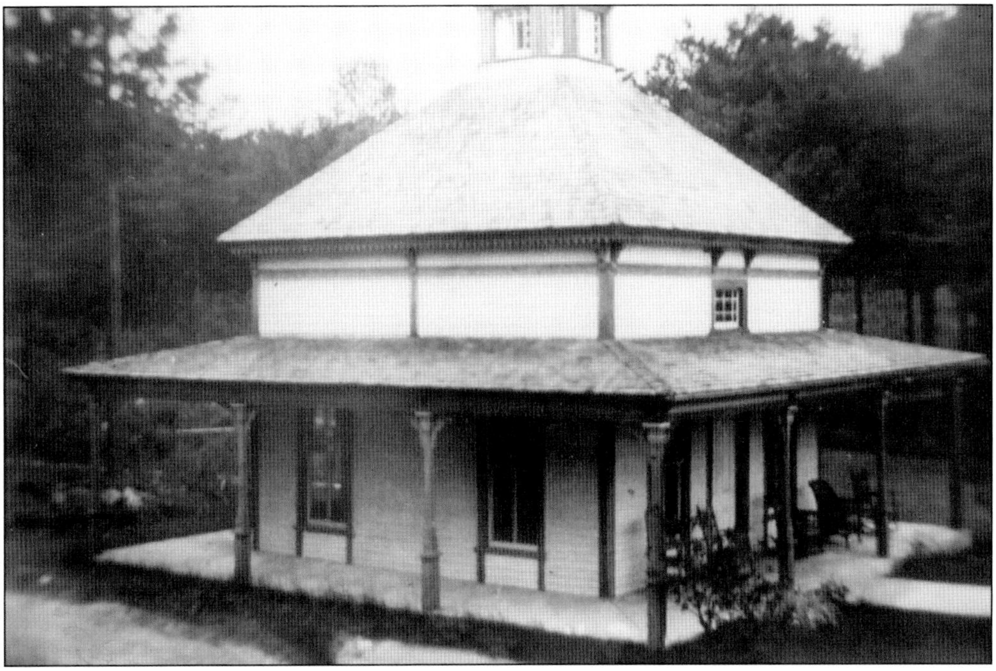

The Wilson Spring House, c. 1885. In an effort to compete with the bottling company at Poland Spring, the Wilson brothers of North Raymond operated this spring house and bottling plant. They installed the latest equipment imported from Belgium and employed mostly British workers to bottle pure spring water and soft drinks.

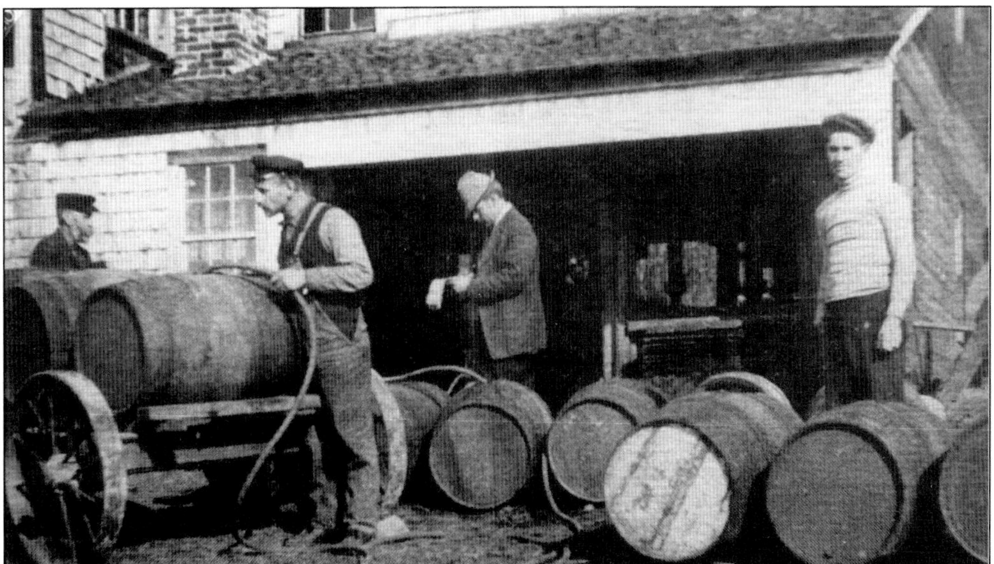

The Gould Brothers' Cider Mill, c. 1910. The glacial hill country around Sebago Lake was ideally suited to the growing of apples, and ready markets in Portland and beyond—made accessible by the building of the Cumberland & Oxford Canal—jump-started the industry. All but the choice apples were pressed into cider at small cider mills similar to this one on Quaker Ridge in Casco. Much of the cider was allowed to ferment into vinegar in casks such as these, very likely made in local cooper shops.

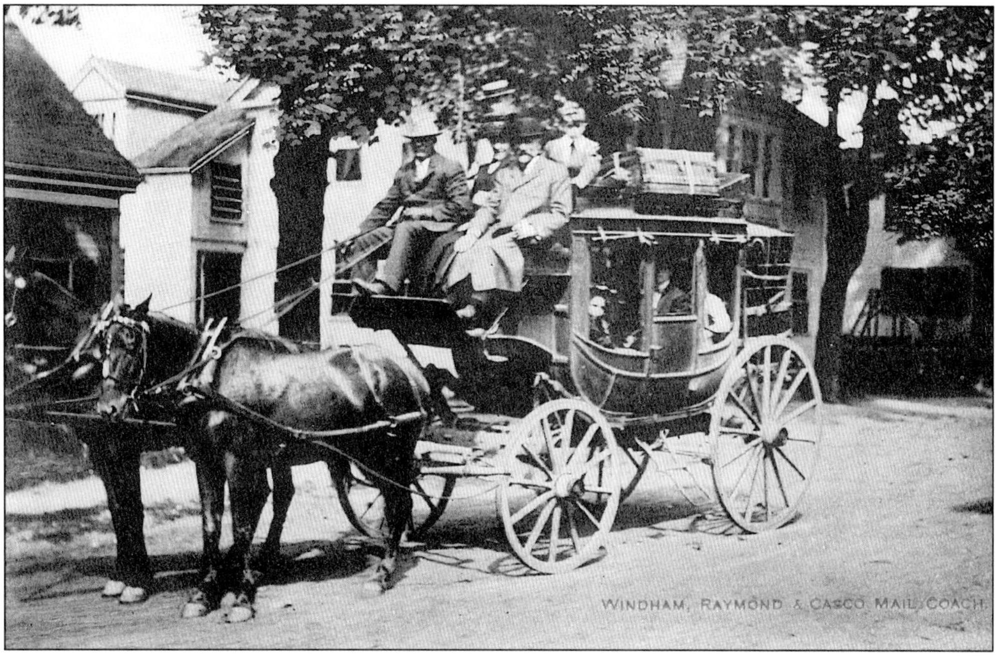

The Windham, Raymond, and Casco Mail Coach. Less than a century ago stagecoaches were still providing passenger service between Bridgton and Portland. This particular thoroughbrace Concord coach was owned by Charles and James Murch, who lived at the Dingley homestead in South Casco. South Windham became the terminus for their run around 1900 when the "electric car" linked South Windham with Portland.

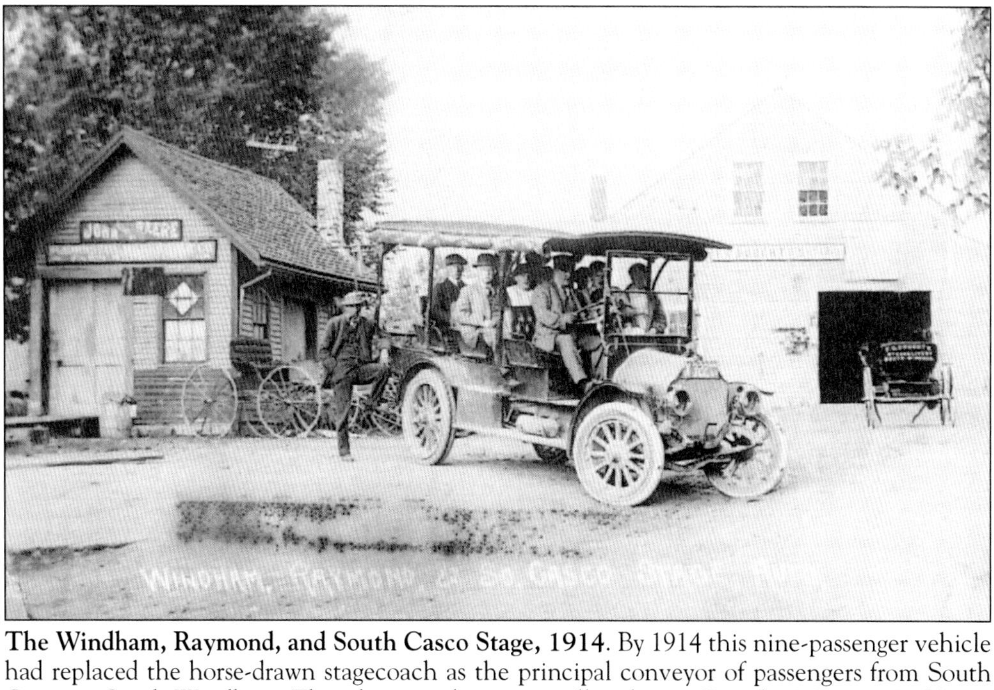

The Windham, Raymond, and South Casco Stage, 1914. By 1914 this nine-passenger vehicle had replaced the horse-drawn stagecoach as the principal conveyor of passengers from South Casco to South Windham. This photograph was actually taken at Doughty's Livery Stable on the Gorham side of the Presumpscot River at Little Falls.

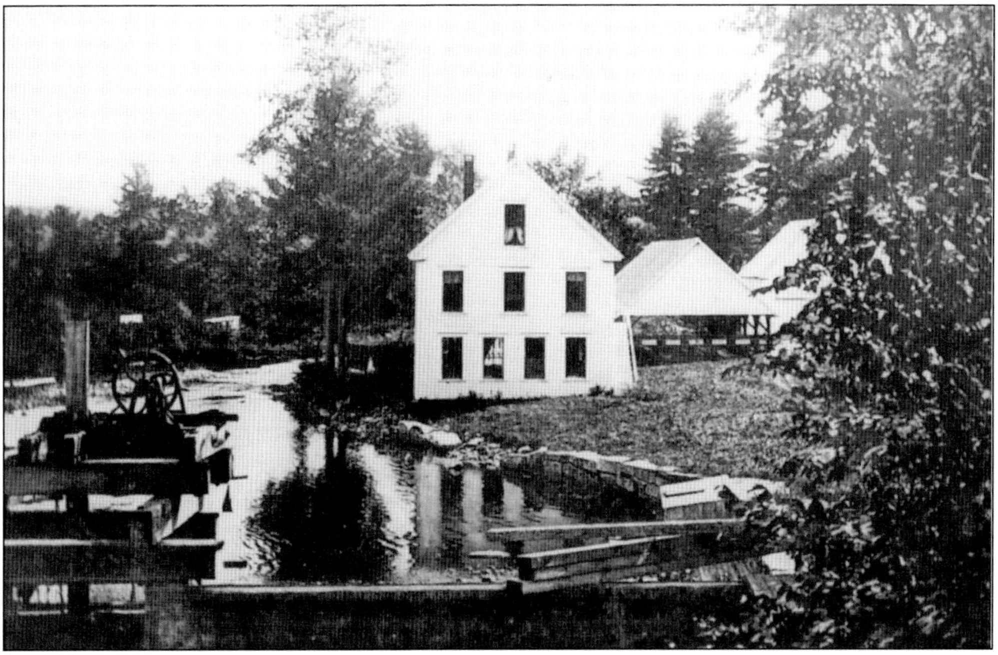

Maine State Fish Hatchery No. 1, c. 1903. The Maine State Fish Hatchery, shown here shortly after it was erected in 1901, was for over fifty years a prominent landmark on the Panther (Jordan) River near Raymond Village. Salmon weighing up to 35 or 40 pounds once migrated to this spot to spawn. Here the salmon were stripped of their eggs and milt, the eggs fertilized artificially, and the young salmon kept in rearing pens until they were big enough to be liberated. The hatchery was moved to Casco in the 1950s, and now only the stripping operation is carried on here.

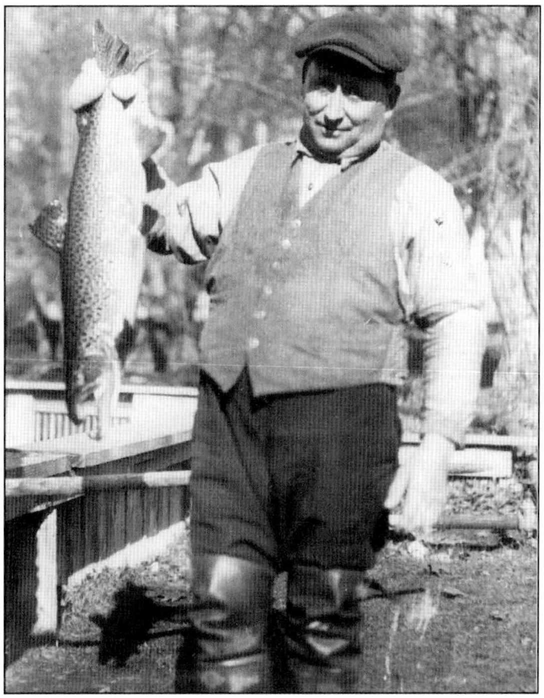

George Libby Holds Up a Big One, c. 1925. George Libby, who lived at the hatchery and managed it for many years, is shown here holding a large male salmon. He is wearing a mitten on his right hand primarily to prevent the coating on the salmon's scales from being damaged. It is claimed that the famous landlocked salmon is native to Maine and that Sebago Lake is one of only four bodies of water in the state where this species, often referred to as Salmo Sebago, originally inhabited. The term "landlocked" is really a misnomer, since there was nothing to prevent these large salmon from returning to the ocean.

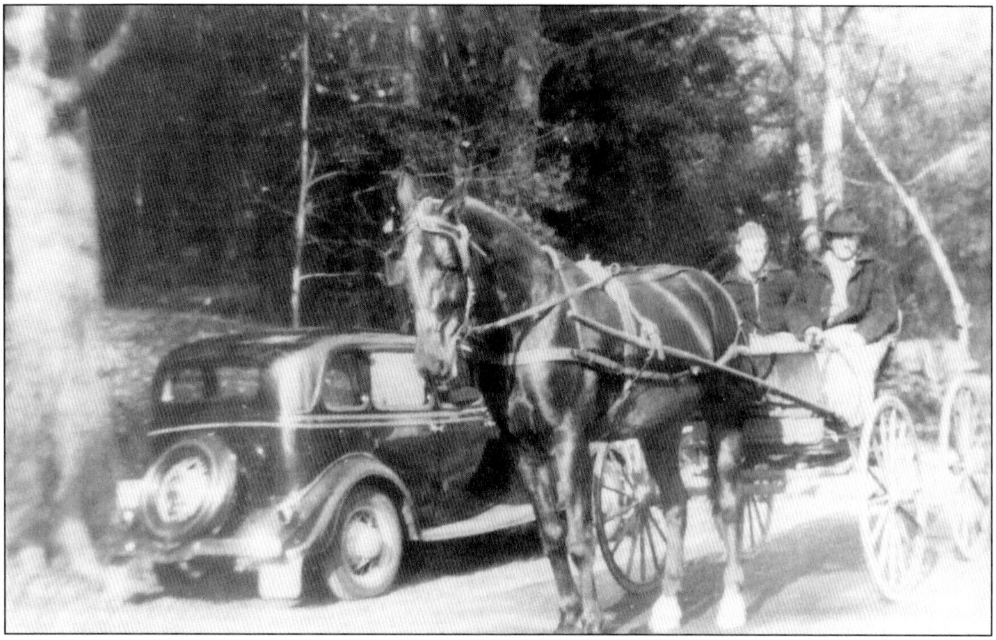

The Passing of Two Eras, c. 1934. The old and the new (a 1934 Plymouth sedan) pass each other on a country road near Pike's Corner in Casco. It was the automobile, more than any other factor by the 1930s, that brought about sudden and rapid changes to the towns around Sebago Lake and elsewhere in Maine. As the roads and highways improved, tourists began pouring into the area in amazing numbers, and more and more people from out of state and urban areas (for the most part) here in Maine began purchasing lots and building camps and cottages along the wooded shores of its many ponds and lakes.

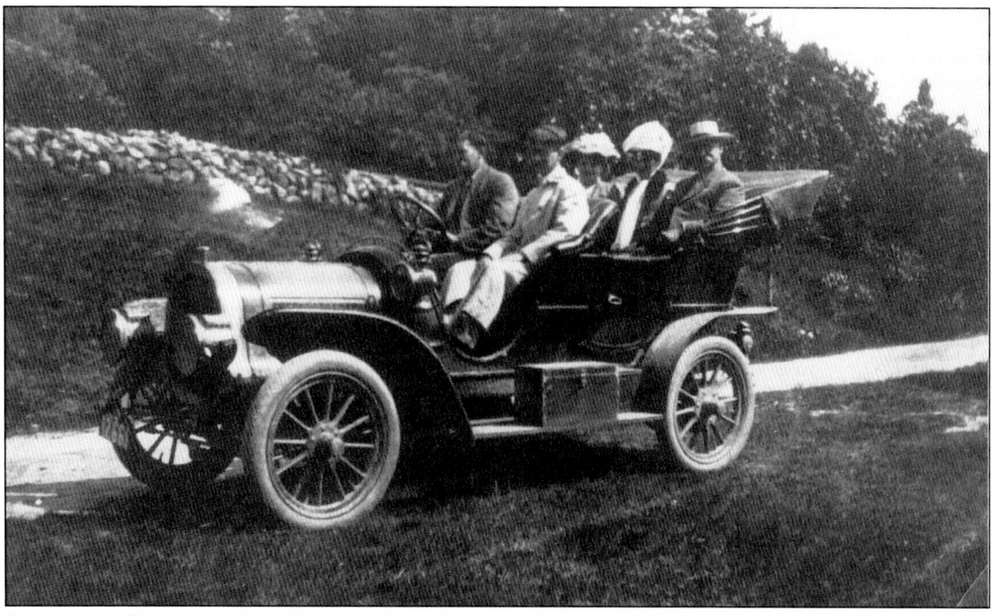

Driving to Boston, 1907. Driving from Casco to Boston in this 1907 Pope-Hartford touring car along meandering dusty roads was a long, arduous ordeal. But Irving and Angie Downing, George Dodd, and Grandma and Grandpa Hall seem to be enjoying themselves.

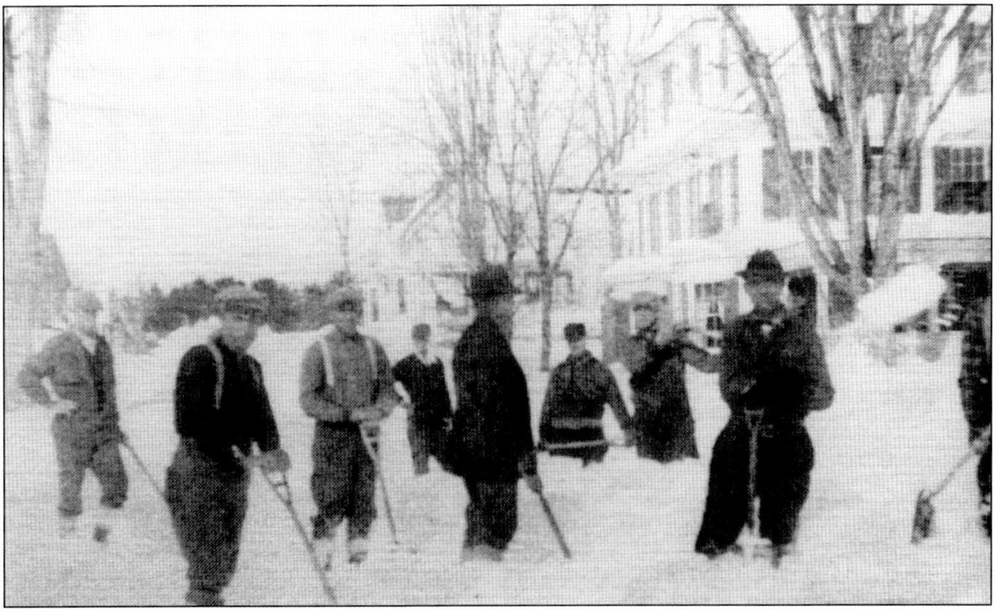

Shoveling the Road at South Casco. This scene of the men of South Casco Village clearing a snow drift from the road near the Thomas House with shovels very likely occurred in the early 1930s. Although the days of the snow rollers had ended and the town of Casco was using a V- shaped plow attached to a truck, apparently the snow had drifted too high here for the plow to penetrate.

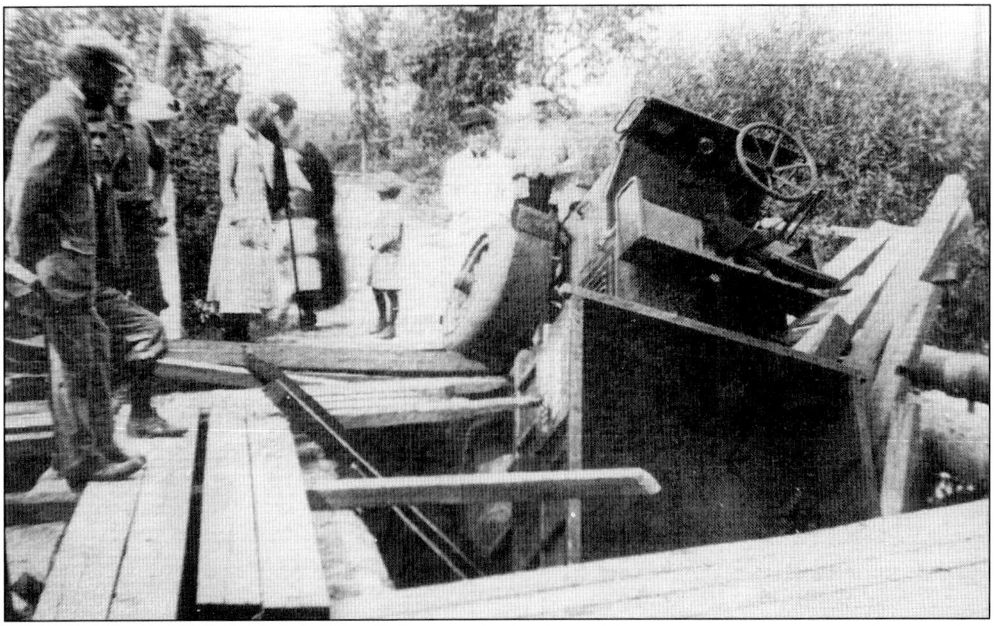

Disaster at Jordan River, c. 1915. Old wooden bridges, like this one that spanned the Jordan River at the junction of what are today Routes 302 and 85 in Raymond, could not endure the pounding they took from vehicles such as what appears to be a two-cylinder truck called an Autocar. Since the wrecker had not been introduced when this mishap took place, either oxen or horses had to be used to pull the truck up and off the collapsed bridge.

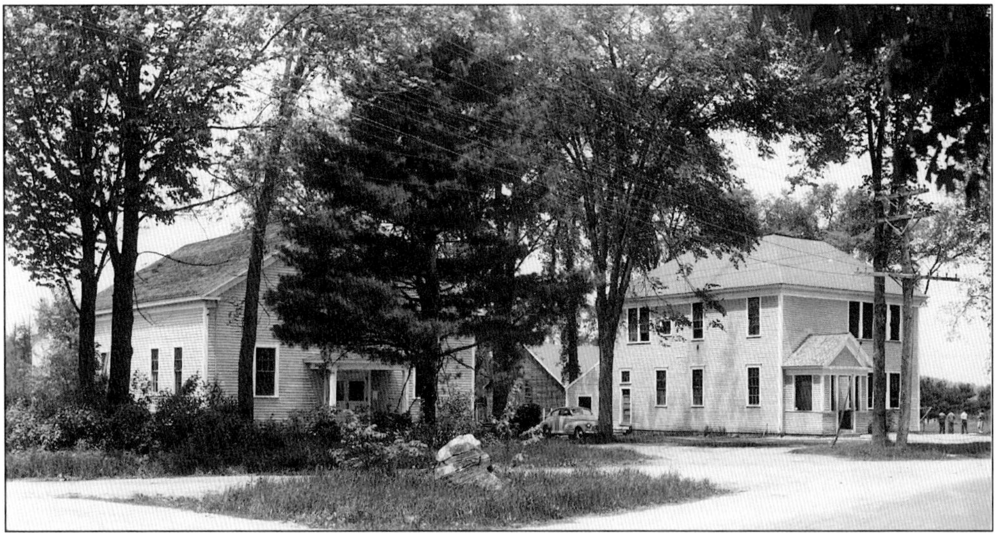

Casco High School, c. 1935. This is a view of Casco High School, which was located in Casco Village. It graduated its first class in 1916. The gym on the left was built in 1929 and made larger in 1937 and again in 1952. The town of Casco over the years has taken pride in its good schools and fine athletic programs. The high school closed in 1969 and most of the Casco's high school students now attend Lake Region High School located on Route 302 in Naples.

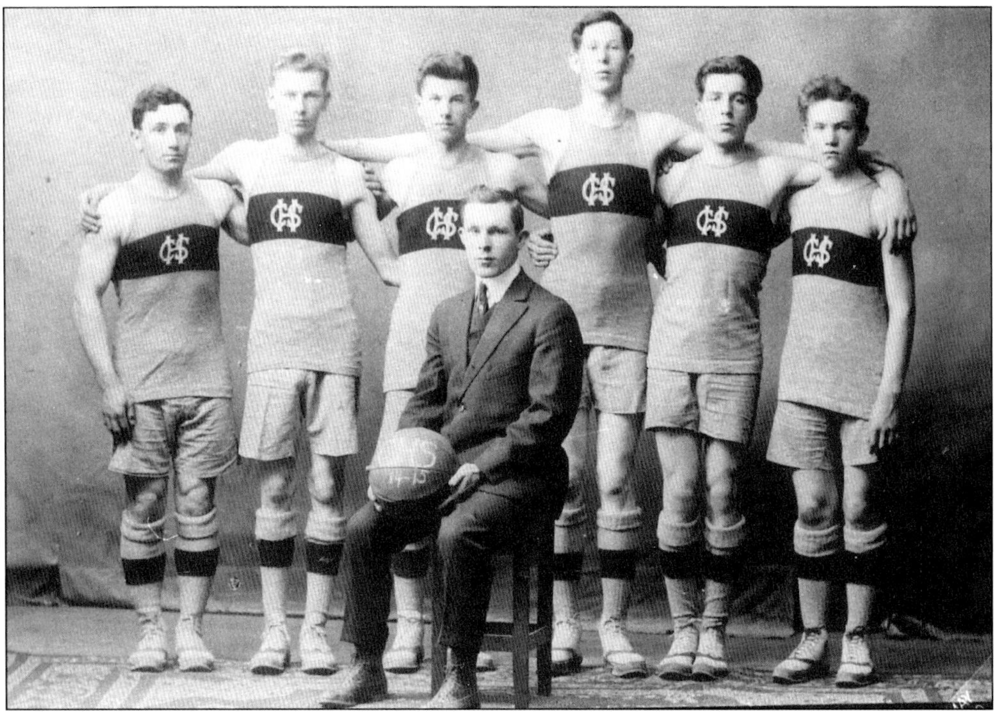

The 1914–15 Casco HS School Basketball Squad. This was one of Casco High School's earliest basketball teams. At least two of these players, Melvin Shaw and George Burgess, were members of its first squad. The Casco HS boys won the coveted Class C State Championship under the tutelage of Conrad Hall in 1964. In 1966 they were the Western Maine Class C Champions.

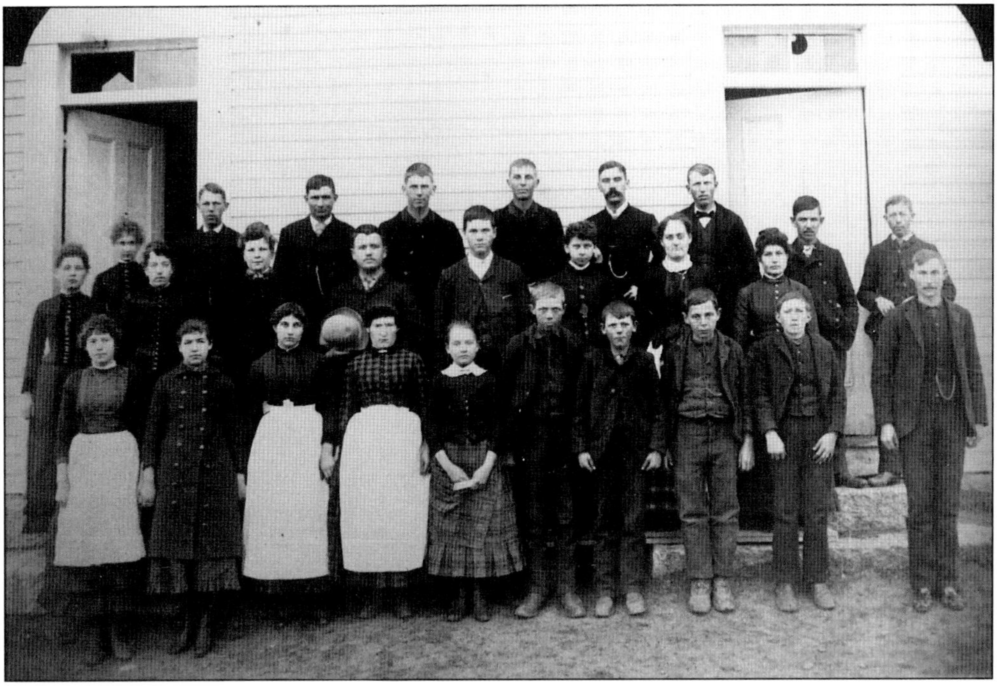

The Raymond Village School, c. 1890. A group of older children pose in front of the old Raymond Village School, which had a double entrance, presumably one for the girls and one for the boys. Although the younger children are missing from the photograph, one teacher taught all grades from sub-primary through the eighth grade. As the broken window panes above their heads indicate, the front yard was primarily the school playground.

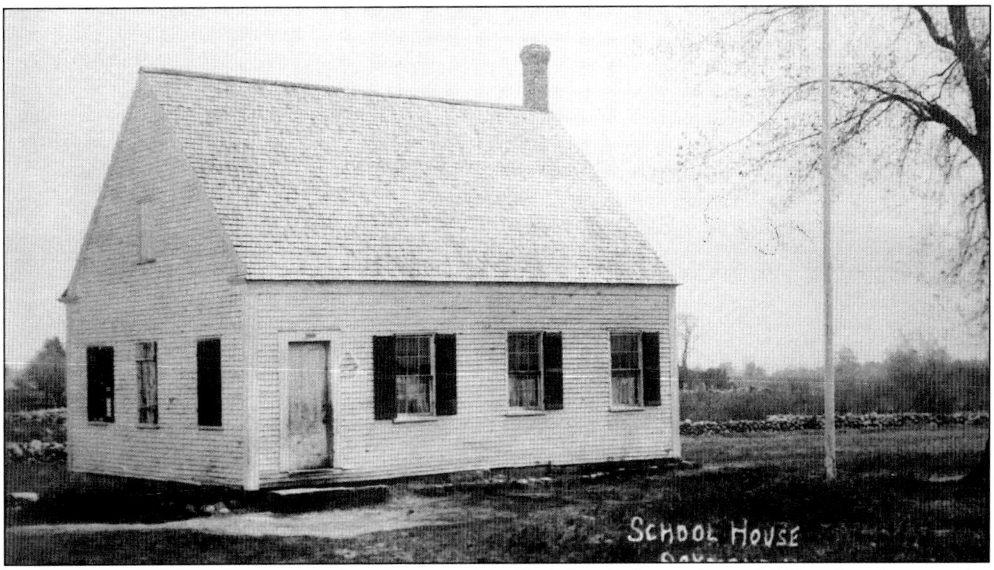

The Raymond Hill School. The Raymond Hill School, located on Valley Road near the Raymond Hill Road, was one of fourteen such schools scattered about the town of Raymond and was typical of the one-room schoolhouses found throughout rural Maine. A box-shaped cast-iron stove heated the room, and usually an older student was paid to carry water from some nearby well to fill a single water cooler, wash the blackboards, and sweep the floor.

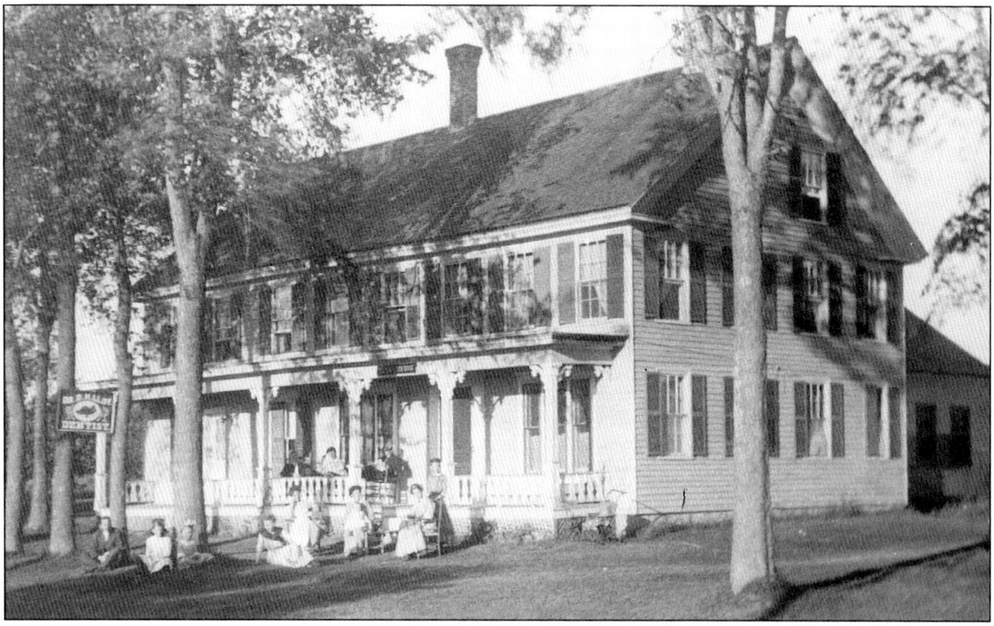

The Pleasant View House, c. 1900. Pleasant View was an excellent name for this large farmhouse, which for many years catered to summer boarders—who could sit on the porch or on the elm-shaded lawn and savor a superb view of Jordan Bay. At the time this photograph was taken, the owner was Dr. Lloy from New York. As the sign in front of the house indicates, he also had a dentist office here. The building, minus the porch, is currently a restaurant featuring French cuisine.

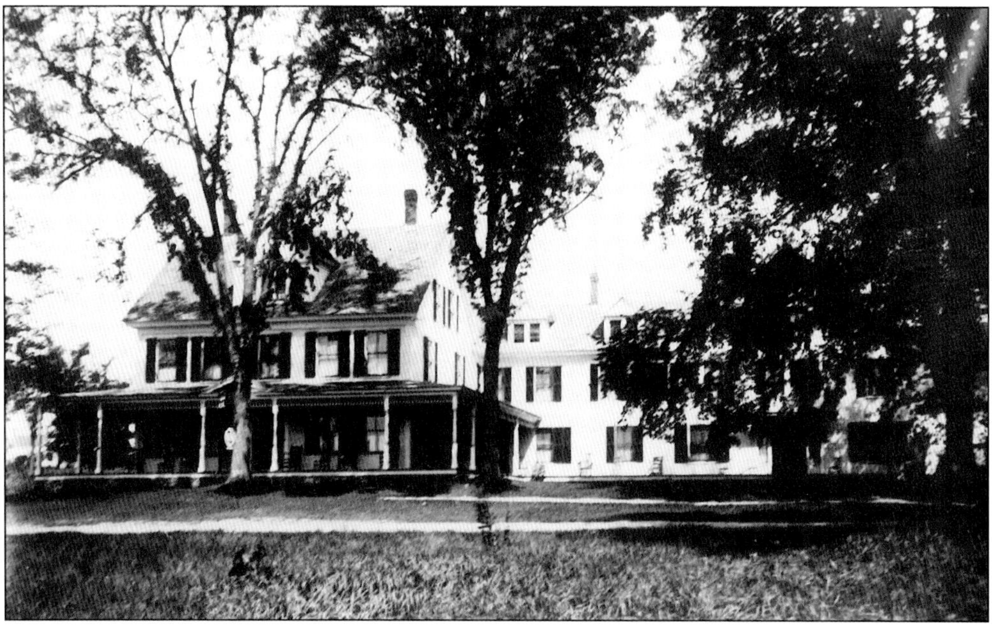

The Elm Tree Inn, c. 1900. At the time this photograph was taken, the home of Jesse Plummer (known as "Mill Jess") had been greatly enlarged and became the Elm Tree Inn—a favorite summer resort for opera singers from New York. Today this is the site of the local firehouse in Raymond Village.

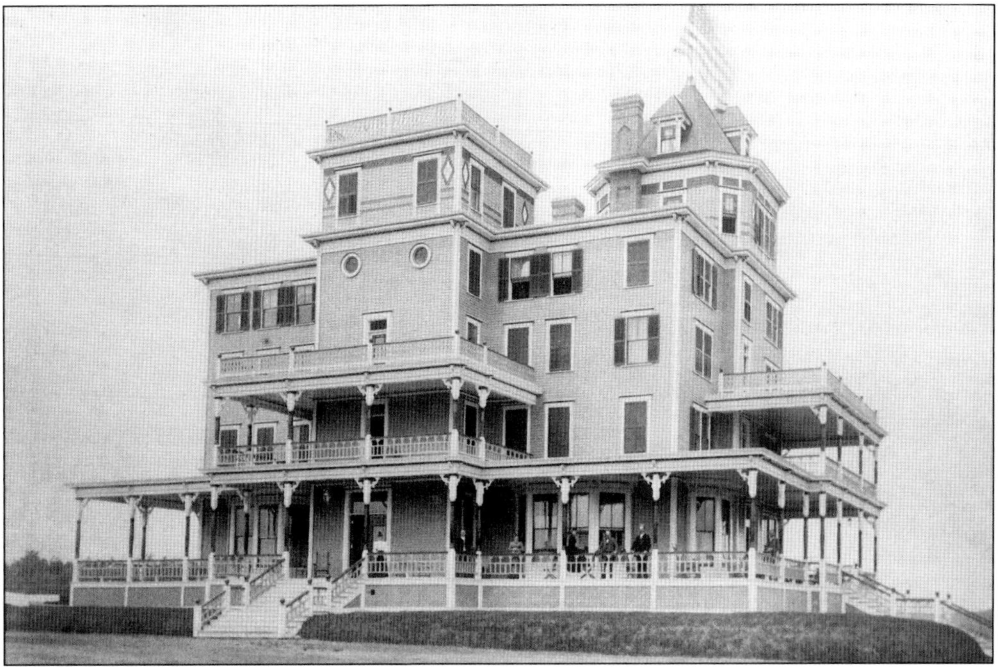

The Wilson Spring Hotel, c. 1885. The Wilson brothers, who had previously farmed this land, built this rather ostentatious Victorian hotel in North Raymond around 1880, along with the Spring House, hoping to successfully compete with the nearby Poland Spring Hotel as a year-round resort. Consequently, they included such modern features as electric bells, spring water for all purposes, steam heat, gas lights, and a tower from which the guests could view a vast, scenic panorama. Their grandiose scheme was aborted when the hotel went up in flames in 1890.

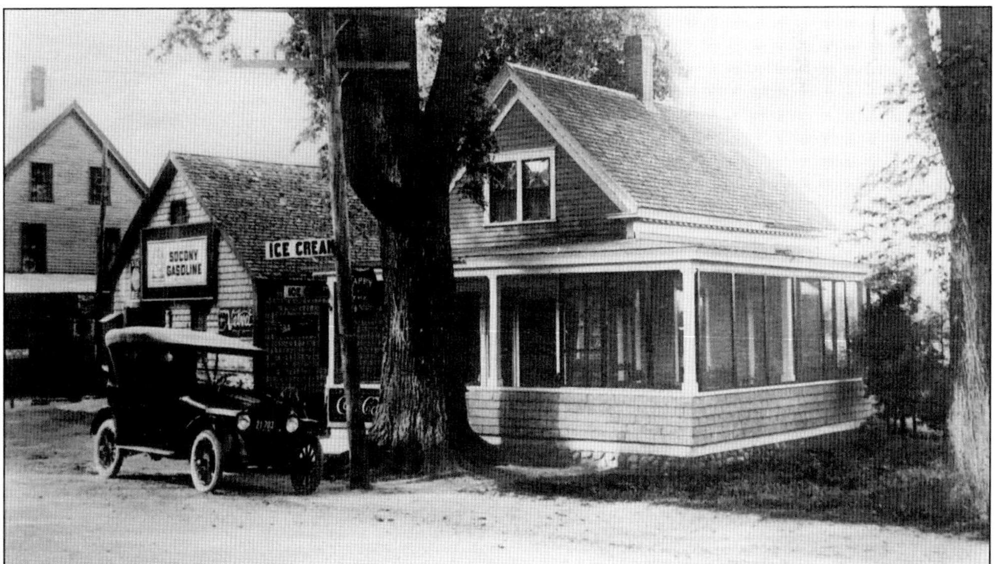

The Ice Cream Parlor, c. 1919. John Leavitt's Ice Cream Parlor in Raymond Village was a favorite meeting place for both the local citizenry and vacationers. The buildings to the left were Scott Morton's blacksmith shop and garage and Jordan's General Store.

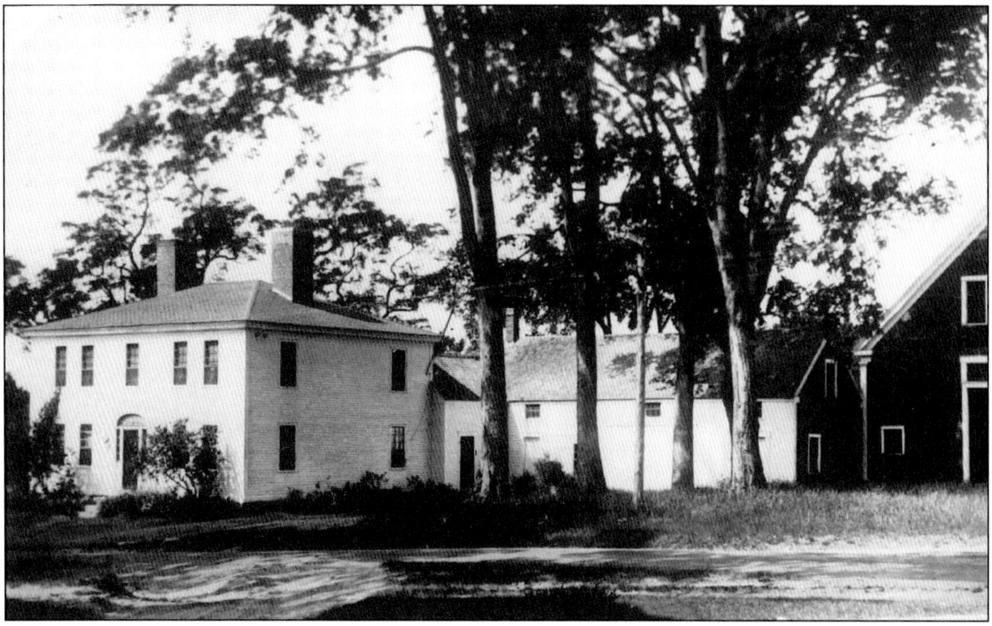

The Manning House in South Casco. John, Richard, and Robert Manning of Salem, the uncles of Nathaniel Hawthorne, inherited around 12,000 acres in Raymondtown from their father. In 1810 Richard, who married Captain Dingley's daughter Susan, built this palatial square hip-roofed house with eight massive fireplaces and imported Belgian glass windows above the sidelights.

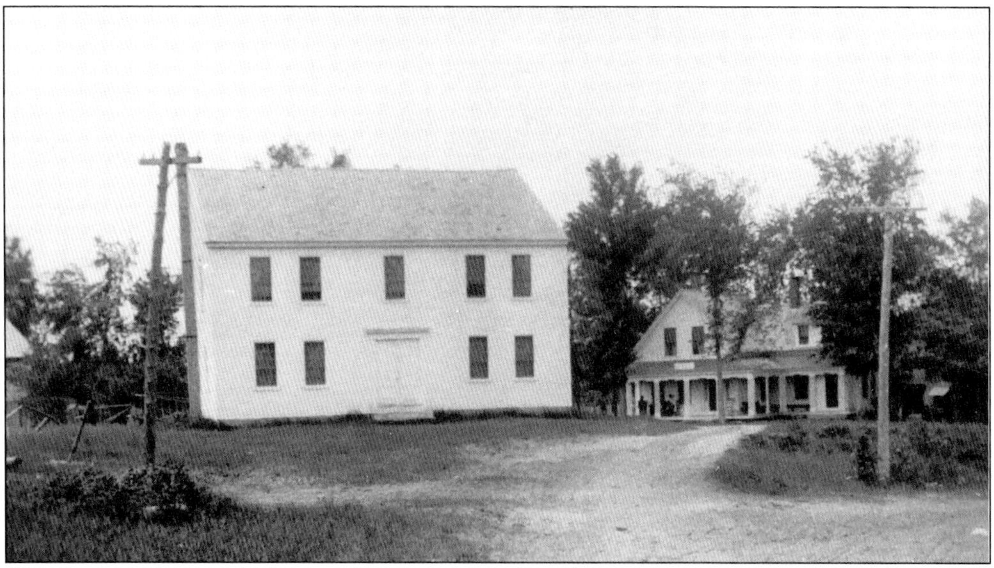

Hawthorne's Boyhood Home in Raymond. Nathaniel Hawthorne was four years old in 1808 when his father, a sea captain, died at sea. His widowed mother—Elizabeth Clark Manning—then moved with her three children (Elizabeth, Nathaniel, and Marie Louisa) to the Manning family home on Herbert Street in Salem. By 1816, Uncle Robert had become so concerned for both his sister's health and his nephew's—who had been using crutches since injuring his foot at age nine—that he shipped the four of them up to board with Richard and Susan while he had this large house built on the other side of Dingley Brook.

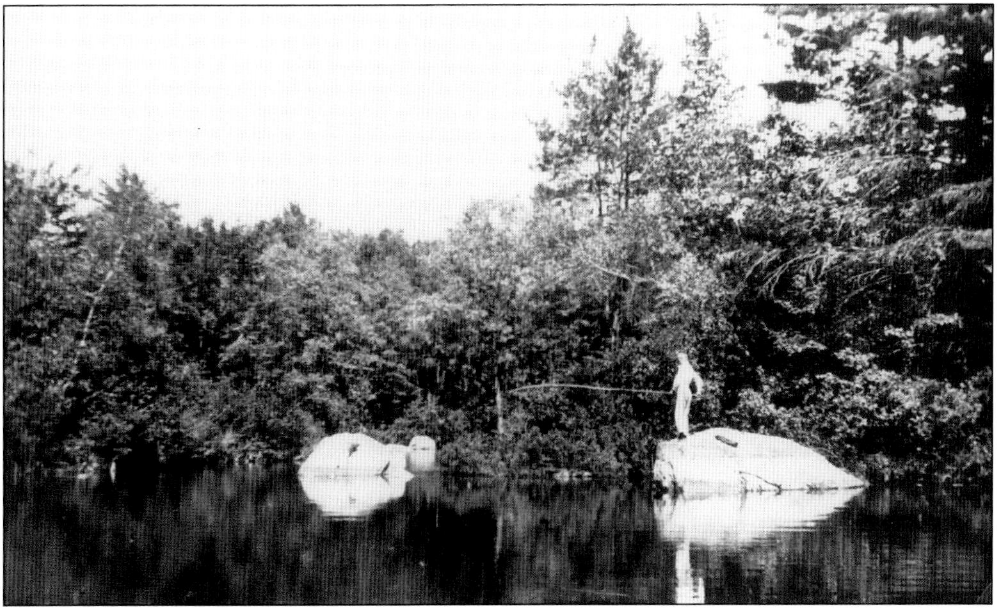

Hawthorne's Rock. Soon after young "Nat" moved to what was then a semi-wilderness, the strange miasma related to his foot injury quickly vanished. He swam and fished by the old gristmill near his house and spent hours fishing from this flat rock still bearing his name where Dingley Brook flows from Thomas Pond. Ed Maines is shown here on Nat's Rock.

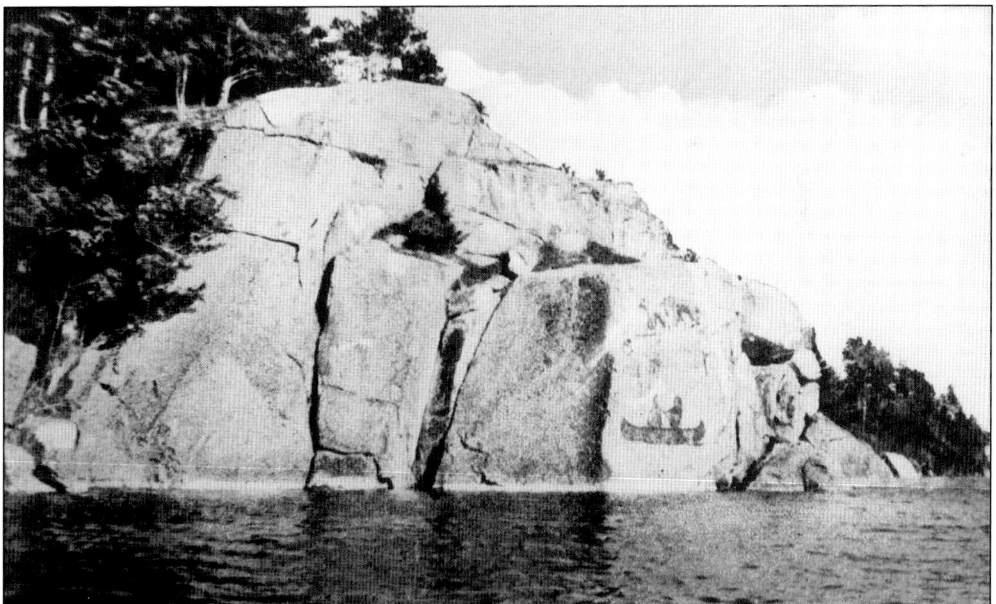

"The Images." Another one of "Nat's" favorite haunts was Frye's Leap or "The Images," opposite Frye Island at the tip of Raymond Cape. From this high vantage point, he would gaze across the opulent waters of Sebago lake to the Baldwin Hills. At other times he would descend the massive ledge to a cave (Hawthorne's Cave) below and to the left. There he would idle away the hours, absorbed in musings which seem likely to have generated characters and plots for some of the romances that would later gain him immortality in the literary world.

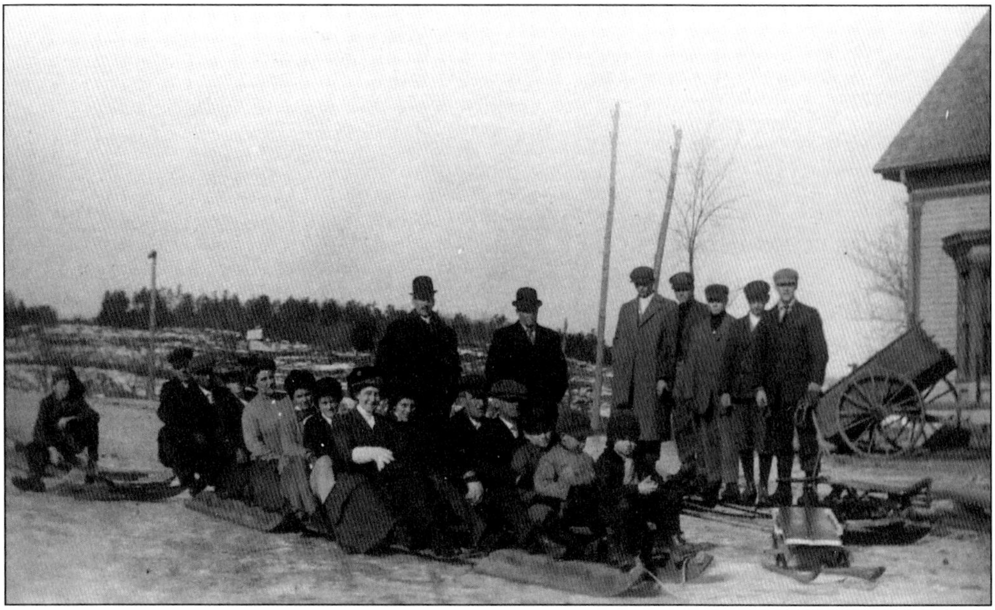

A Coasting Party in South Casco, c. 1910. It was not until the late 1920s that crawler tractors with built-in cabs and trucks began being used to plow the local roads. Consequently, both villagers and farm families lived relatively isolated and often quite lonely lives during the long hiatus from late autumn to early spring. But as long as the snow rollers were used to pack down the roads, such coasting parties as this one in South Casco were popular social events shared by families and friends of all ages.

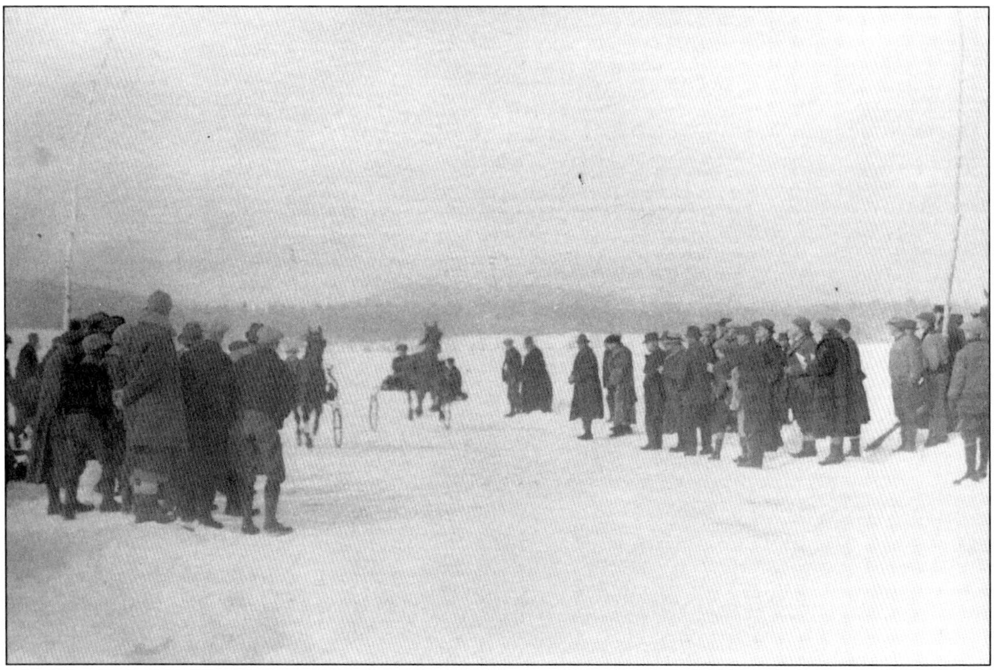

Horse Racing on Thomas Pond, c. 1910. Horse racing in winter on the frozen ponds and lakes in the Raymond-Casco area obviously was a popular winter sport that attracted a sizeable number of male spectators. These races were being held on Thomas Pond in South Casco.

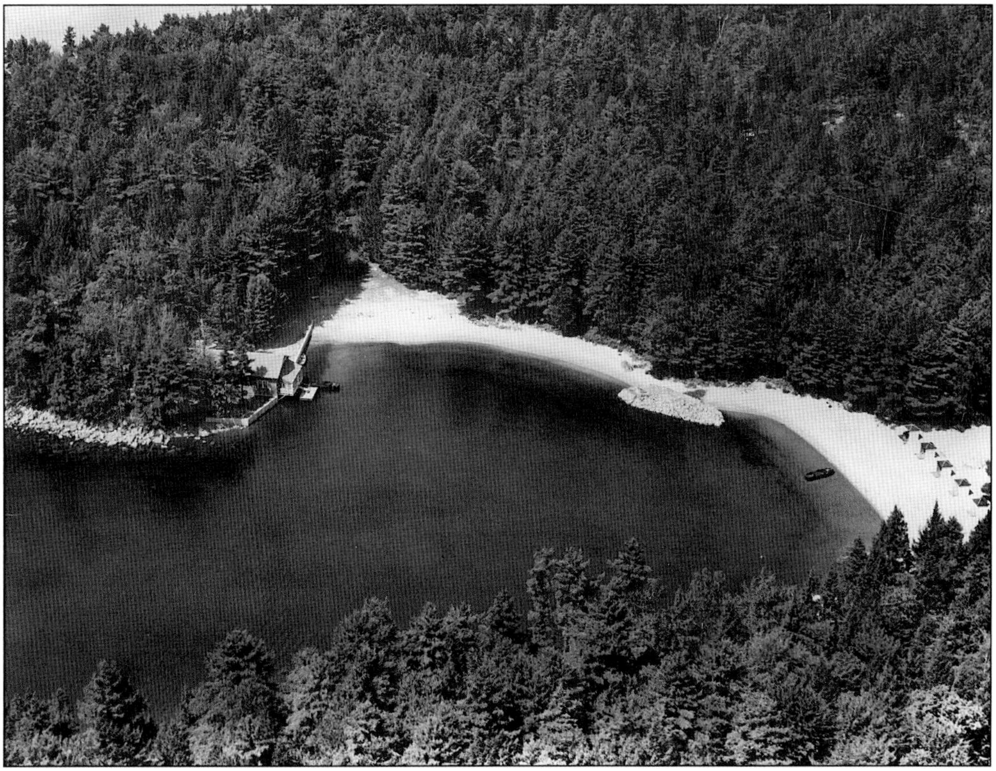

The Cabana Beach Club, c. 1938. This casino was tucked in between a dense growth of young conifers on the Raymond Cape at a point where the rocky shore in Shingle Cove gives way to a pearlescent stretch of sandy beach. It was owned and operated by Fred Gilliatt from about 1933 and featured live music and dancing. Since Gilliatt was known to be an inveterate gambler, it seems very possible that some gambling was done here also. A row of cabanas is visible along the beach to the right. Shortly after this aerial photograph was taken, the casino burned. Today a boathouse built by William Stroud sits upon the former site of the casino. Otherwise, this quiet little cove thus far has escaped the scars of development.

Located in the foreground and extending out to the lake is a portion of the 300 acres owned by The Luther Gulick Camps (Sebago Wohelo and Little Wohelo), founded in 1907 by Dr. and Mrs. Luther Halsey Gulick. For many years Dr. Gulick was director of the physical department of the International Committee of the YMCA and was the originator of the internationally-recognizable YMCA triangle. His wife Charlotte was the founder of Camp Fire Girls. The Luther Gulick Camps were just one of many boys' and girls' camps that were developed shortly after the turn of the century along the shores of Sebago and other bodies of water in the area. Many of these camps were built on large tracks of land that had been previously farmed. Boys and girls of all ages, mostly—but certainly not entirely—of middle and upper-class families from urban areas, were afforded an excellent opportunity to spend all or part of a summer enjoying a broad spectrum of outdoor as well as indoor activities including sports of all kinds, nature study, music, and arts and crafts taught by well-qualified personnel. At first, most campers slept in large tents, usually supervised by two counselors. Soon, however, more permanent cabins were constructed.

These camps provided a wholesome, family-like atmosphere for young people—many of whom returned year after year and eventually became counselors, instructors, and even directors. Camps such as Wohelo continue to maintain the high standards of their founders.

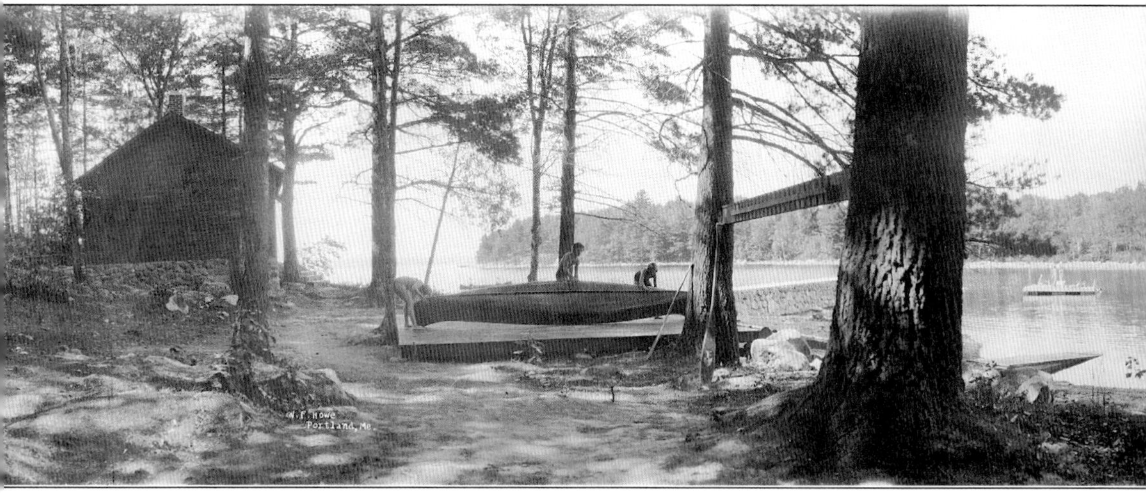

The Waterfront at Camp Wawenock, 1936. This scene of some of the cabins and the waterfront at Camp Wawenock on the Raymond Cape is a paradigm of what boys' and girls' camps are all about. Canoeing, horseback riding, and swimming are camp activities represented in this photograph. Camp Wawenock—founded in 1910 as a camp for girls from

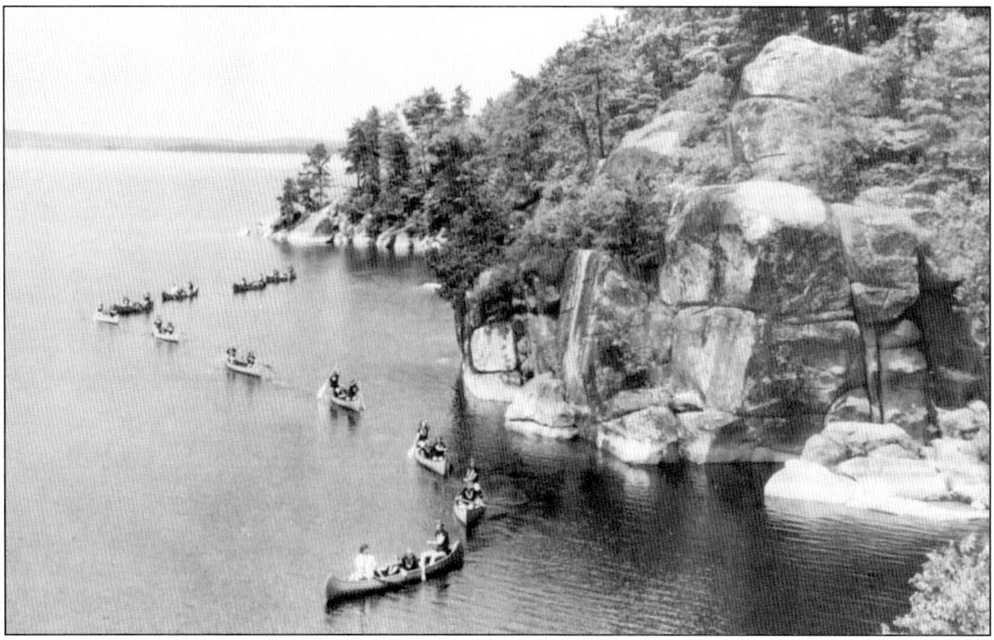

Canoeing on Sebago Lake. A group of campers and their counselors from Camp Wawenock hardly stir up a ripple as they quietly paddle by Hawthorne's Cave where The Notch separates Raymond Cape from Frye Island. These glacial megaliths were a favorite haunt of the young Hawthorne. It was here that he also came in summer to swim and to sail his boat as far as Muddy River and up the Songo and Crooked Rivers. In winter he enjoyed skating.

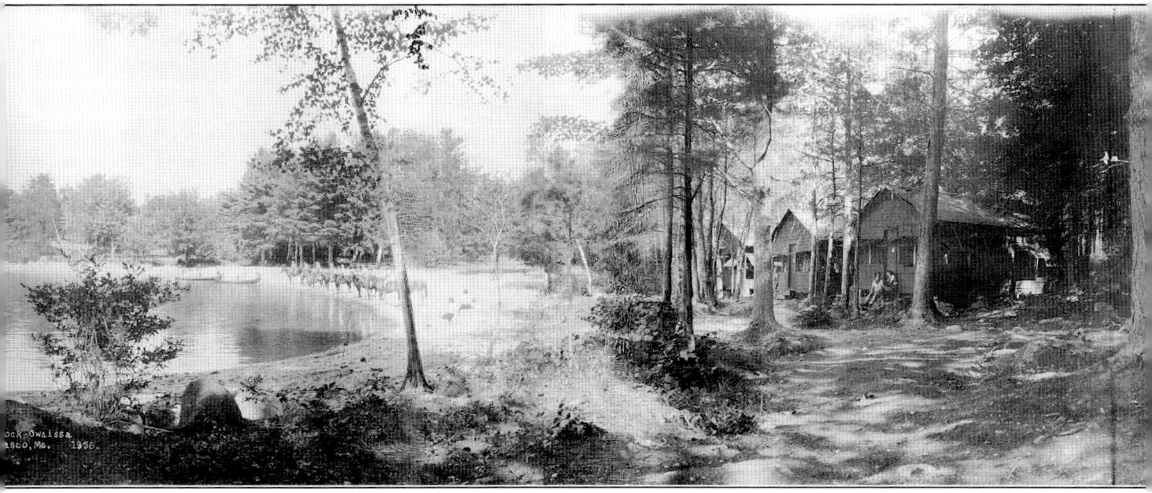

ages eight to seventeen—encompasses 75 acres of woodland and shore property on Sebago Lake, including one of the great landmarks on the lake—Frye's Leap. Today this fine camp for girls, under the directorships of June Gray and Patricia Smith, continues to operate in the spirit in which it was founded.

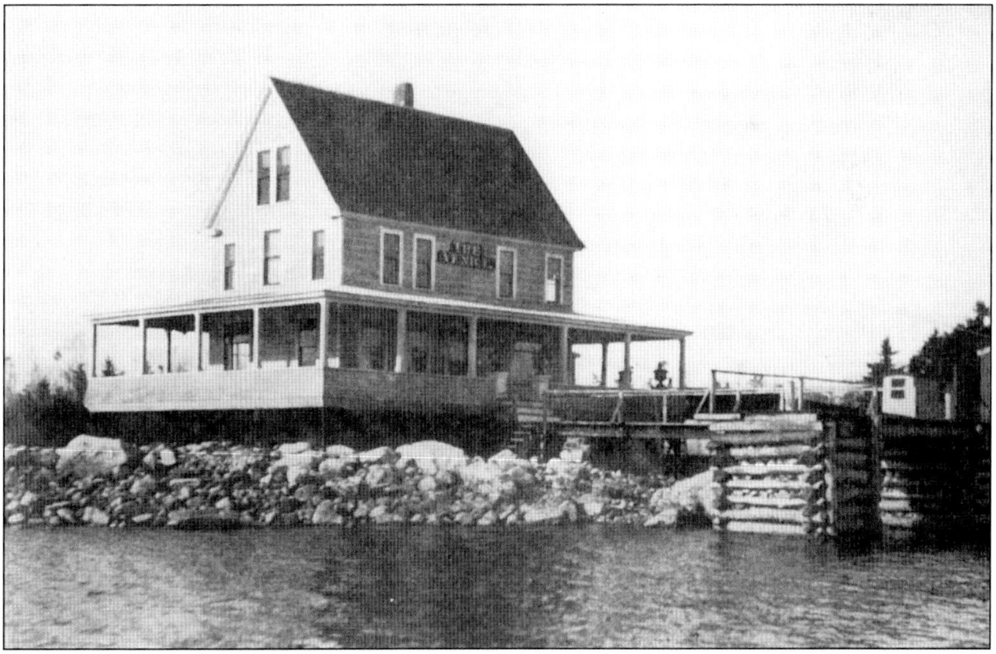

"The Venice," c. 1912. "The Venice," which until quite recently perched on a tiny rocky island in Jordan Bay, was one of two camps that comprised the Raymond Camps for Girls, founded shortly after the turn of the century near Raymond Village. The other camp was at Deep Cove. Steamboats conveyed campers and counselors on the 10-mile trip from Sebago Lake Station to the Raymond Camps.

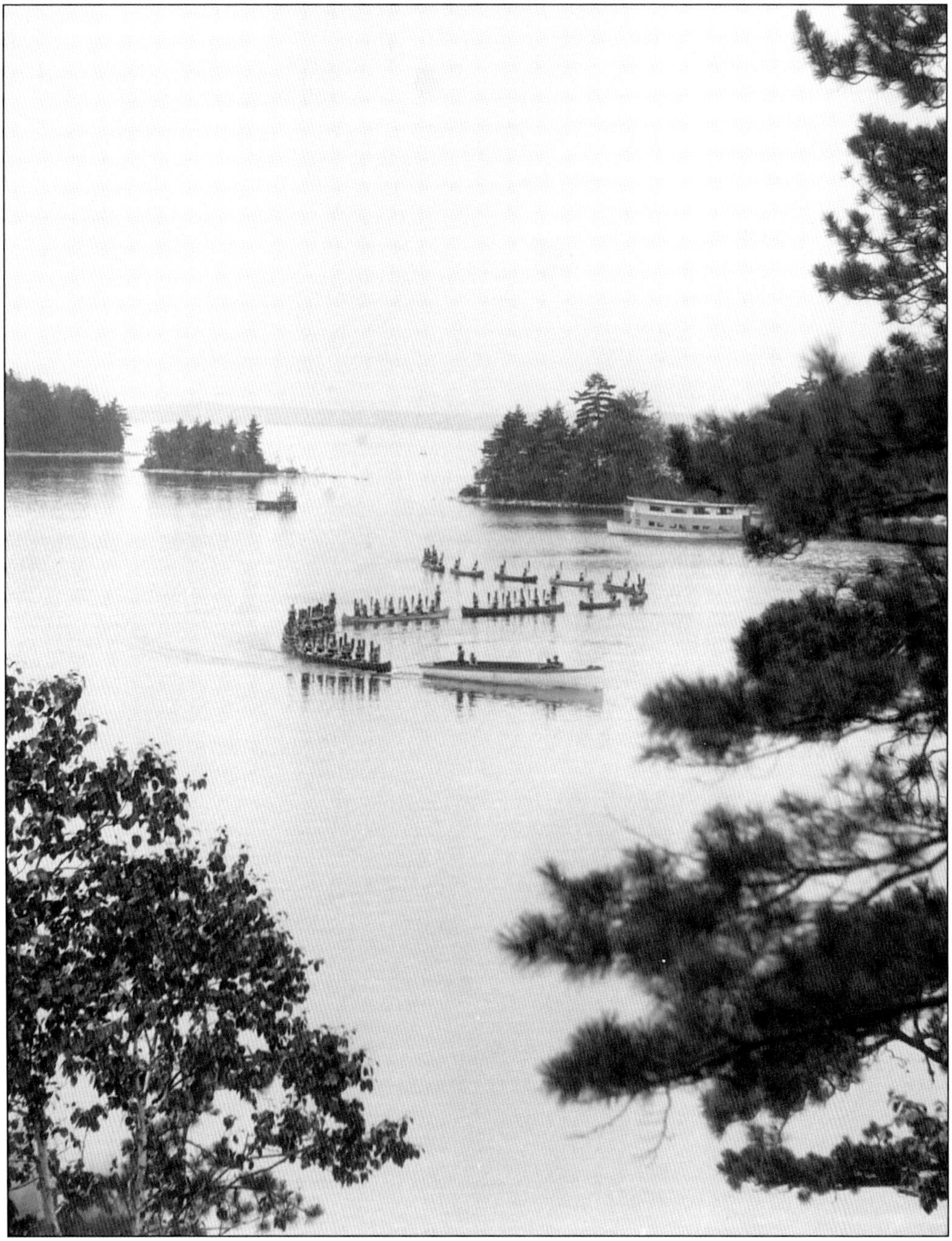

The Luther Gulick Camps, c. 1928. This scenic cove is a portion of the mile-long shore front and three small islands (Blueberry, Rookies, and Battleship) owned by The Luther Gulick Camps (Wohelo) on the Raymond Cape. The towing of camp boats and canoes, which is performed annually on Water Sports Day—held shortly before the closing of the camps at the end of summer—has been a camp tradition since the 1920s.

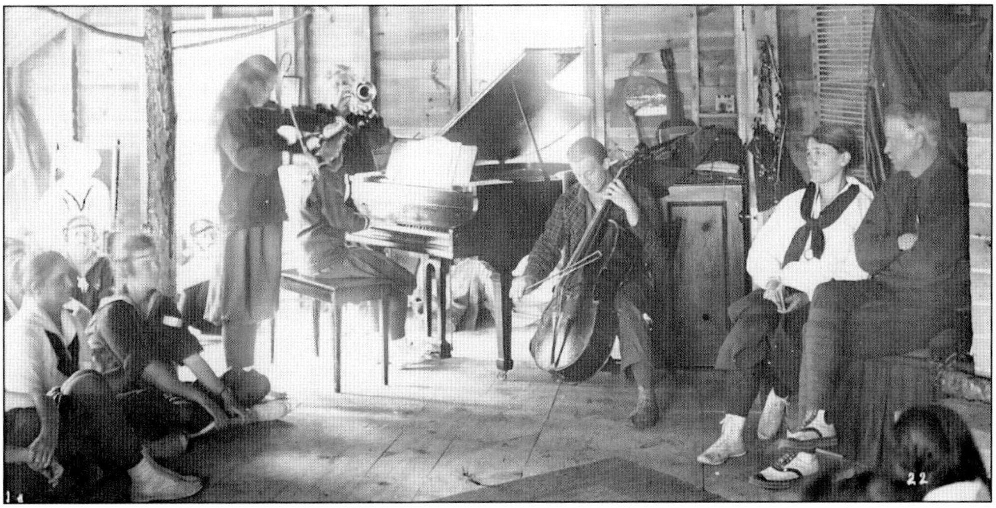

A Concert at Wohelo, c. 1916. It was a part of the tradition of Sebago-Wohelo (girls age twelve to seventeen) and Camp Timanous (the adjacent camp for boys founded by the Gulicks) to join together each morning for singing and a musical recital, followed by short talks and the raising of the flag. The founders, Dr. and Mrs. Luther Gulick, are shown here sitting to the right next to the fireplace. Their son, J. Halsey Gulick, who directed the camps from 1928 to the late 1960s, is playing the cello. The founders' granddaughter, Louise Gulick Van Winkle, and her husband Davis currently direct the camps on a year-round basis.

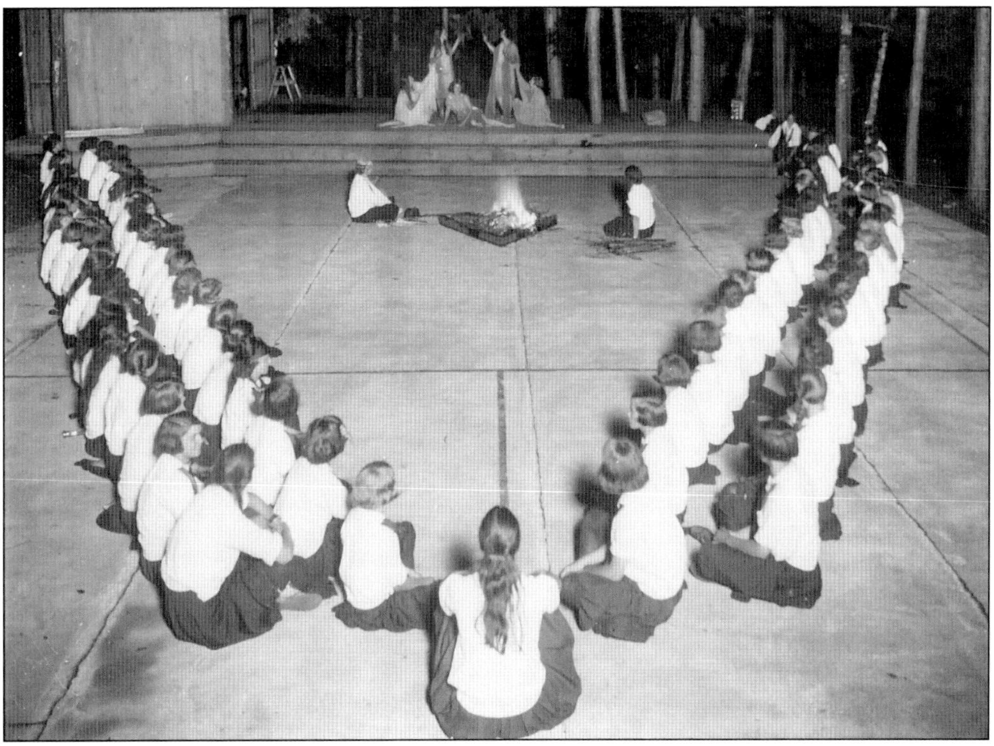

The Council Fire, 1922. The older girls at Sebago-Wohelo appear to be captivated by the annual pageant-drama being performed on stage in front of the council fire in the ambiance of tall, lithe conifers.

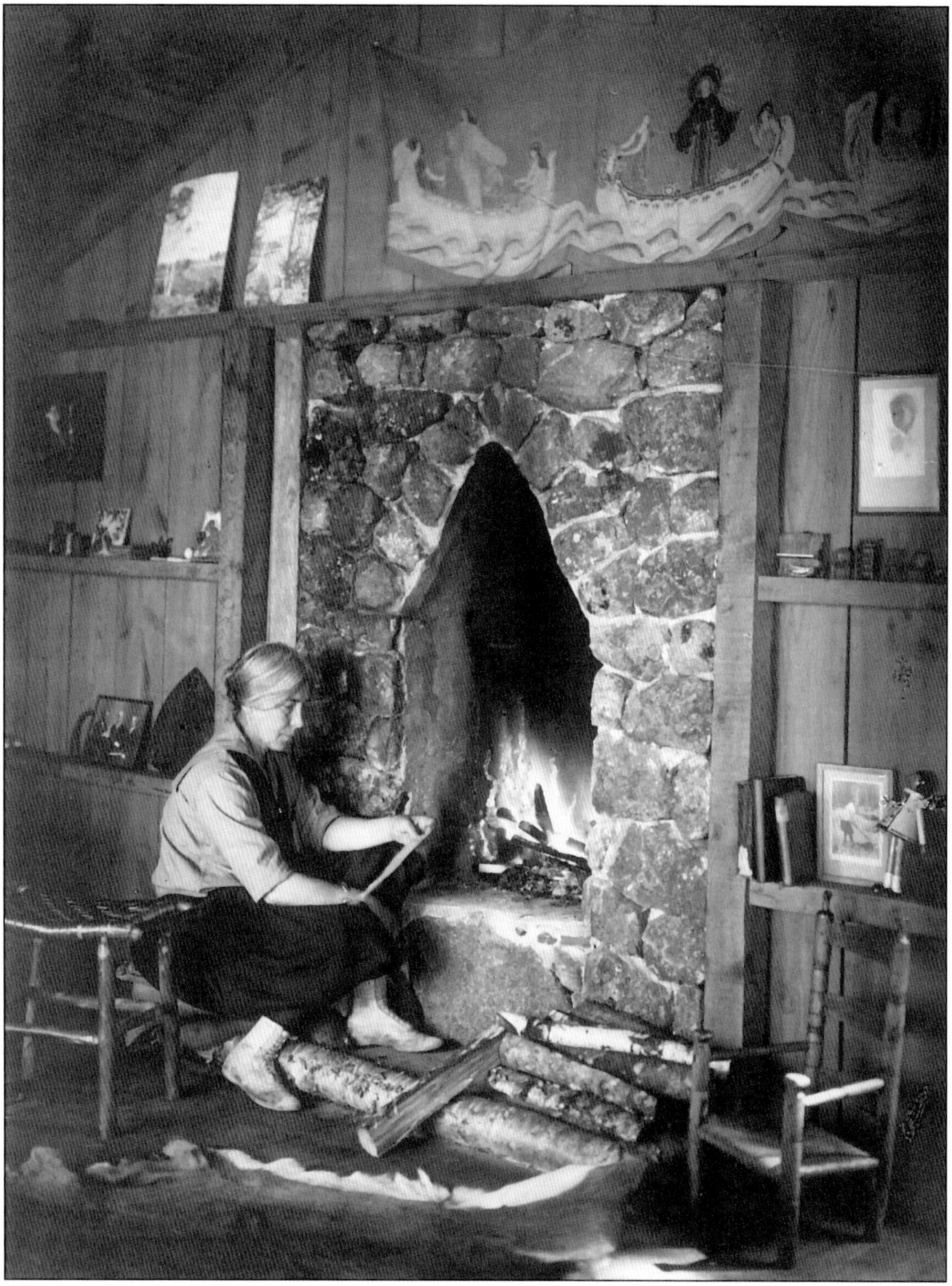

Charlotte Vetter Gulick, 1923. Charlotte V. Gulick, the co-founder of the Gulick Camps and the founder of Camp Fire Girls, was reading by firelight at Sebago-Wohelo Camp when the now-famous Maine photographer Chansonetta Stanley Emmons (1857–1937) took this photograph. Chansonetta spent several summers at the Gulick Camps, where she taught photography. Closely entwined with Mrs. Gulick's work at the Gulick Camps and Camp Fire Girls was her pioneer work in child development and sex education. The Gulick Camps became an extension of her own family relationship.

Four

Sebago

First Settled: 1750
Incorporated: 1826
Population: 974
Area: 43.6 square miles
Principle Settlements: Long Beach, East Sebago, North Sebago, Sebago Center, Convene

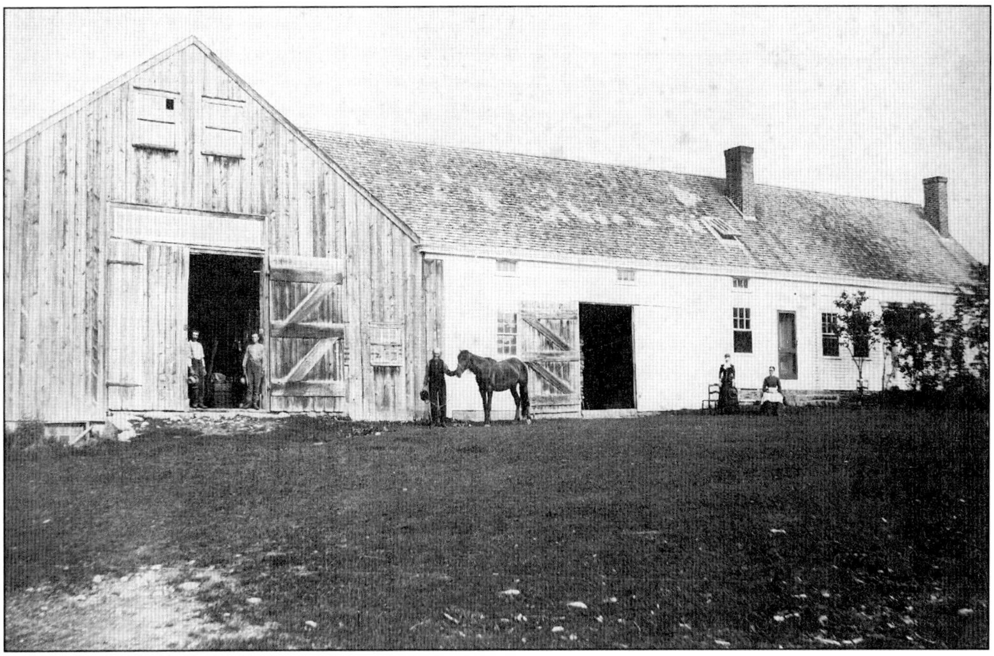

The Thomas Jackson Farm, c. 1910. The Thomas Jackson Farm, one of the older farms in the town of Sebago, is located at the foot of Poor's Hill on Route 107 near the site where Joseph Lakin, Sebago's first settler, cleared land and built his cabin. This lovely vintage set of buildings, a sort of blending of English and early nineteenth-century New England farm architecture, exudes charm. The elderly gentleman holding the horse is Thomas Jackson, who died in 1939; the woman seated is probably his wife Ella, who died in 1927. The two men standing at the entrance to the barn seem to be their son Daniel, who years later was accidentally shot by a deer hunter and died in the house a few days later, and his uncle Gene. Alfred and Mariemma Jordan now own the farm.

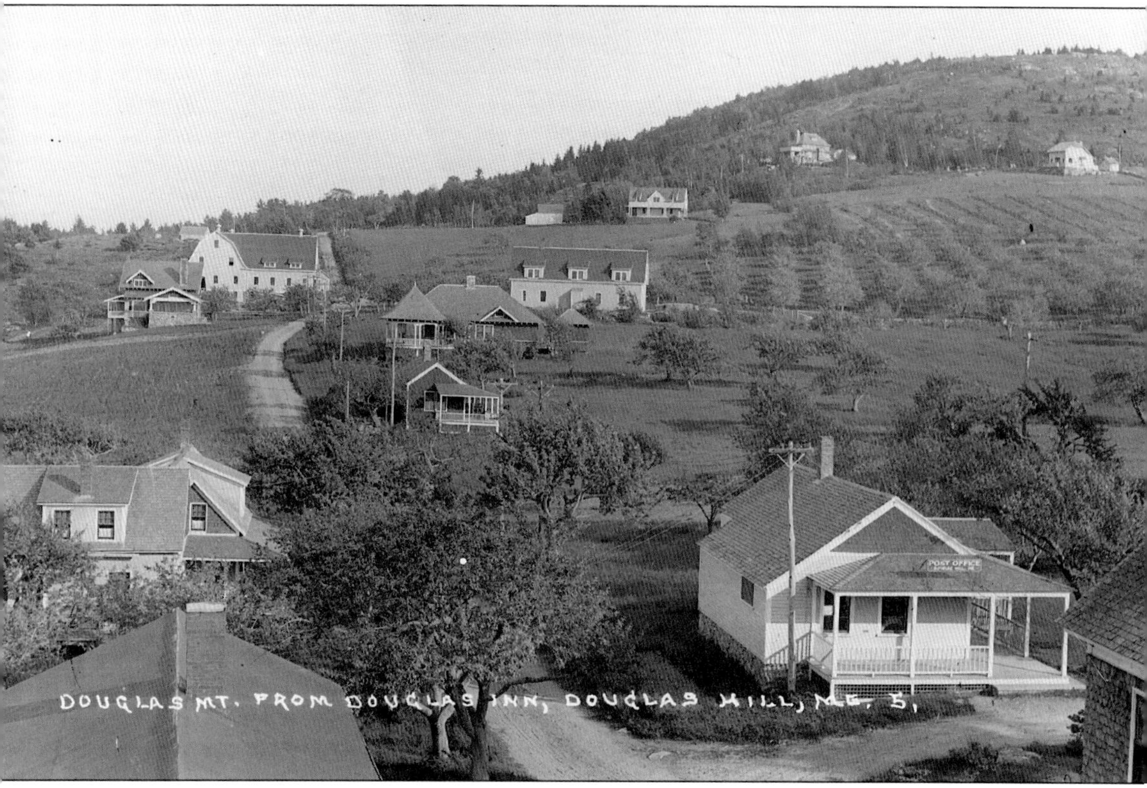

Douglas Hill, c. 1910. There is a tremendous amount of history captured in this pre-World War I photograph of Douglas Hill, the highest portion of the Saddleback Mountains (Baldwin Hills). Until 1826 Sebago was essentially a part of the town of Baldwin (originally called Flintstown), first settled in 1735 and incorporated in 1802. A small section of the town of Denmark was added to Sebago in 1830. Like most of what became the town of Sebago, Douglas Hill and the adjacent hills known as Dike Mountain and Winn Mountain were a vast undulating sea of colossal white pine. Ineluctably the loggers were the first to arrive. Soon the sound of axes and the boisterous halooing of teamsters, goading their oxen as they pulled heavy loads of logs down toward the Northwest River to be floated down to Sebago Lake, reverberated throughout the hills and across the lake. And as abruptly as they appeared upon the scene, when there were no more trees of value to harvest, the woodsmen evanesced—leaving the hills littered with brush, jagged stumps, and protruding glacial outcroppings. But in their wake came the first settlers with a desire to sink roots into the rocky soil, build permanent dwellings, and raise families.

Not long after the building of the Portland & Ogdensburg Railroad, Douglas Hill, Dike Mountain, and Hog Fat Hill began attracting vacationers. Farmhouses evolved into summer boarding houses. Vacationers came by train as far as the railroad station in Mattocks (East Baldwin) and then were conveyed, for example, to this hill by carriage. Home-cooked food and a spectacular view of Sebago Lake, the White Mountains, and even Portland Harbor on a clear day from the summit of Douglas Hill were irresistible attractions.

Even before the first cottage was built on the shores of Sebago Lake, Dr. Blackman had the magnificent stone cottage (the uppermost structure) built on the side of the hill. Soon summer cottages outnumbered the farms. And it is because Douglas Hill and Dike Mountain attracted summer people that these hills were not eventually abandoned the way most hills in Maine were once farmers either began moving west or down into valleys more suitable to mechanized agriculture.

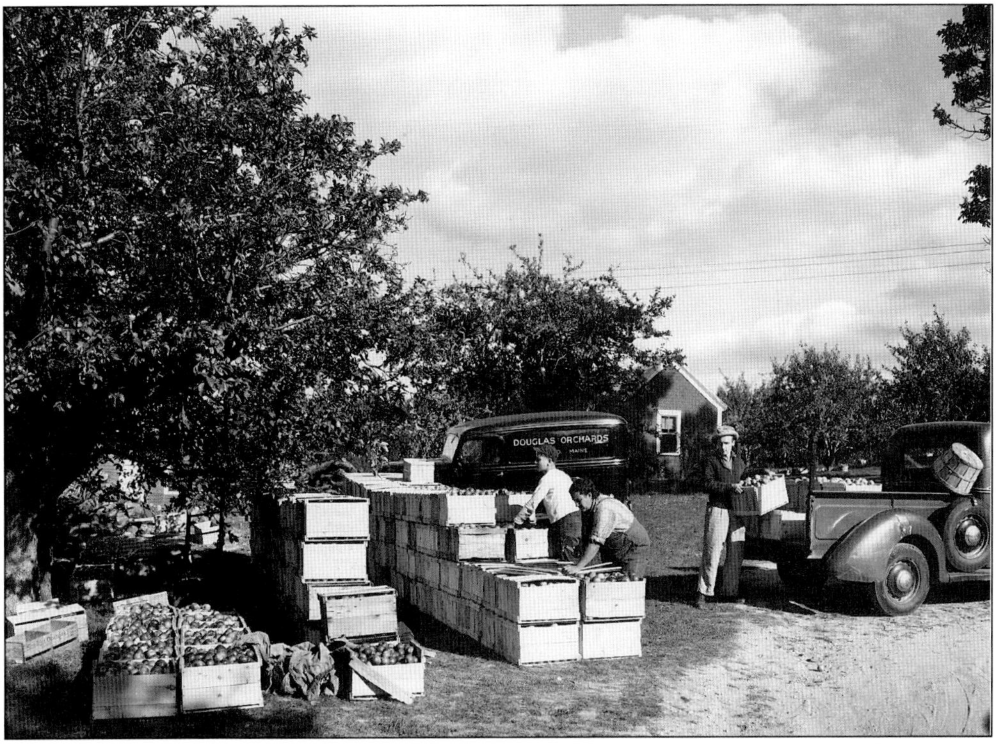

The Apple Harvest, c. 1940. Douglas Hill was ideally suited to the growing of apples. Sometime in the 1930s Ed Douglas purchased this land and set out this fine orchard that continues to be productive today. Dwight Greene is loading a crate of apples onto the pickup truck.

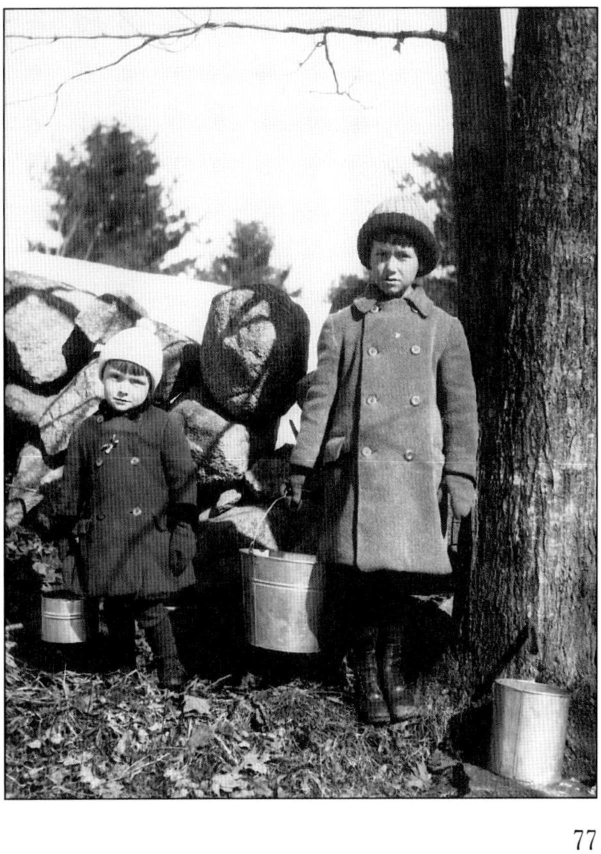

Gathering Sap, 1917. Until a few decades ago, tapping sugar maples soon after the first real warm breath of spring began to melt the snow and boiling the sap down to maple syrup were welcomed activities throughout rural Maine. Here Robert and Edward Dyer are collecting sap at the Dyer Farm at Mac's (MacDonald's) Corner. Five years after this photograph was taken, Robert succumbed to typhoid fever, a disease almost unheard of today. Theodore Greene, their nephew, continues to tap the trees at the farm and sell maple syrup.

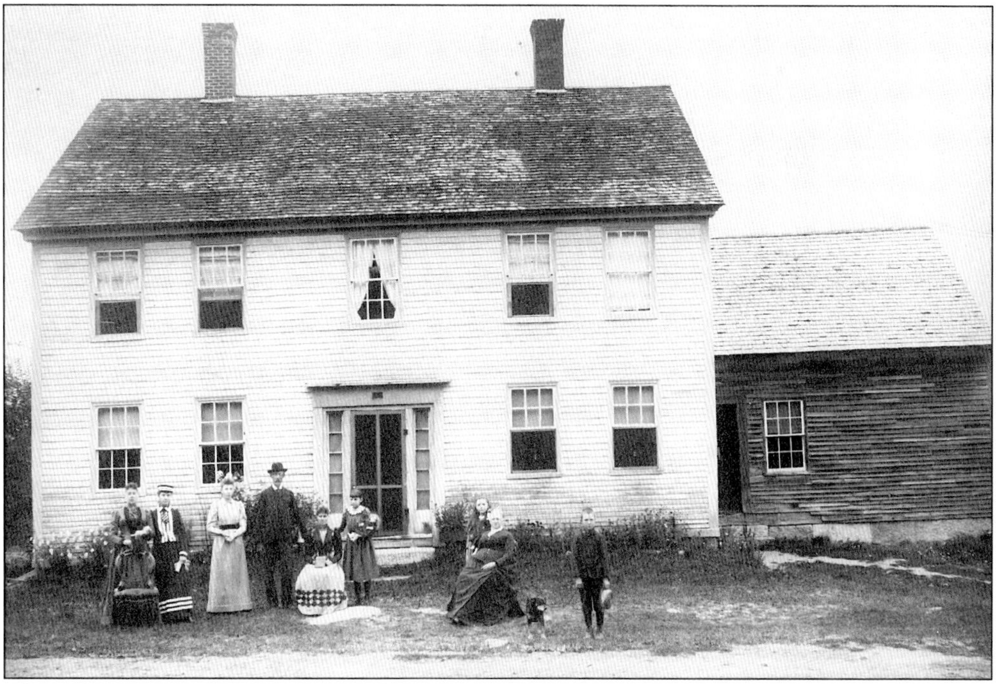

The Sebago House, 1891. One of the oldest houses remaining in Sebago is the Sebago House at Mac's Corner, built in 1848 and operated by J. Rowe as a tavern—the only one in the history of Sebago. Arthur Dyer ran a store in an adjacent building to the left of the house from 1865 to 1920. Shown here are, from left to right: Ada Walker, Mary Dyer, Alice Dyer, Arthur Dyer, Alice H. Dyer, Edna Dyer, Cora Kelly, Emma Dyer, the dog Fido, and Arthur Edward Dyer. Leona Greene, Arthur Edward's daughter, lives in the house today.

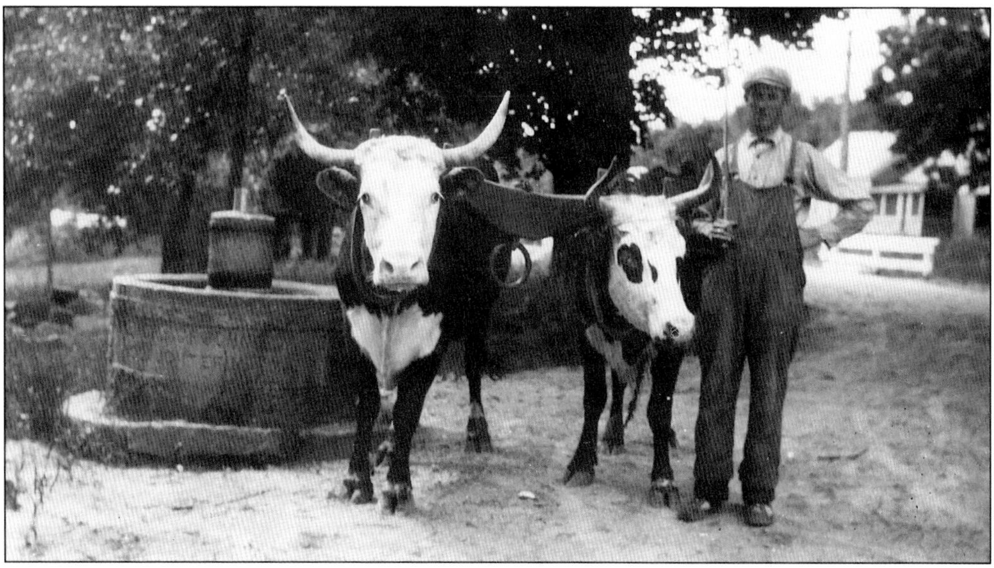

Edward Dyer and His Oxen, c. 1920. Edward Dyer and his team of oxen pose beside the watering troth at Mac's Corner, dedicated to the memory of John E. MacDonald in 1899. No water has run into the troth since 1937, when workman exploded dynamite on the hill above the road.

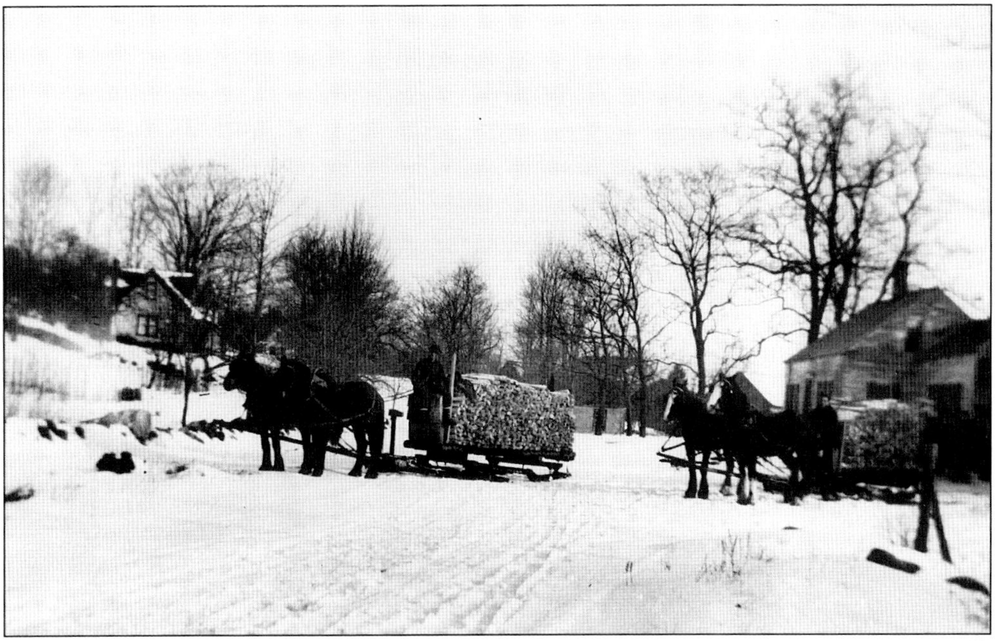

Hauling in Cordwood, 1913. This was a familiar sight in rural areas soon after the first snowfall. Ed Douglas (to the right) and Arthur Dyer (to the left) have just arrived at the Dyer Farm at Mac's Corner with their bobsleds stacked high with split hardwood logs. Arthur's grandson, Theodore Greene, lives here today.

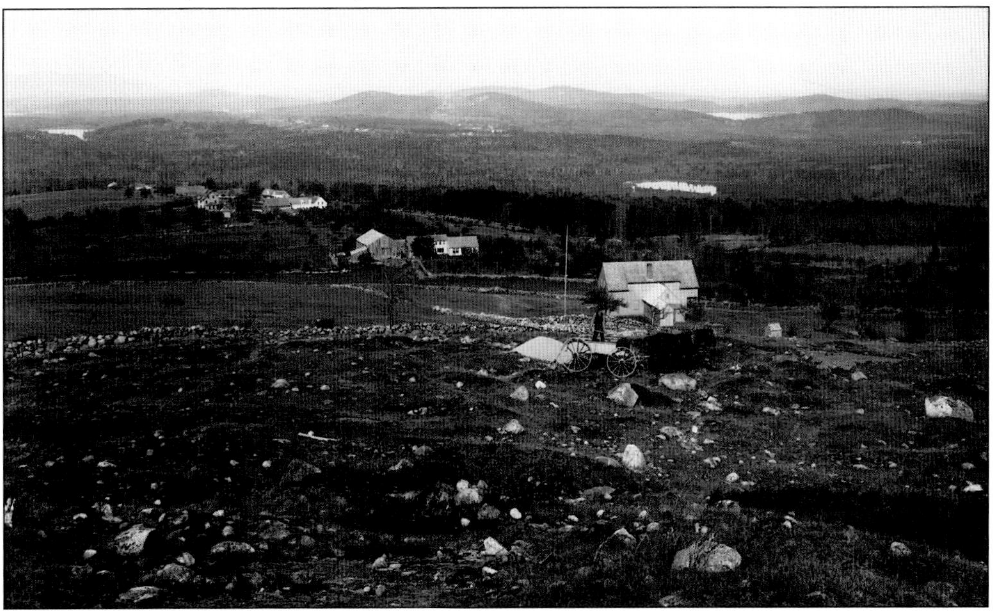

Douglas Hill, 1896. By the turn of the century Douglas Hill was still farming country, but its scenic panorama had been discovered by vacationers. The Douglas Farm (far down the hill) was converted to the Douglas Inn, and here in the foreground George Douglas is unloading sand in preparation for the building of Dr. Blackman's magnificent stone cottage. Several ponds are visible including the Mud City and Peabody Ponds (beyond on the right), and the Hancock and Brown's Ponds (to the left).

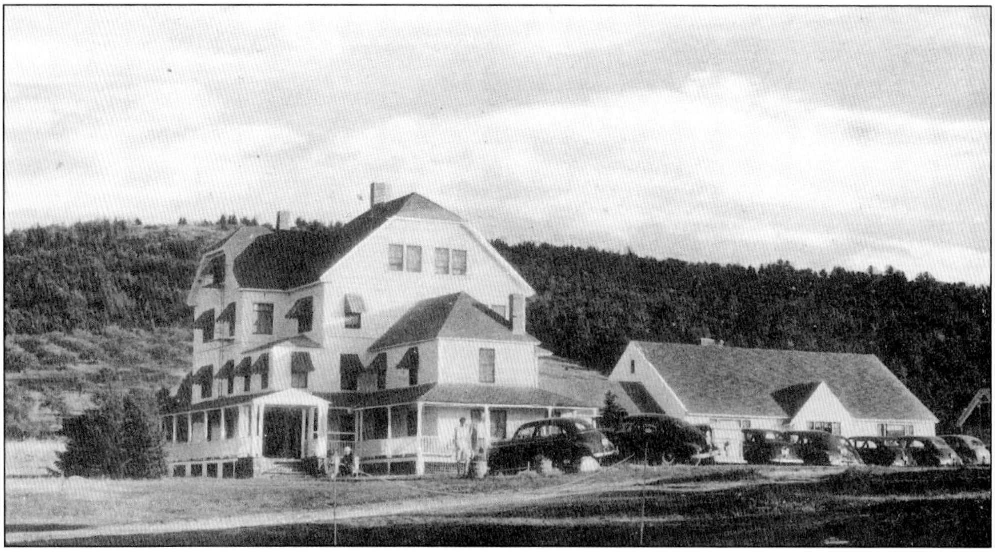

The Douglas Hill (Mountain) Inn, 1940. The Douglas Hill Inn was the largest hotel in Sebago. For many years the inn maintained a bathhouse at Long Beach on the lake side of Naomi Street and provided transportation for its guests to and from the lake. The inn, except for the annex, burned in 1928. A series of new owners added onto the annex and the inn continued operating through much of the 1940s. It was torn down around 1959.

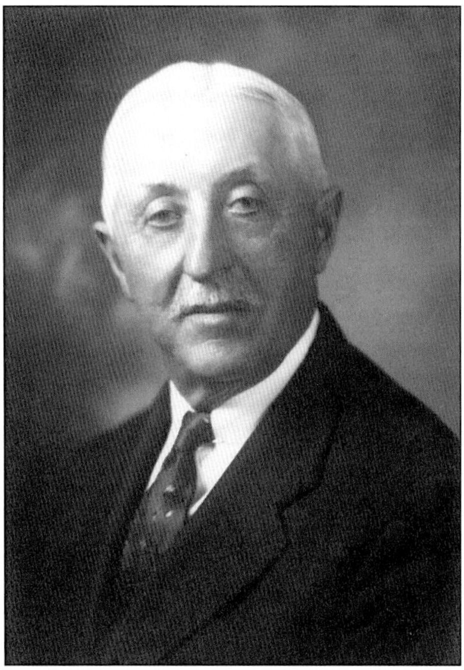

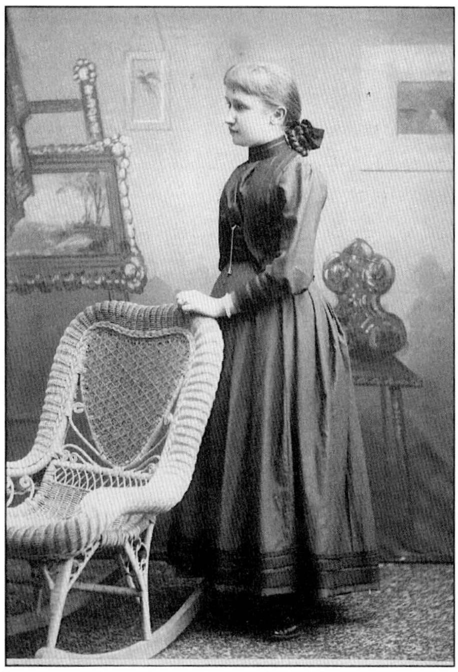

Left: Edward S. Douglas, c. 1940. Edward S. Douglas owned and operated the Douglas Inn for many years before selling it to Edward Post in 1924. He also owned the Douglas Hill Orchard. He died in 1945.

Right: Vesta Chadbourne Douglas, 1890. Vesta Chadbourne, who was the first wife of Edward Douglas, had deep roots on Douglas Hill. She was sixteen when this photograph was taken. She died in 1933 at the age of fifty-nine.

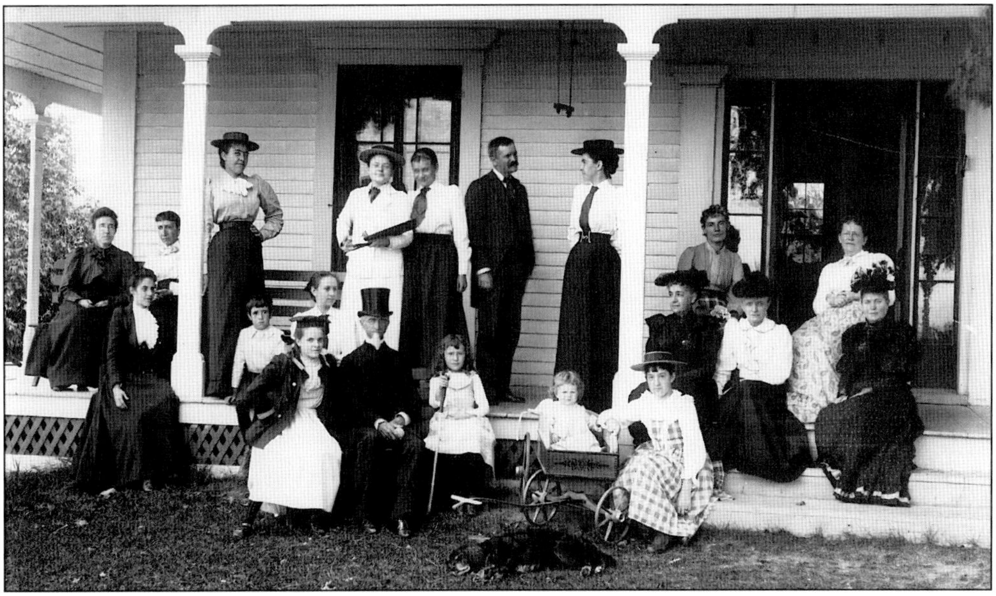

A Tea Party at the Douglas Farm, c. 1888. A group of summer guests was gathered on the porch of the Douglas Farm, owned and run as a summer boarding house by Stephen and Carolyn Douglas, when John Haley took this photograph. Later Edward Douglas, the son of Stephen and Carolyn, added onto the farmhouse, along with nine cottages, and operated it as the Douglas Inn.

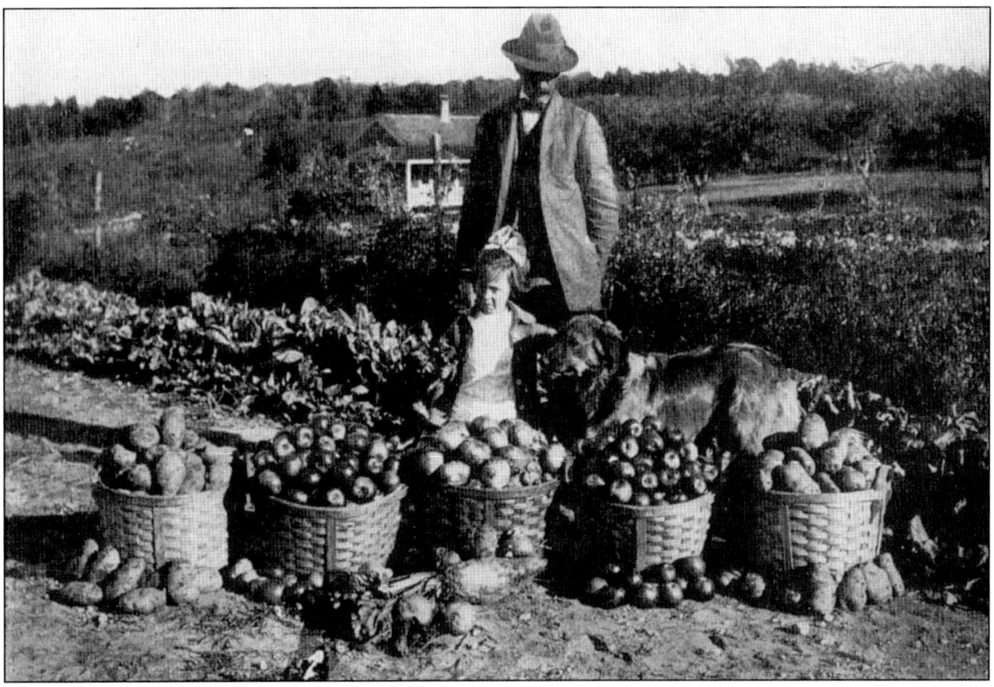

Assuring a Satisfactory Table, 1917. Edward S. Douglas, with his daughter Helen and dog Rex, stands in the garden behind baskets heaped with potatoes and apples. He prided himself in being able to serve his guests fresh milk, cream, butter, eggs, vegetables, and fruit produced on his 125-acre farm on Douglas Hill.

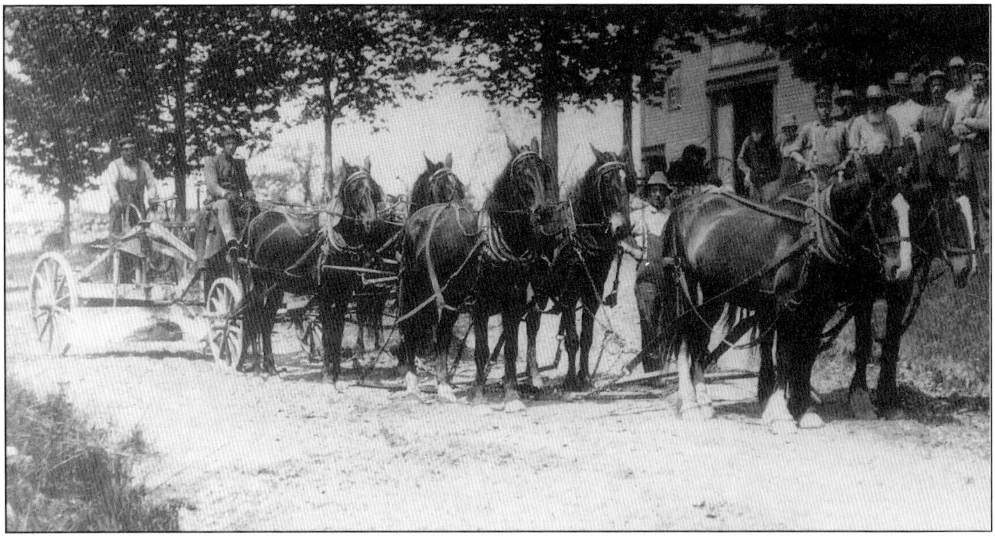

Grading the Road, c. 1890. Three pairs of well-matched horses are pulling a grader along the narrow road that passed by the Haley residence in Convene. It was a major task after mud season to grade the deeply rutted roads. The group of onlookers was very likely working on the roads in their area in lieu of paying taxes.

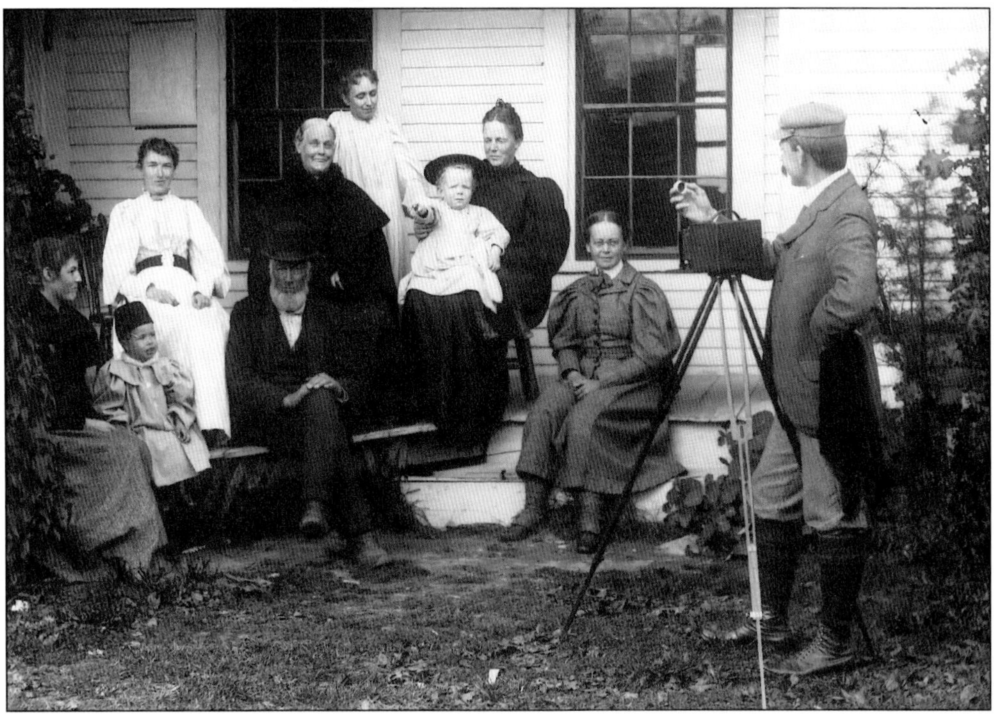

John Haley at Work with His Camera, c. 1890. John Haley, who lived in a section of Sebago known as Convene (New Limington), was a noted photographer in the area in his day. Here he is taking a group photograph at the Chadbourne Farm on Douglas Hill. He is holding the lens cap while exposing the photograph and will put it back on the lens when the exposure is finished. The gentleman with the beard is George Douglas. Sitting closest to the tripod is the photographer's sister, Elzira. Note the little boy wearing an exotic fez.

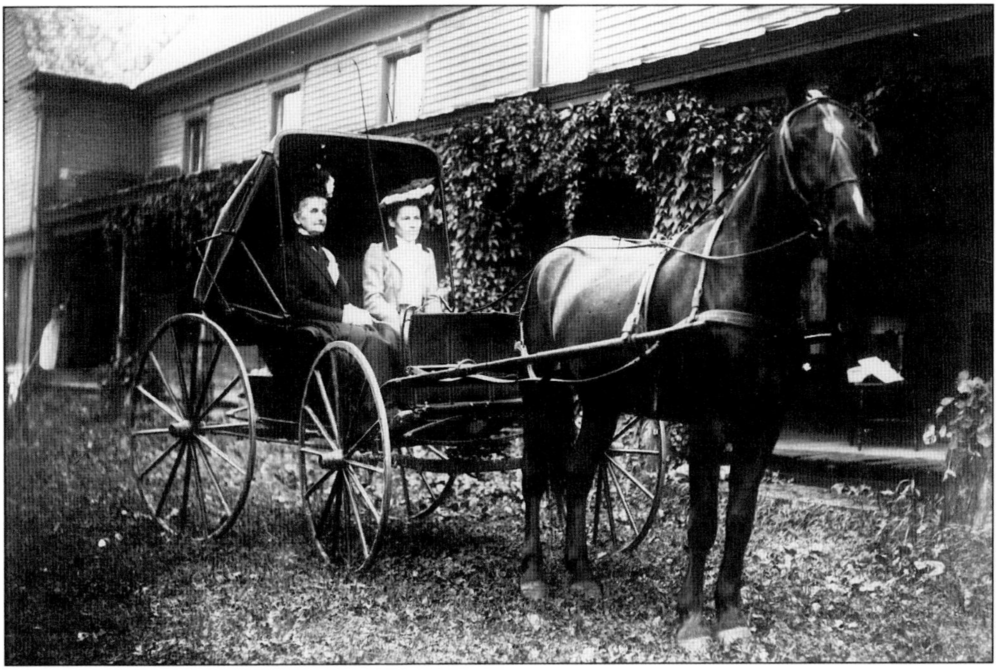

Going for a Drive, c. 1895. Two Haley women, Rose (left) and Sarah (right), are preparing to head down the driveway and onto what is known today as the Sebago Road. This lovely set of farm buildings in Convene has weathered the years and remains easily identifiable. Only recently did the Haley property pass out of the family. John Haley took this photograph.

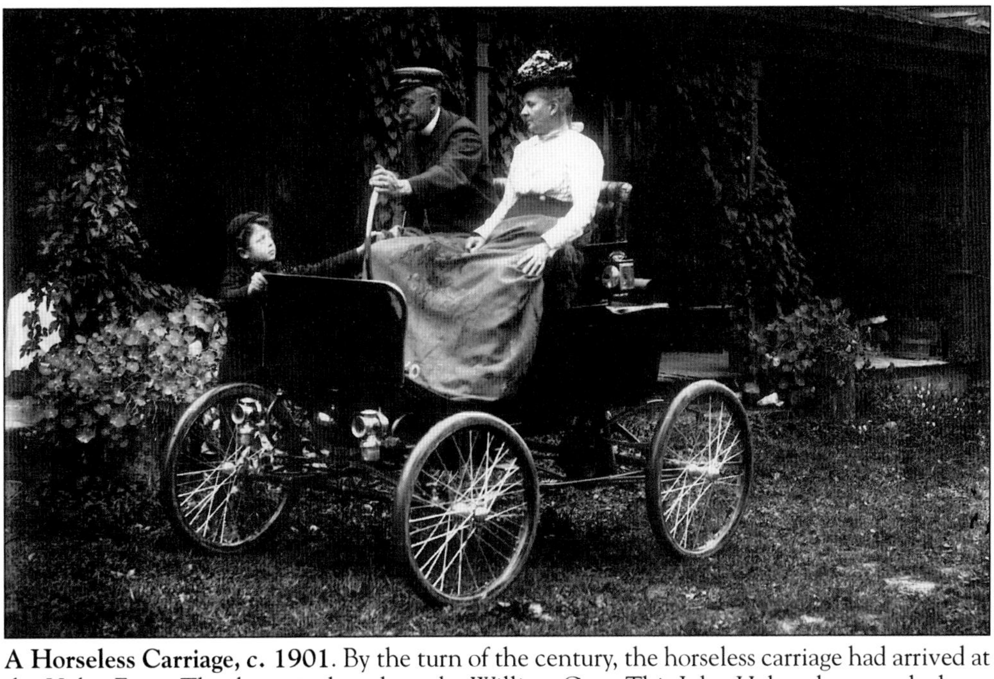

A Horseless Carriage, c. 1901. By the turn of the century, the horseless carriage had arrived at the Haley Farm. The driver is thought to be William Gray. This John Haley photograph shows a 1901 Geneva Steam Car model-A runabout that was manufactured in Geneva, Ohio. It has self-generating bicycle lights in the front with a kerosene light on the side.

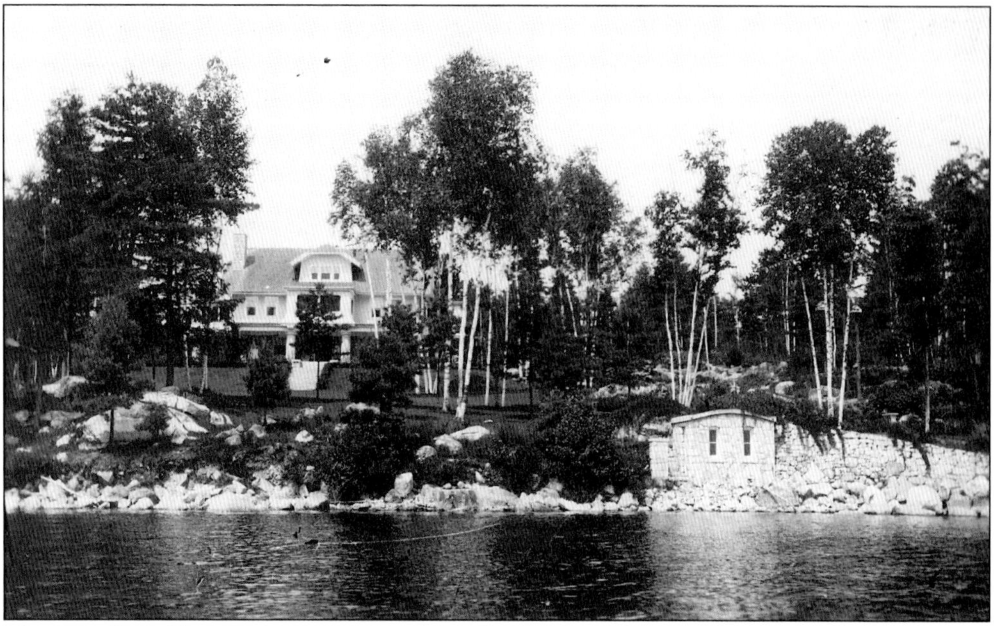

The Leon Spaulding Estate, c. 1930. This palatial summer home, built in 1917 in East Sebago between Long Beach and the West Shore, was part of the 100-acre Spaulding estate. Both Leon Spaulding and his wife Dorothy were nouveaux riches, Leon having amassed a fortune operating the Spaulding Fiber Company in Rochester, New Hampshire. He died in 1924.

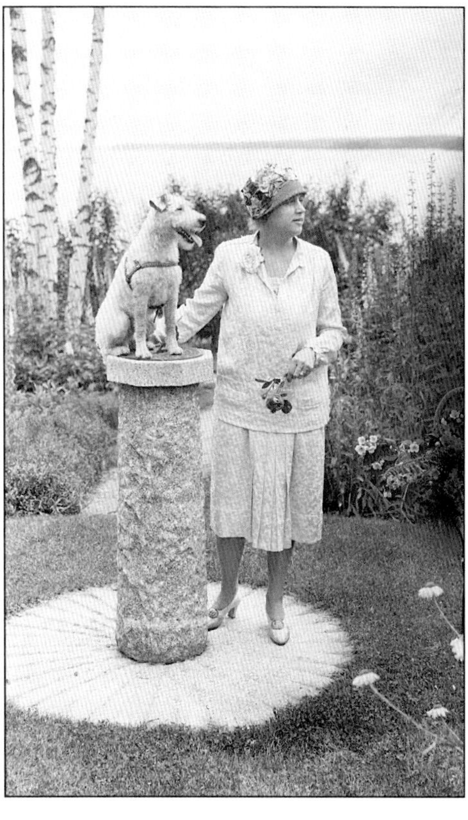

Dorothy Spaulding, c. 1920. Dorothy Spaulding traveled in style to some of the most exotic places in the world, but the place dearest to her heart was her home overlooking Sebago Lake. Her generosity knew no bounds. Besides providing employment for a host of local citizens, every child in East Sebago received a gift from her each Christmas. Among her many other gifts to the community were the Spaulding Memorial Library in East Sebago (1927), the gymnasium and town hall in Sebago Center (1941), and the East Sebago Elementary School (1951). She died here in 1963. The Spauldings are entombed on the estate (now Rockcraft).

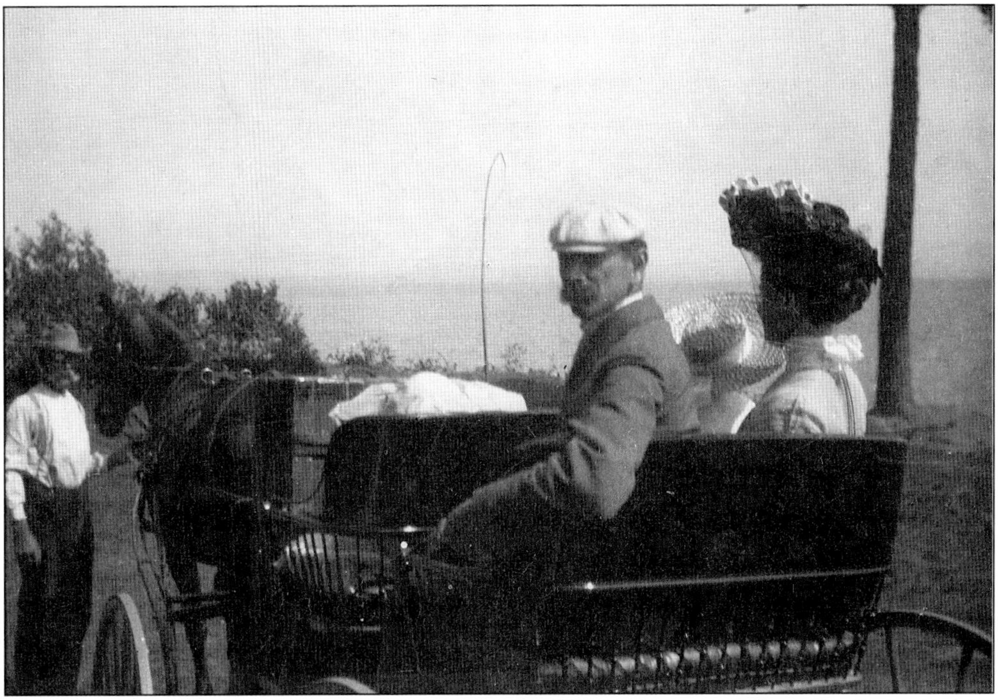

A Leisurely Drive, 1901. Waldo Elliott Pratt and his wife enjoy a leisurely drive in their horse-drawn carriage in front of their spacious cottage, located high up on the embankment overlooking Sebago Lake near the mouth of the Northwest River in East Sebago.

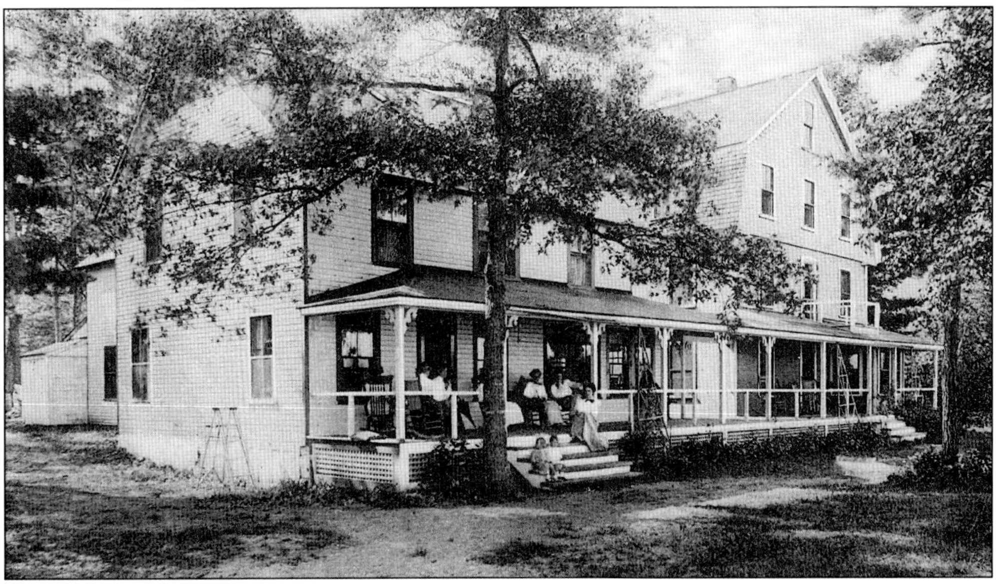

The West Shore Hotel, c. 1920. For over a half century the West Shore Hotel and Camps in East Sebago attracted summer vacationers and tourists from all over the United States and abroad. The original owner was A.L. Brackett. Later it was owned and operated by Mr. and Mrs. Kernan. Horseback riding, dancing, swimming, and other aquatic activities were just a few of the major attractions. The hotel has been closed for over quarter of a century and the camps are now individually owned.

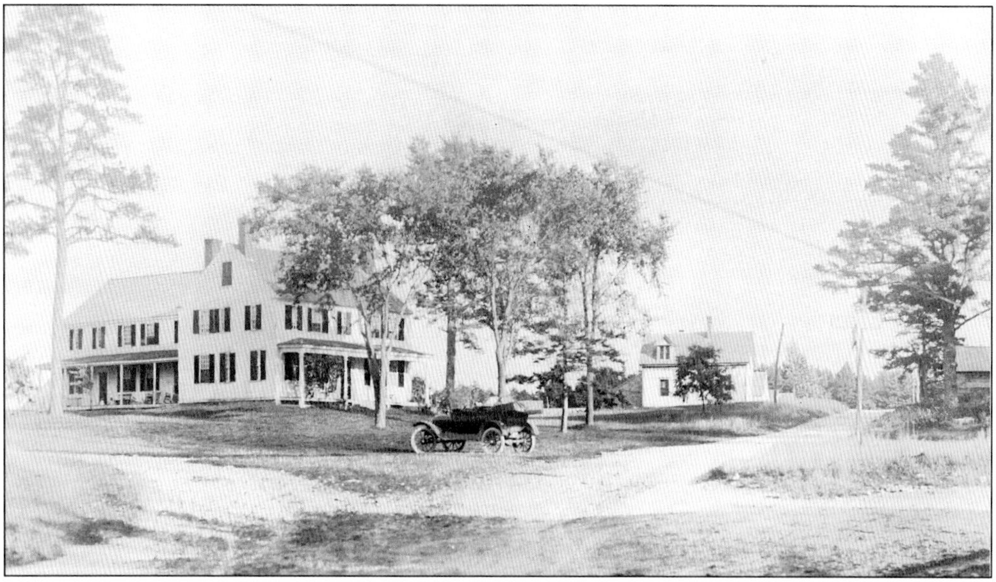

The Fitch Homestead, c. 1920. William Fitch, the progenitor of one of Sebago's most distinguished families, built this impressive home in the center of East Sebago in 1792. It was last lived in by his great-grandson, Harry H. Fitch, who died in 1948. Mrs. Spaulding purchased the property and gave it to the town in 1951 to be made into a consolidated elementary school.

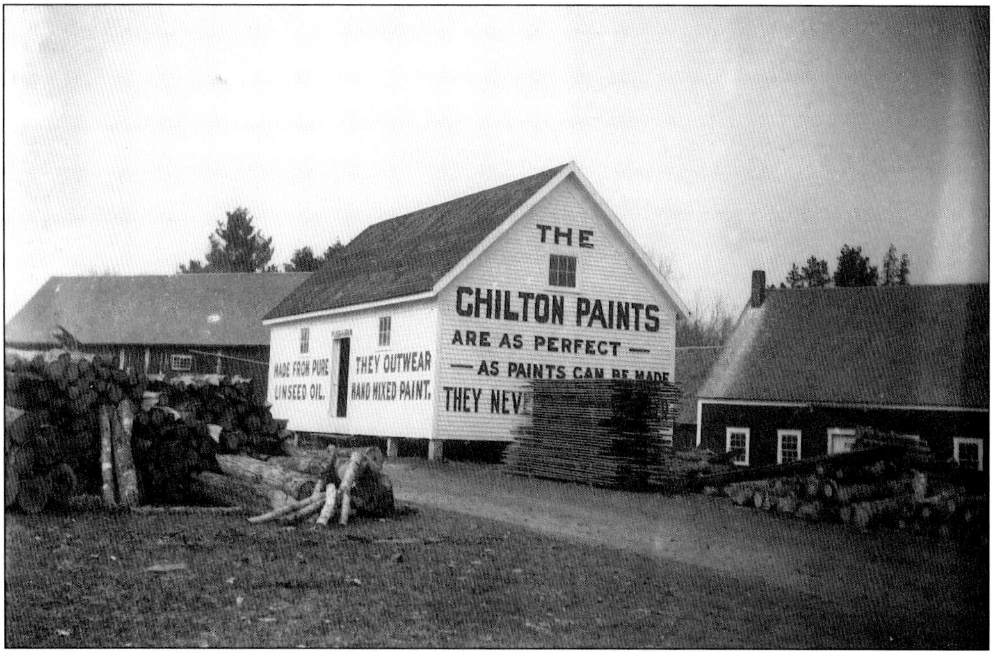

The Fitch Brothers' Sawmill, c. 1930. The Fitch Brothers' Mill, built in 1866 on the original site of the gristmill built by the first William Fitch, was for nearly a century the economic mainstay of East Sebago as well as much of the remainder of the town. It provided, among other things, steady employment for several generations of local men, and was last operated by Harry Fitch as the Fitch Lumber Co.

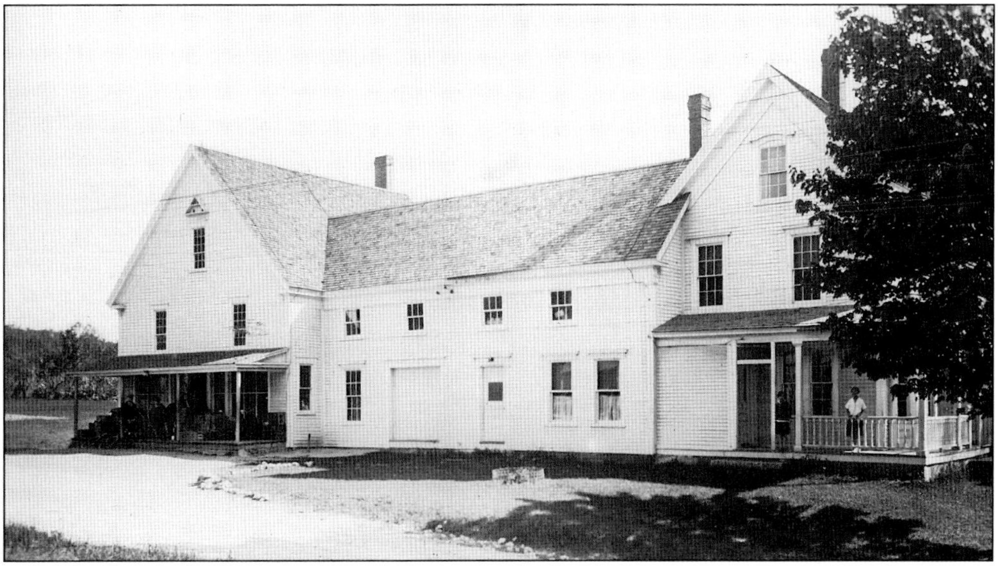

Fitch's Store, c. 1925. Ever since Luther Fitch built a store across the road from the sawmill in 1830, there has been a store in East Sebago run by Fitches. The first store was hit by lightning and burned in 1864 and was promptly rebuilt. In 1872 Luther's three sons—John, William, and George—purchased it from him. When they died, William's son Harry took over the mill, and in 1919 George's son Montford took over the store. That same year lightning again struck, and once again the store burned. Nonplussed, Montford ("Monty") set up business in the barn at his house shown here across the road.

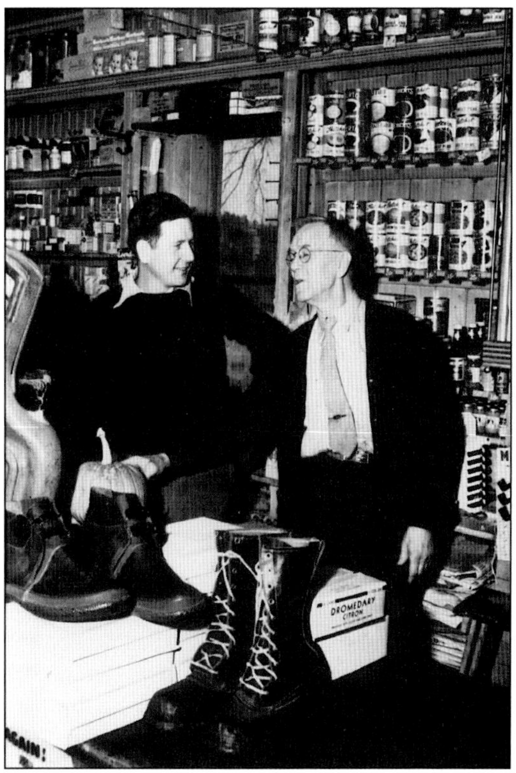

Monty and His Son Laurence, c. 1946. When Monty's son Laurence returned from World War II, he began assisting his father in the store; and when his kindly father died in 1957, Laurence and his wife Vera carried on. And just as his father had done, Laurence (now seventy-five) continues to sell just about everything imaginable. On March 10, 1995, Fitch's General Store and house was entered in the National Register of Historic Places.

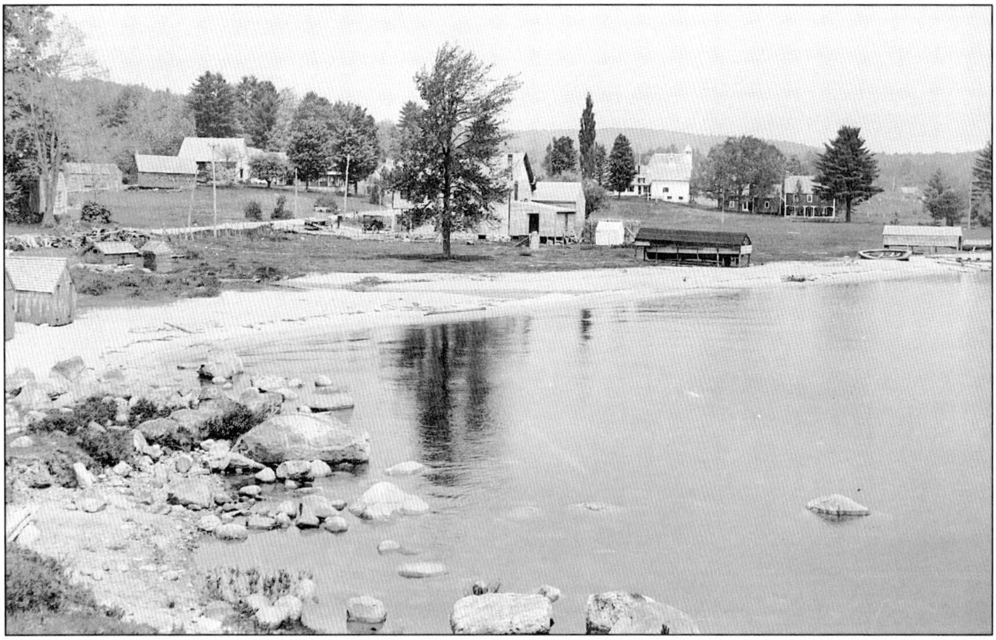

Nason's Beach, North Sebago, c. 1920. Amazingly, little has been altered here at North Sebago since this photograph was taken, except that in the late 1950s the Nason field to the right of Shaw's Store (now owned by Billy Nason), which served as a baseball field for so many years, was developed into a trailer park and camp grounds by Marion and Henry Nason. The buildings on the edge of the beach were privately owned boathouses.

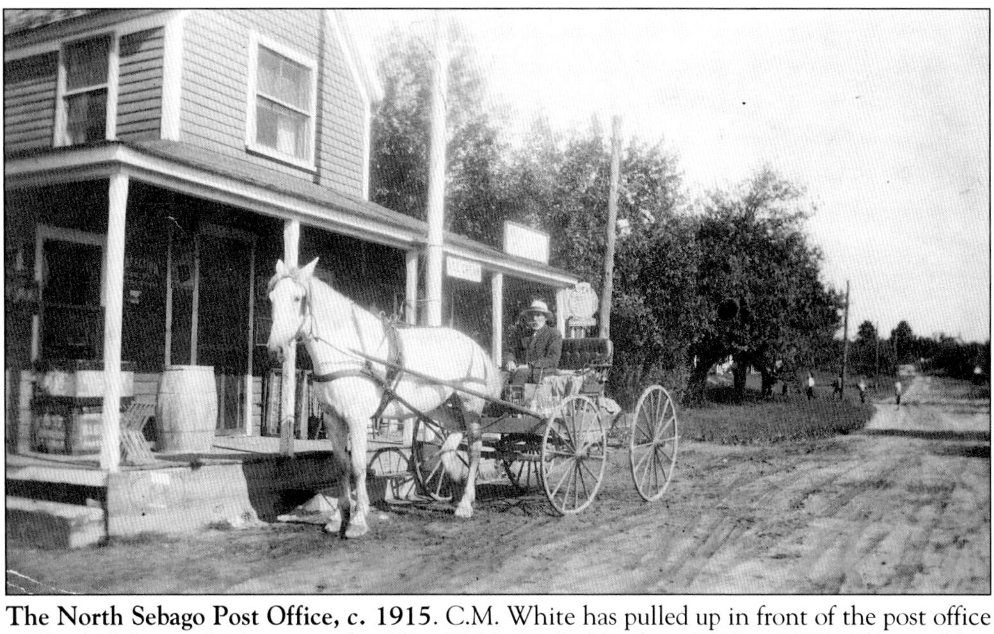

The North Sebago Post Office, c. 1915. C.M. White has pulled up in front of the post office at North Sebago, which was run by Alice Hobbs Bacheldor from 1910 to 1932. Alice and her husband Walter, who lived upstairs, also ran an ice cream parlor here for several years. The building, located on Route 114, was torn down in the 1970s.

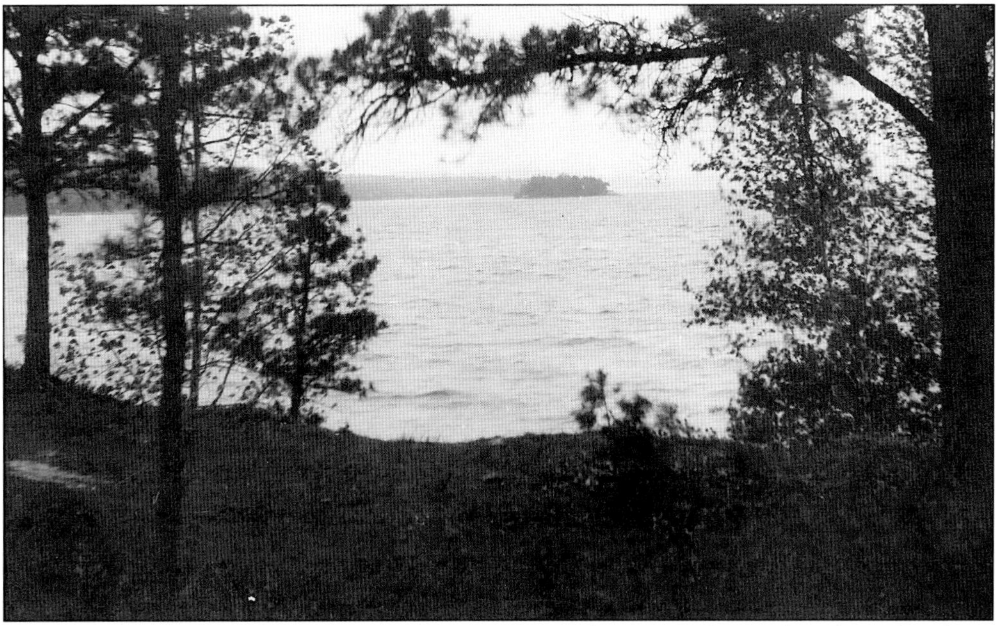

Spider Island. Spider Island, located off Cox's Point (Star Point), North Sebago, has been artistically framed like a Japanese woodblock by pine trees. It is said that Spider Island once changed ownership in a poker game. The island and cottage are owned by Frank and Charlotte Schell. The foreground is probably the area of Goodwin's Lodge.

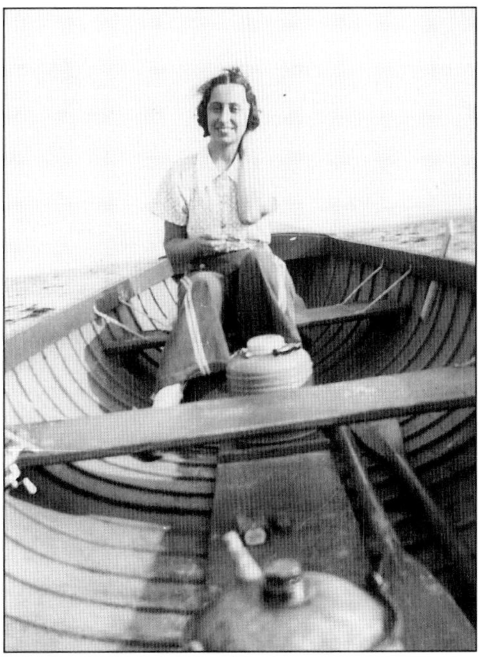

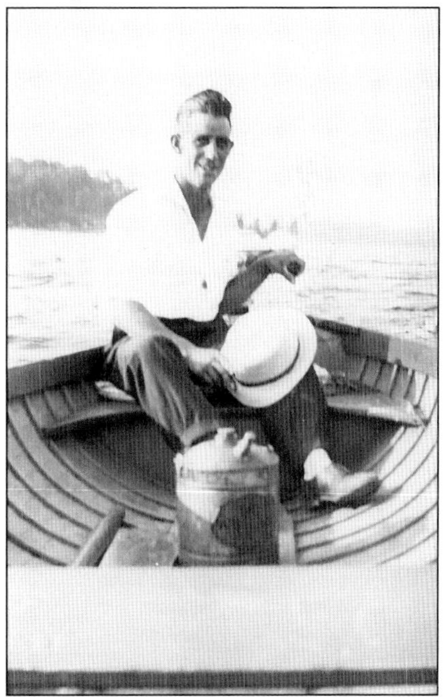

Homeward Bound, 1937. Franklin and Helen Irish are headed toward Nason's Beach in North Sebago in their outboard motorboat from a day's outing and picnic on Sebago Lake. Visible behind Franklin is Star Point and Spider Island. Helen is the daughter of Edward and Vesta Chadborne Douglas, who ran the Douglas Inn. The couple still resides on Hillside in Sebago near the site where Franklin was born.

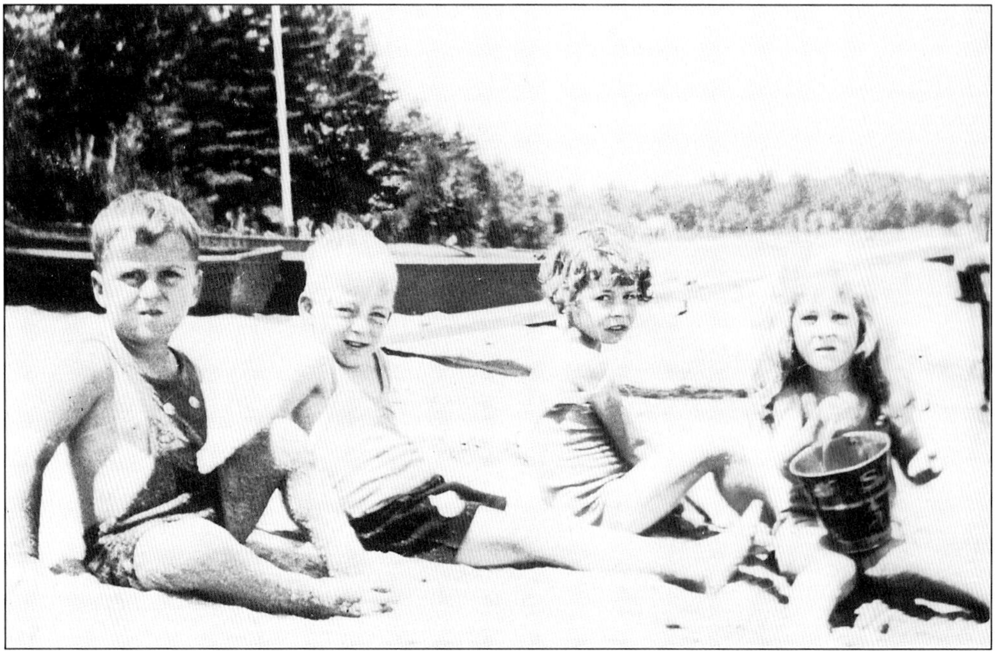

Carefree Days, 1932. The extraordinarily long stretch of sandy beach at Long Beach, East Sebago, was a splendid place for young children to play. Shown here on the beach near the old steamboat wharf at the foot of Long Beach are, from left to right: Tyler White (Milton, Massachusetts), Jack Barnes (Long Beach), Cherry Breton (Massachusetts), and Cherry Locker (Pennsylvania).

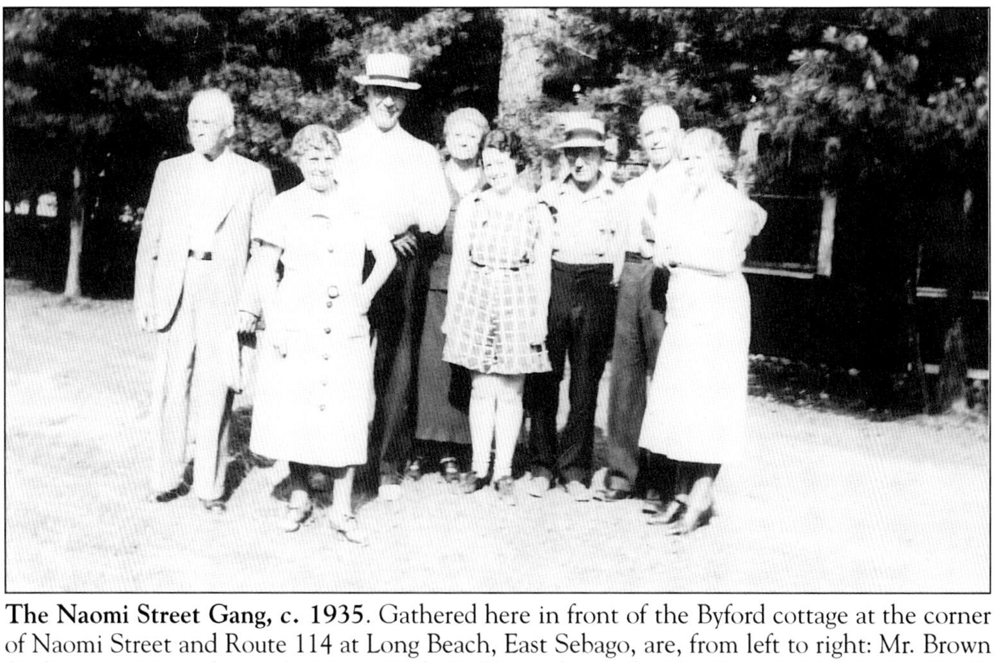

The Naomi Street Gang, c. 1935. Gathered here in front of the Byford cottage at the corner of Naomi Street and Route 114 at Long Beach, East Sebago, are, from left to right: Mr. Brown (Arlington, Massachusetts), Mrs. Mitchell (Massachusetts), Mr. Russell (South Portland), Mabel Byford (Massachusetts), Grace Barnes (Long Beach), Bert McKenney (Portland), Alfred Byford (Massachusetts), and Mrs. Russell.

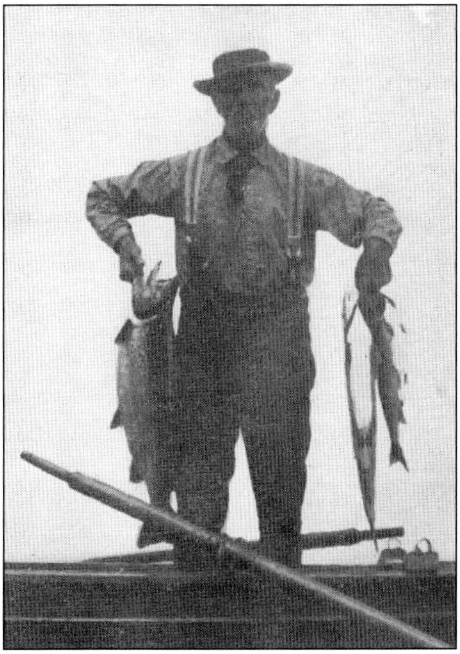

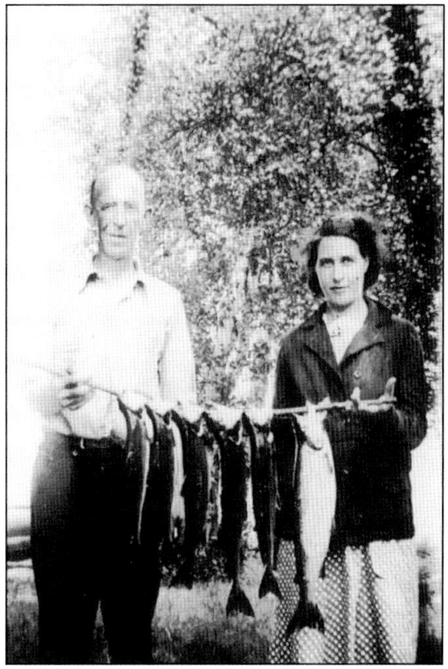

Left: A Good Catch, c. 1909. George E. Fitch of the Fitch Brothers' Mill in East Sebago and the father of Montford Fitch of Fitch's Store, stands in his row boat displaying three large landlocked salmon weighing 17, 10, and 7 pounds.

Right: Another Great Catch, c. 1937. Arthur Layler and his daughter Beatrice from the Portland area, who owned a cottage on Naomi Street at Long Beach, caught their limit while out trolling on Sebago Lake. By this time the famous landlocked salmon were but a legend.

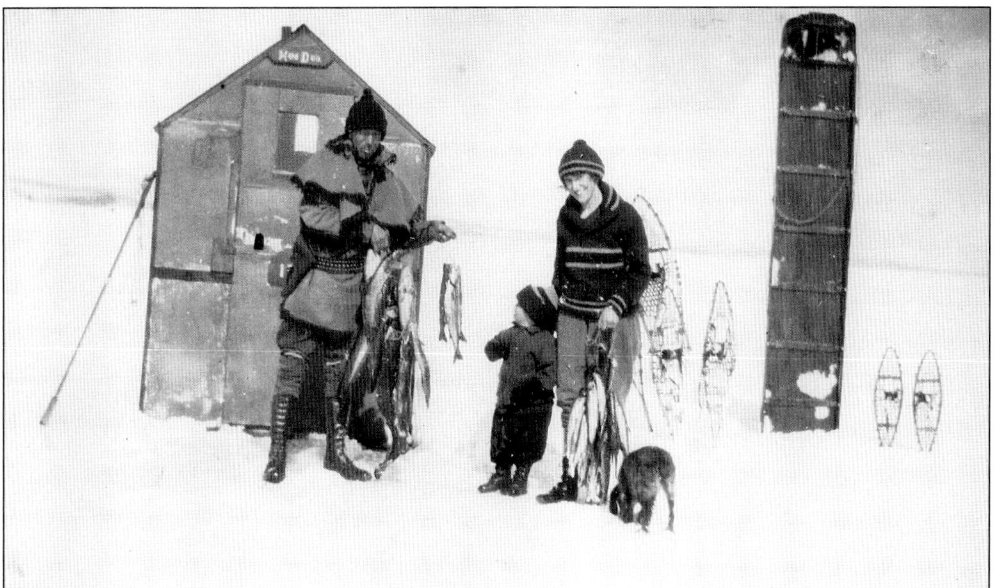

Ice Fishing off Long Beach, 1925. Cecil Lowell Barnes, his wife Rose (granddaughter of famed Mellie Dunham), and their son Buddy (Dr. Lowell Barnes) certainly needed the toboggan (standing upright) to haul home this catch. Mellie Dunham made the snowshoes.

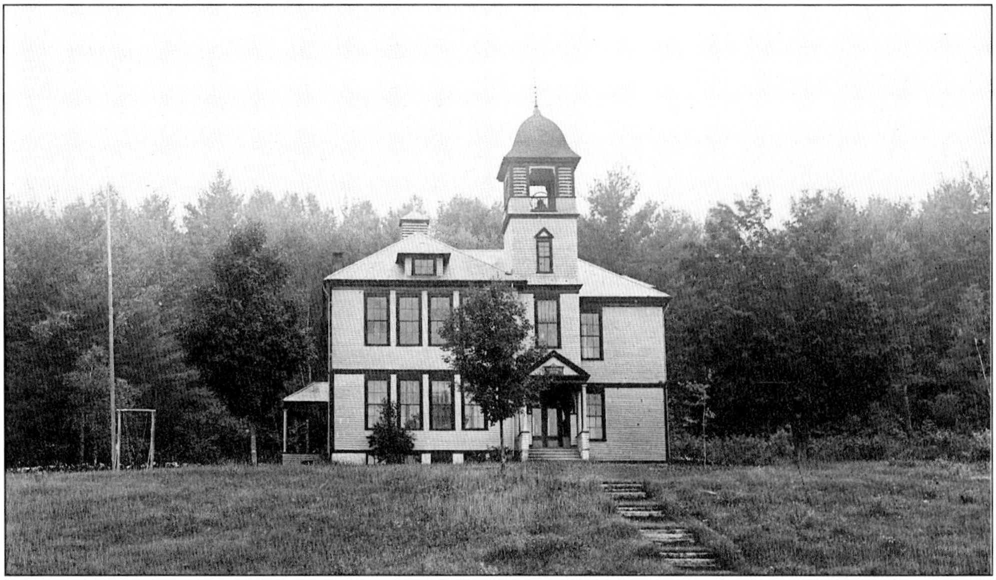

Potter Academy. Potter Academy was erected on this prominent hill surveying Mud City (Sebago Center) in 1895, thanks to the generosity of Joseph Fitch Potter—who was born in Sebago in 1808 and later moved to Cincinnati, Ohio.

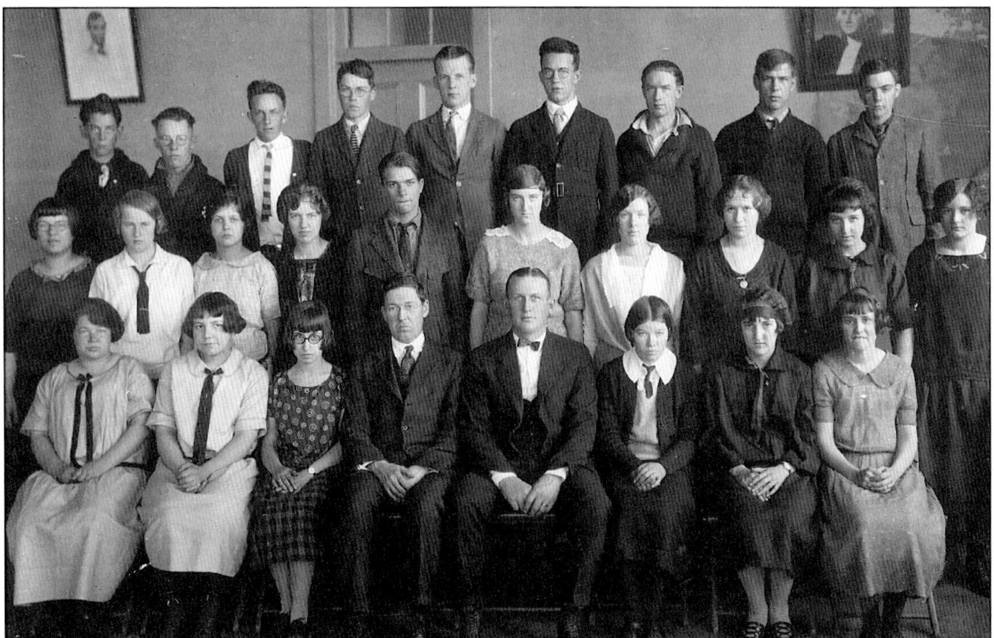

Potter Academy, 1924. From left to right are: (front row) Martha Robinson Burnell, Edna Douglass Hale, Helen Douglas Irish, Mr. Barber, Paul Marston, Elizabeth Nason Getchell, Alice Warren Pelletier, and Marion Dolloff Nason; (middle row) Marion Ward Graffam, Doris Weed Douglass, Doris Dolloff Hamilton, Alice Gray, Eula Larrabee Lewis, Elva Murch Sanborn, Isabelle Gray Usher, Alice Merrifield Bauchman, and Olive Murch Sanborn; (back row) Franklin Irish, Merle Douglass, Alton Warren, Everett Chadborne, Harold Warren, Dennis McKenney, Henry Nason, Arnold Ward, and Clifford Douglas.

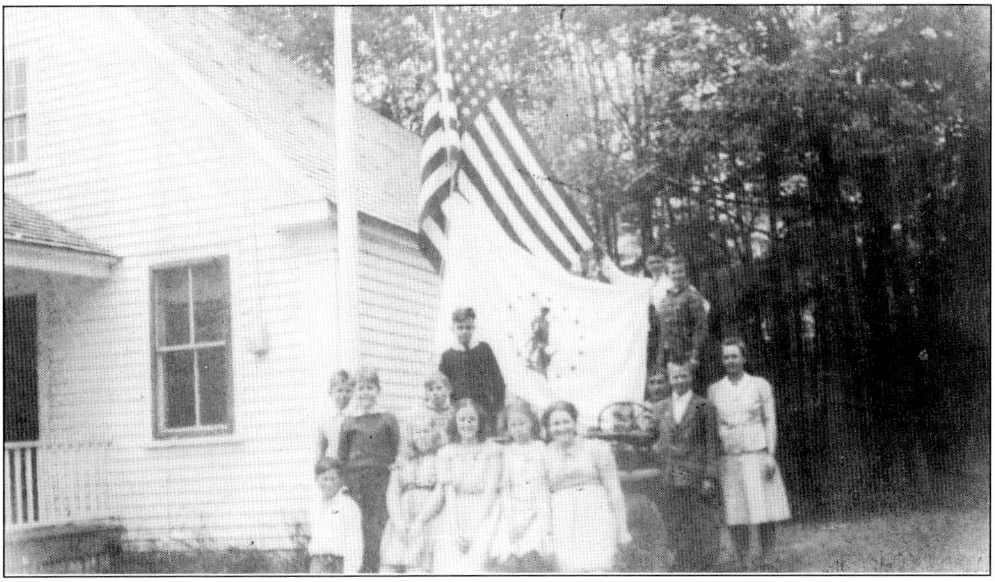

The North Sebago School, 1945. The following members of this little one-room schoolhouse celebrating the purchase of a $25 war bond are, from left to right: (front row) Donald Gregory, Pat Coleman, Gloria Day, Evelyn Skillings, and Carlene Wright; (middle row) Hartley Shaw, Ed Richards, and Merlin Shaw; (back row) Ray Anderson, Milton Skillings, and Helen Stickney (the teacher). Behind the jeep are Joyce Day and Clarence Chute.

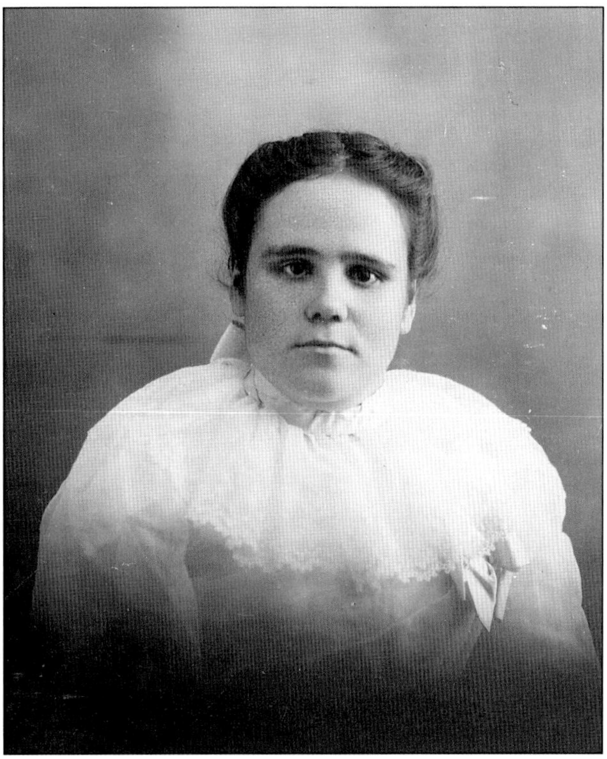

Mamie White, c. 1895. Mamie White, who taught in the Sebago school system for much of her long life, was a young lady when this portrait was taken. For many years she taught all nine grades from the primary through the eighth grade at the two-room schoolhouse near the foot of Long Hill in East Sebago, in the proximity of her grandparents' graves, close to the Northwest River where they had once farmed. She was a remarkable woman who commanded the respect of all her students and who left an indelible impression upon most. When she retired, she went to live with her two bachelor brothers—Grover and Leon, who were very successful farmers at Hillside. Mamie White (Miss White to all her students) died in 1960.

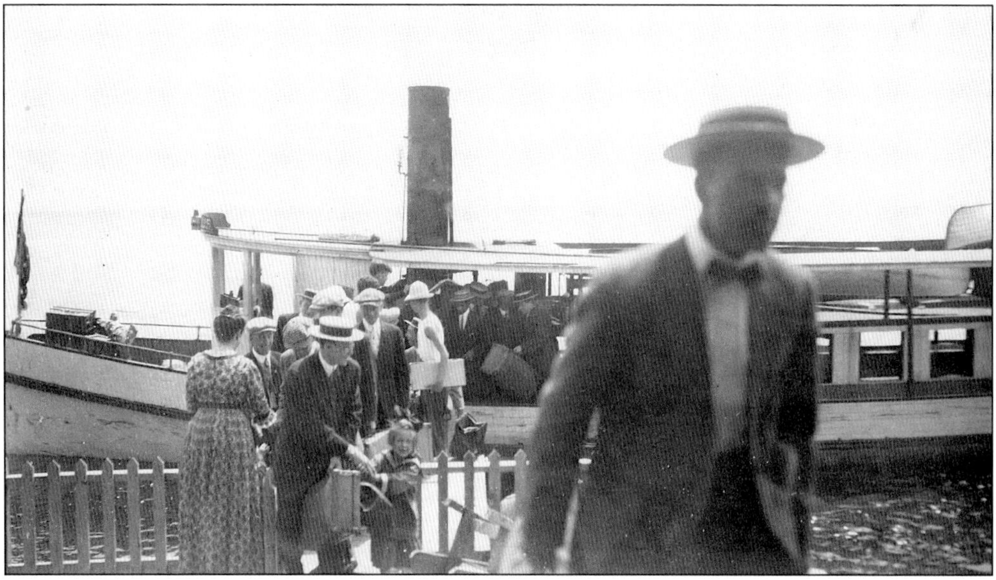

Arriving at Camp O-At-Ka, c. 1918. Ever since 1906, when Camp O-At-Ka was founded, boys have been arriving each summer to spend either half or the full season at this 75-acre boys' camp on the west shore of Sebago Lake between East and North Sebago. In the early days the boys arrived at Sebago Lake Station by train and then transferred to one of the steamers owned by the Songo River and Bay of Naples Company (after 1912 the Songo River Line). Here, boys are shown disembarking from the *Worrambus* at the O-At-Ka dock. Today they arrive by private cars at the camp or by bus or plane in either Portland or Boston, where they are met by camp staff.

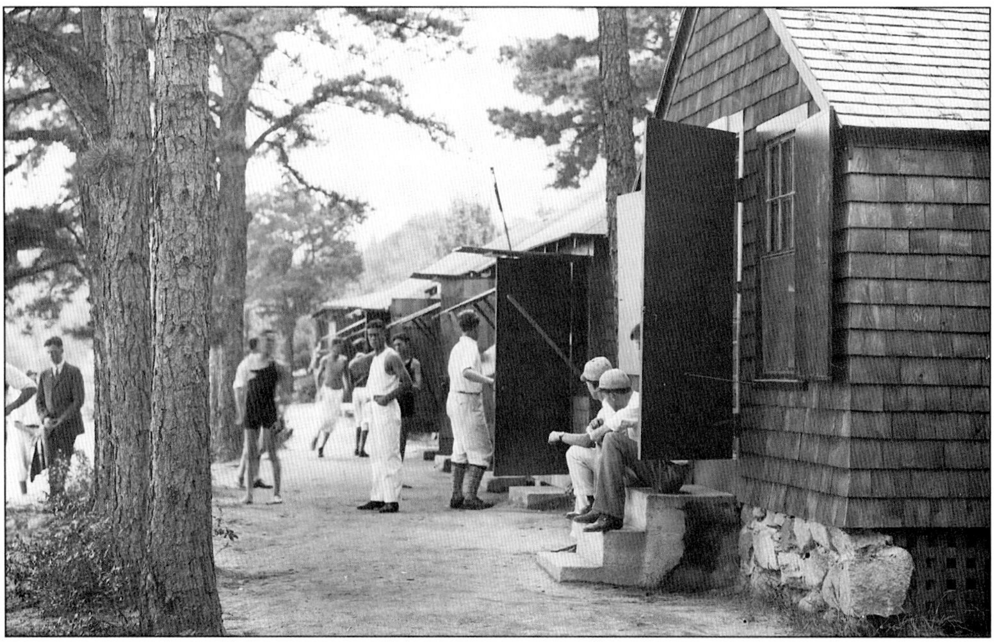

O-At-Ka's Senior Unit, c. 1935. These boys in the senior unit on the edge of Sebago Lake are probably waiting for the bugle to sound for them to come to the dining hall or to report for camp activities.

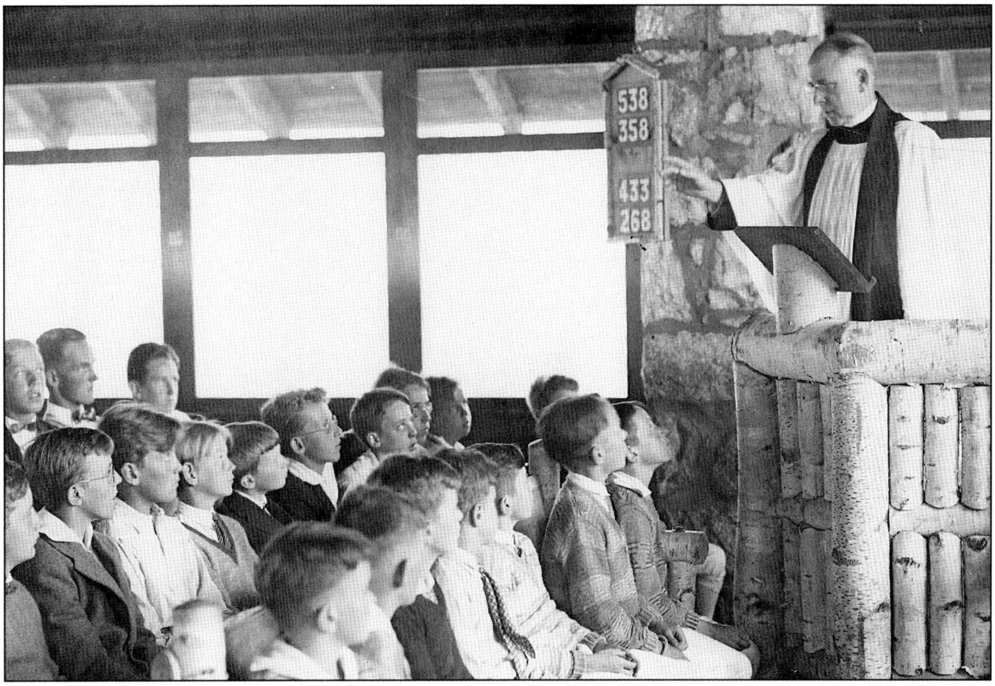

A Sunday Service in the Chapel, c. 1935. Reverend Ernest J. Dennen, the founder of Camp O-At-Ka, is conducting a Sunday service in the rustic chapel, built in 1920. O-At-Ka operates within the Episcopalian tradition, and unlike most boys' and girls' camps in the area that are based on various traditions and lore of our American Indians, O-At- Ka is steeped in the rich legends of King Arthur and the Knights of the Round Table. Besides the great hall and the castle, each cabin in the junior, middle, and senior units bears the name of a mythical English castle. Such Arthurian values as chivalry, obedience, and truth are stressed.

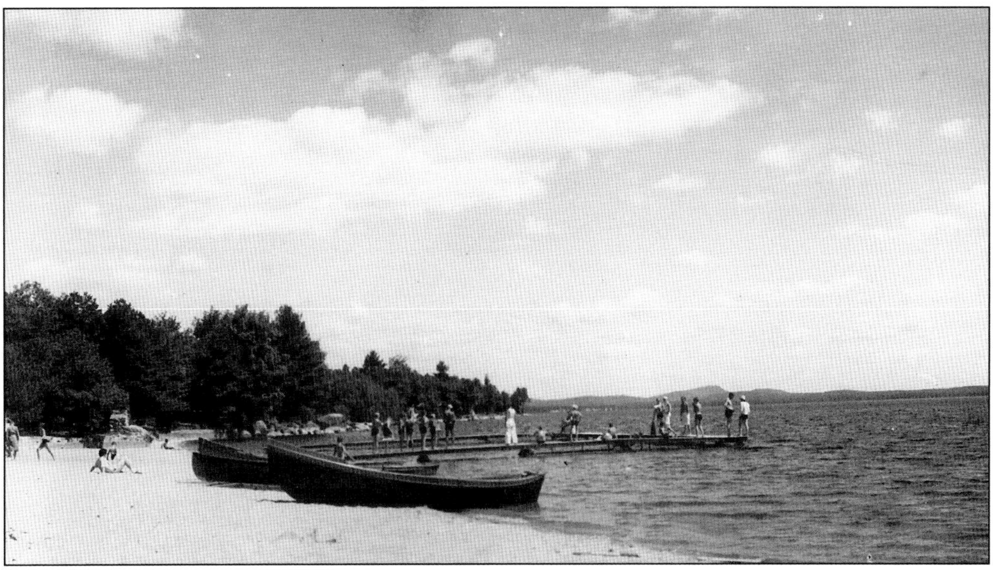

O-At-Ka's Waterfront, c. 1935. O-At-Ka is blessed with a half-mile waterfront, including this capacious sandy beach where groups of boys are receiving swimming and possibly life-saving lessons.

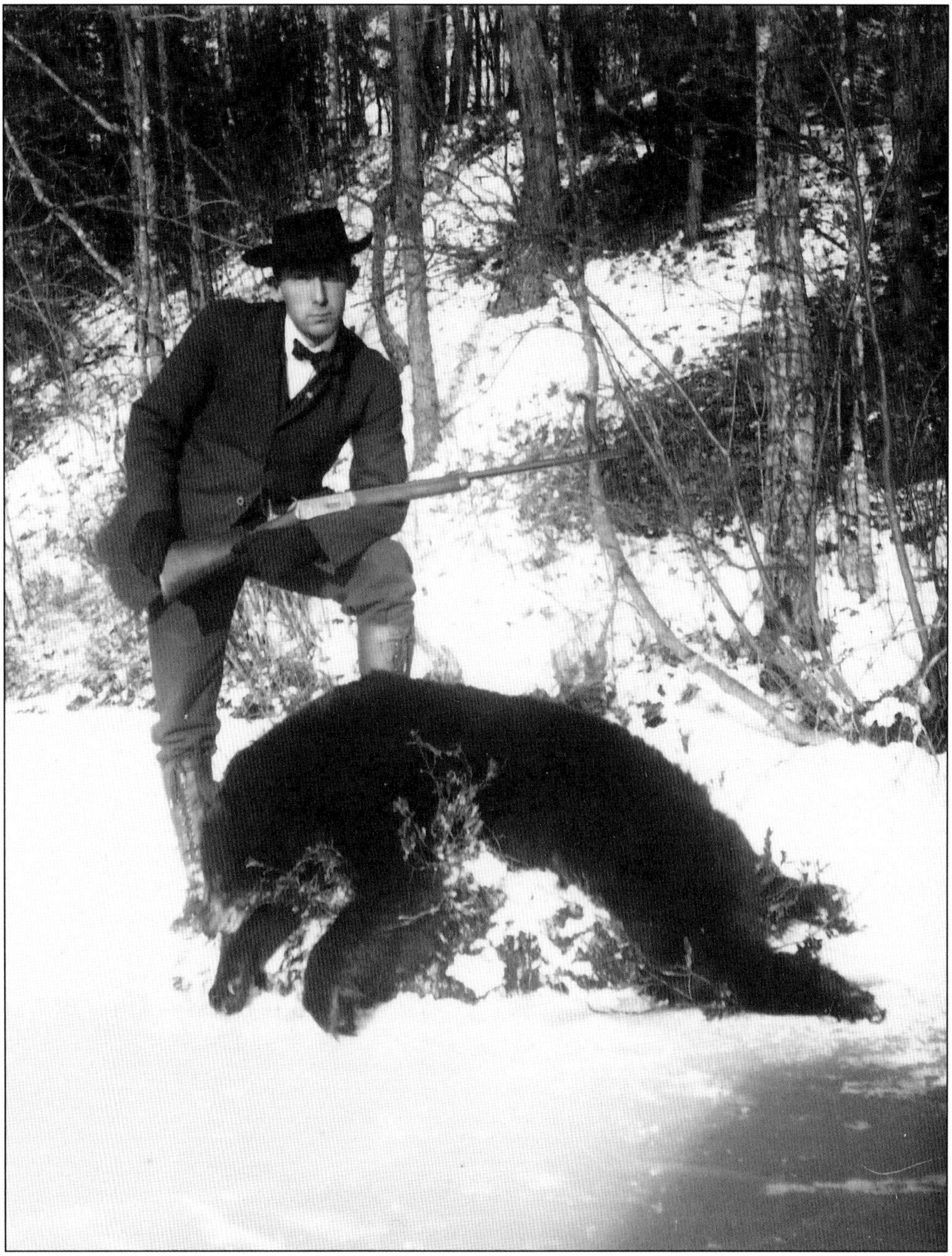

Carlton Martin and His Bear, 1908. Carlton Martin was a dapper young man, who must have changed into his finest clothes to be photographed with this 257-pound black bear he shot on January 13, 1908. For many years Carlton lived with his wife Inez and daughter Julia in a house up on the hill from the road to East Baldwin (Mattocks), at the end of East Sebago Village. He owned a boat shop down the hill and across the road, and enjoyed the reputation of being one of the finest builders of wooden boats of all sizes in the entire Sebago Lake region. He built the much-admired *Ramona I* and *II*, which were used by the Spauldings to take guests on cruises around Sebago Lake.

Five

Naples

First Settled: 1774
Incorporated: 1834
Population: 3,000
Area: 31.25 square miles
Principle Settlements: Naples, Edes Falls

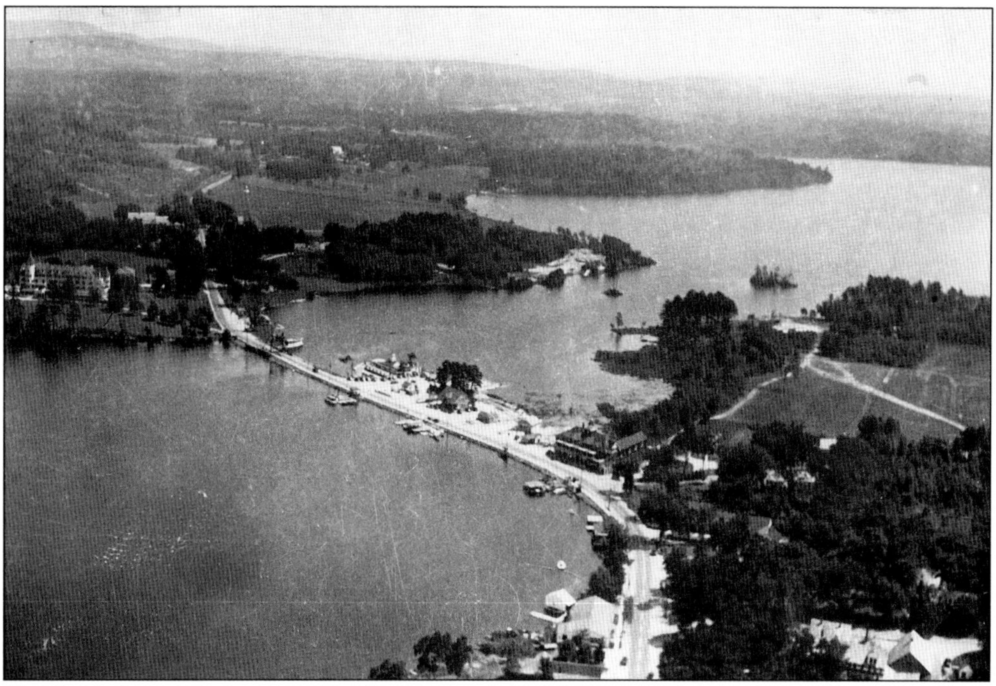

The Bay of Naples, c. 1940. This bird's-eye view of the beautiful Bay of Naples clearly evinces why Naples very early developed into a mecca for summer visitors. The body of water to the right is Brandy Pond (the Bay of Naples), which is linked to Sebago Lake by the Songo River. Chute's River (said to be the world's shortest river), spanned by a swing bridge, joins Brandy Pond with Long Lake (Long Pond). In the left-hand corner overlooking Long Lake is the Bay of Naples Inn (Hotel), which was by far the largest hotel in the Sebago Lake region. The road that is visible is Route 302 or the old Roosevelt Trail (Highway), a vital artery linking much of the hinterland with Portland and consequently hastening the development of Naples, as well as Casco, Raymond, and Windham.

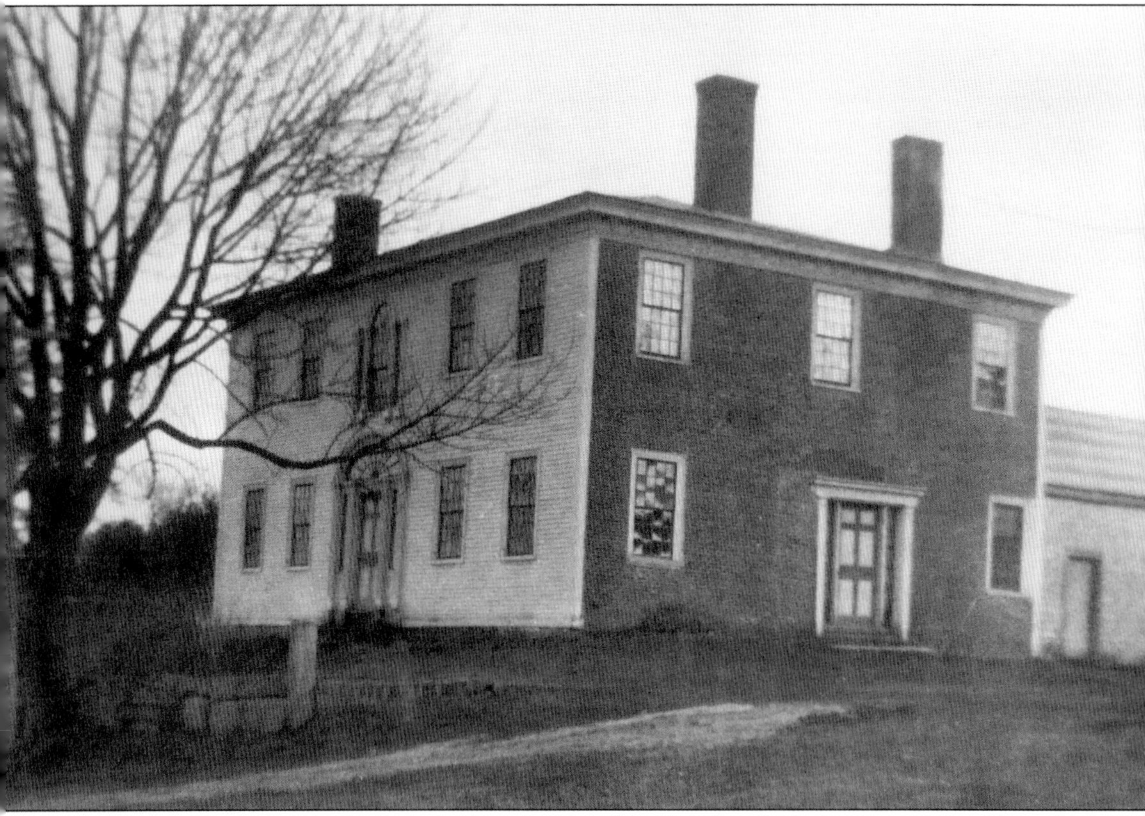

"The Manor," 1918. This outstanding historical landmark, which has been entered in the National Register of Historic Places, is thought to be the oldest house in Naples. Built between 1792 and 1799 by Squire George Peirce, a distinguished businessman and civic leader credited with having been the first permanent settler in Naples at Edes Falls, it is partially brick, has four massive chimneys, a hip roof, twenty-four light windows, and a beautiful Palladian window. Being located on the major route from Bridgton to Portland, this impressive Federalist dwelling served as a popular hostelry and inn for several decades. Behind "The Manor" is Skid Hill, so named because choice pine logs were skidded down by oxen to Mast Cove on Long Pond, and then floated down to Falmouth (Portland) in pre-Revolutionary times to be used as masts by the British Navy.

The town of Naples, which was incorporated on March 4, 1834, was created out of segments of the towns of Otisfield, Bridgton, Harrison, Raymond, and Sebago. Like the other towns that surround Sebago Lake, it was logging and sawmills that set what eventually became Naples in motion. Then came the farms. Apple growing in particular became profitable after the building of the Cumberland & Oxford Canal. Eleazer Bartlett and his two sons, John and Isaac, settled at Bartlett's Corner near Edes Falls and were the first to clear a sizeable tract of land extending to Long Pond. Other early families were the Jacksons, Kimballs, Chaplins, Leavitts, Chutes, Goodridges, Sanborns, Perleys, and Leaches.

Because of its extraordinary setting, Naples began attracting summer visitors even before it was incorporated as a town. Thomas Chute opened the Elm House in 1816. Fire destroyed it in 1822, but he rebuilt only to have it go up in flames again in 1876. Other hotels and inns opened in its wake. However, it was Charles L. Goodridge, the grandson of Benjamin Goodridge, who really put Naples on the map as a summer recreational area when he built the Bay of Naples Inn and established his "little white fleet," known as the Songo River Line. Some sources also mention him in terms of the Casino.

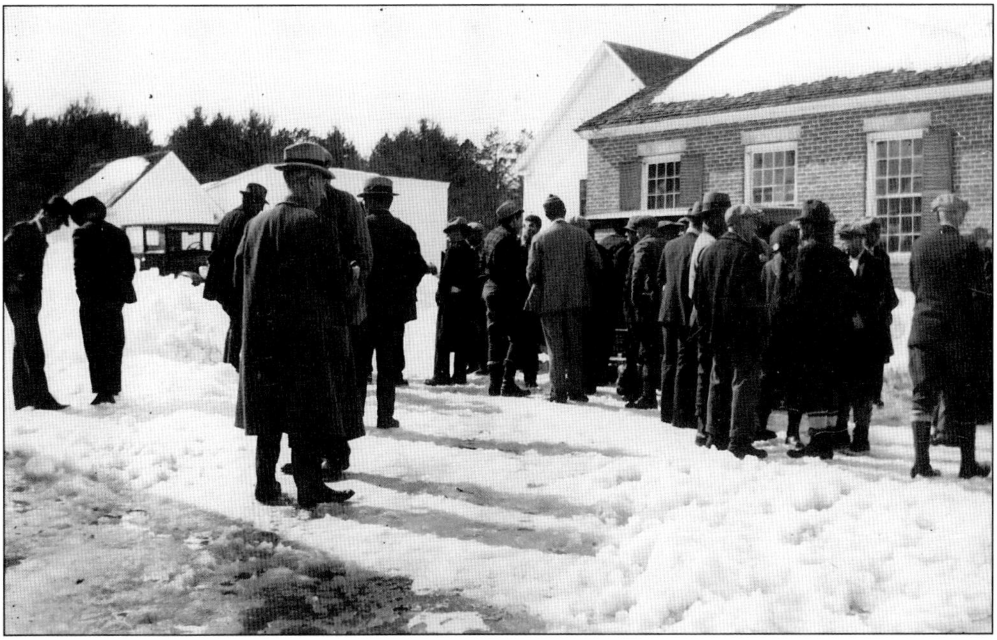

A Town Meeting, c. 1928. The local men airing their views during the noon recess at an annual town meeting at the Naples Town Hall (now the town office). The first town meeting held in Naples was on April 1, 1834, at the village school. The New England town meeting is one of the few surviving pockets of pure democracy in the world, thus contributing a unique seasoning to the rural communities—especially in the tri-state area.

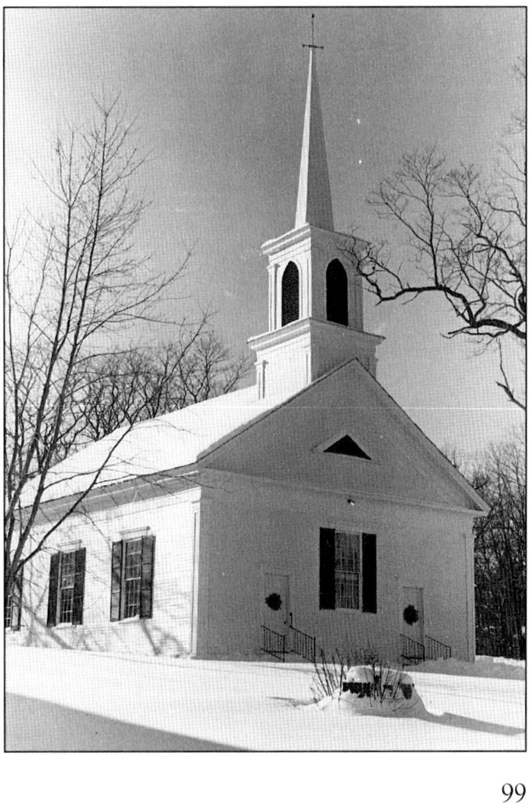

The Union Church. Like the town meeting, the small, white clapboard churches, with their pyramidal steeples pointed skyward, are an integral part of New England rural landscapes and help to provide a cohesiveness to small communities such as Naples. This sedate and lovely little church amidst the chiaroscuro surroundings of winter was built in 1857. The ministers of both the Congregationalists and the Freewill Baptists conducted services here.

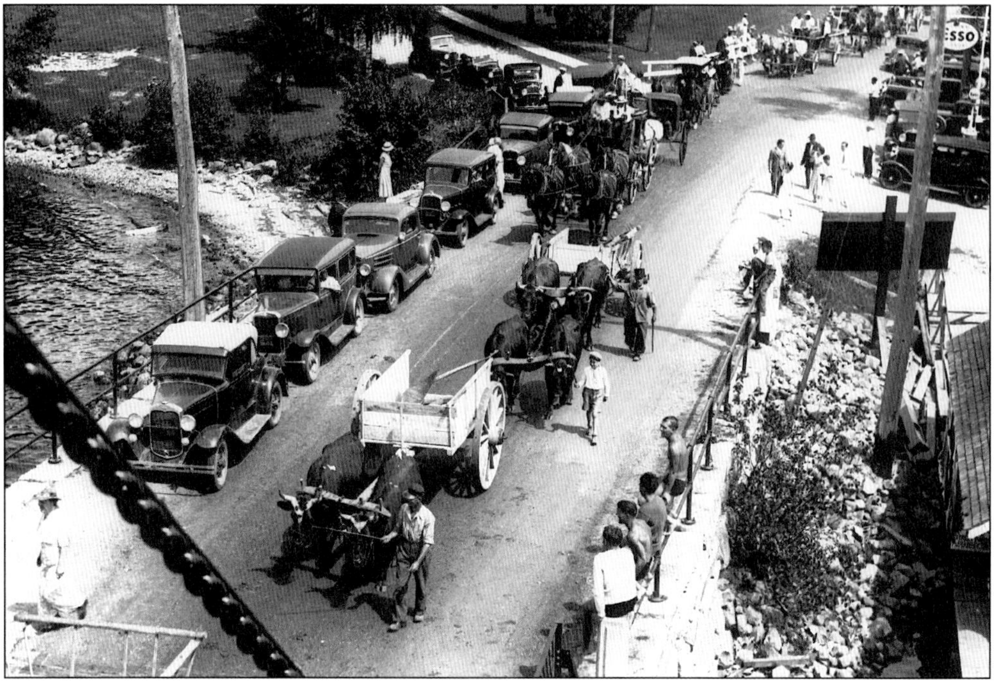

The Naples Centennial Parade, 1934. The high point of the Naples Centennial celebration during the summer of 1934 was this parade, viewed from what was then the draw bridge spanning Chute's River between Long Lake and the Bay of Naples. Heading the line of automobiles, which today would be precious antiques, is a 1930 model-A Ford and a 1928 Chevrolet. Following behind the two ox carts is a fine Concord coach.

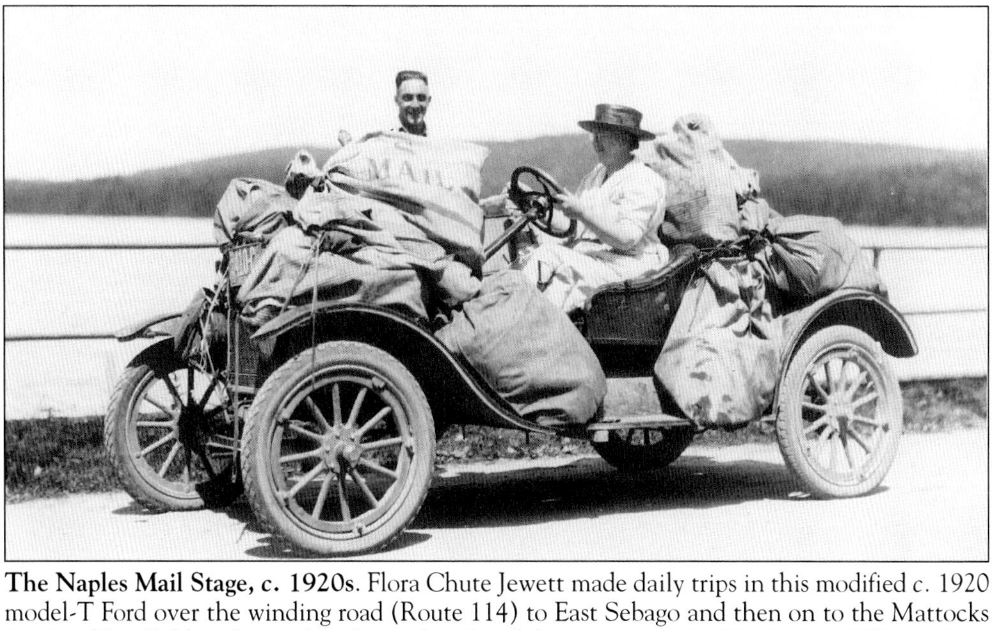

The Naples Mail Stage, c. 1920s. Flora Chute Jewett made daily trips in this modified *c.* 1920 model-T Ford over the winding road (Route 114) to East Sebago and then on to the Mattocks Station (East Baldwin) to pick up bags of mail and then return to the Naples Post Office, where the mail would be sorted and much of it delivered by mail boat on Long Lake, Brandy Pond, and down the Songo River to Sebago Lake. Long Lake is visible in the background.

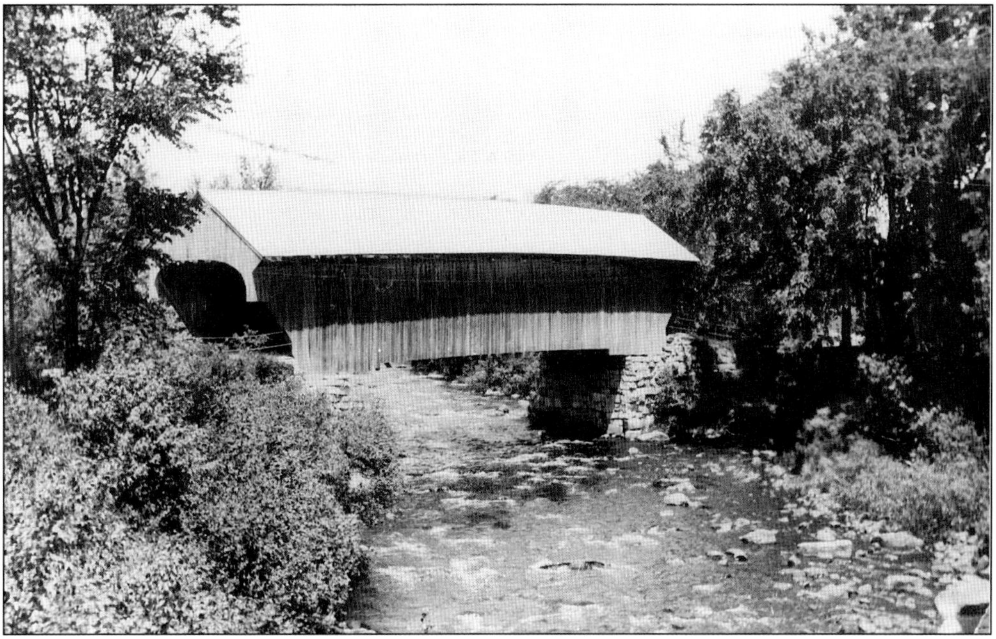

The Covered Bridge at Edes Falls, c. 1900. This picturesque covered bridge once spanned Crooked River at Edes Falls. Unfortunately it was washed away in the flood of 1936.

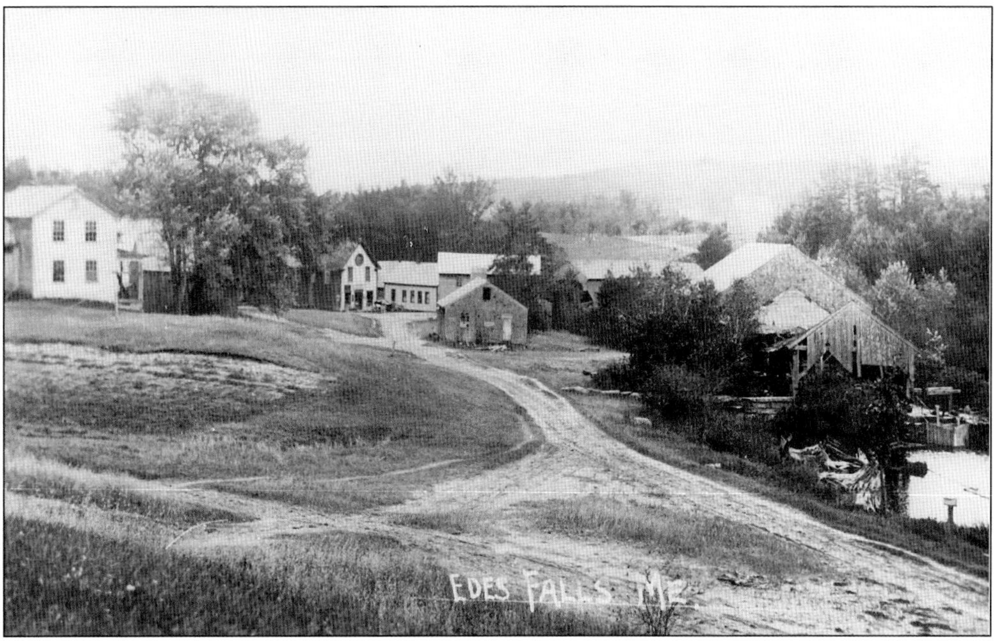

Edes Falls, c. 1895. It was here that George Peirce of Groton, Massachusetts, first settled in 1774 and built a cabin, sawmill, and gristmill—and initially the area was called Peirce's Falls. Shortly before and for several decades after the Civil War, Edes Falls was a bustling little commercial and manufacturing community of around forty houses, supporting six stores and boasting a pants shop, a wool carding mill, a milling company, and two sawmills. By the time this photograph was taken looking down Jug Town Road, Edes Falls was on the decline. Visible beyond the old mill is the covered bridge.

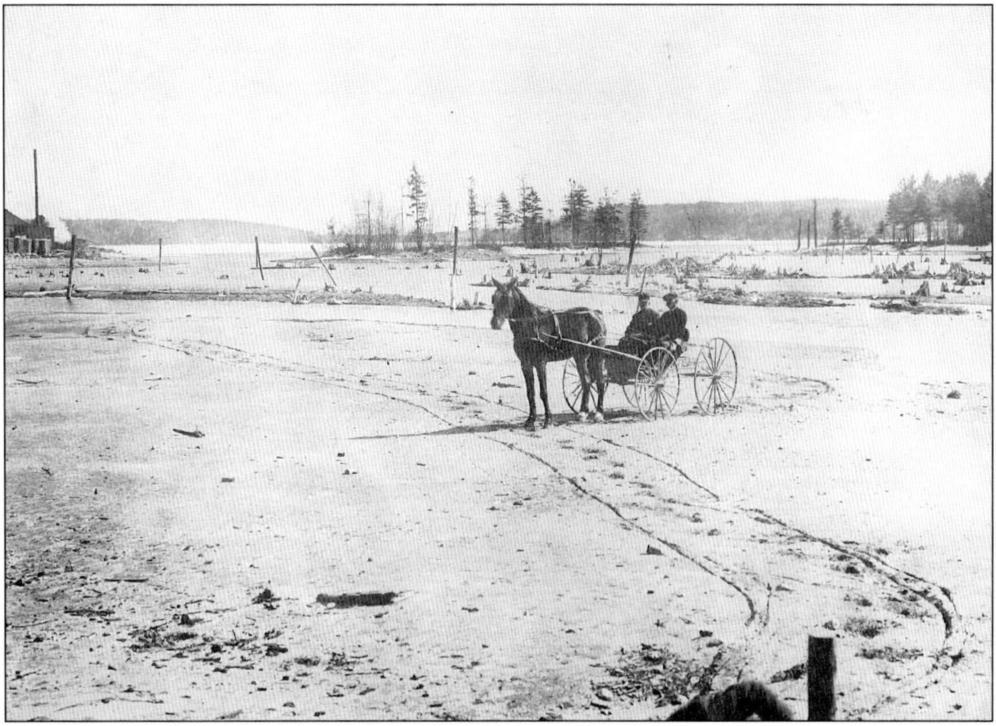

Lewis Knight's Mill, c. 1895. Lewis Knight owned and operated the large steam-powered sawmill (visible to the left in the distance) on the edge of Brandy Pond near the mouth of Chute's River. Captain Mel Brackett, one of the famous canal and freight boat captains and a partner with Lewis Knight in the freight boat business, is enjoying a buggy ride on the beach with an unidentified companion.

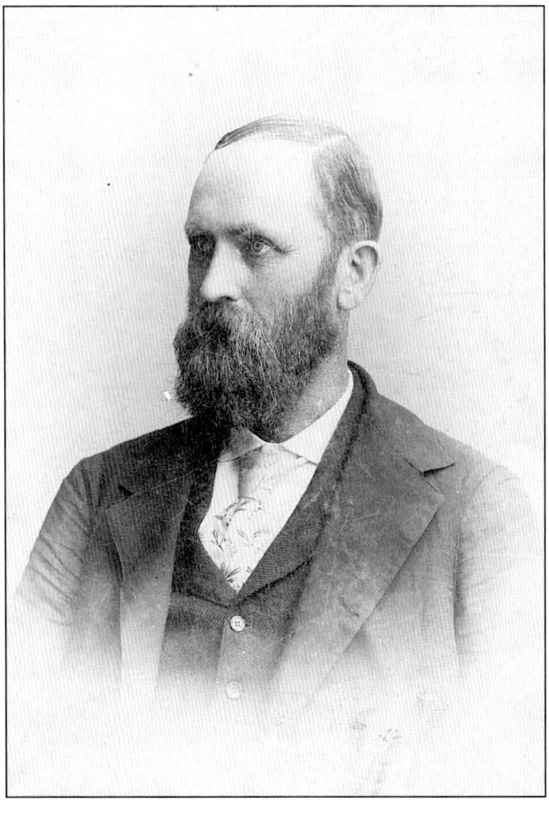

Lewis P. Knight, c. 1910. Lewis P. Knight (1852–1926), the son of Major W. Knight and the grandson of Nathaniel Knight (the progenitor of the Knight family of Naples), was a prominent lumber man and freight boat owner (Knight and Brackett). In addition to operating the permanent steam mill on Brandy Pond where he specialized in manufacturing shooks, he also operated portable mills on the large tracts of timberland which he acquired.

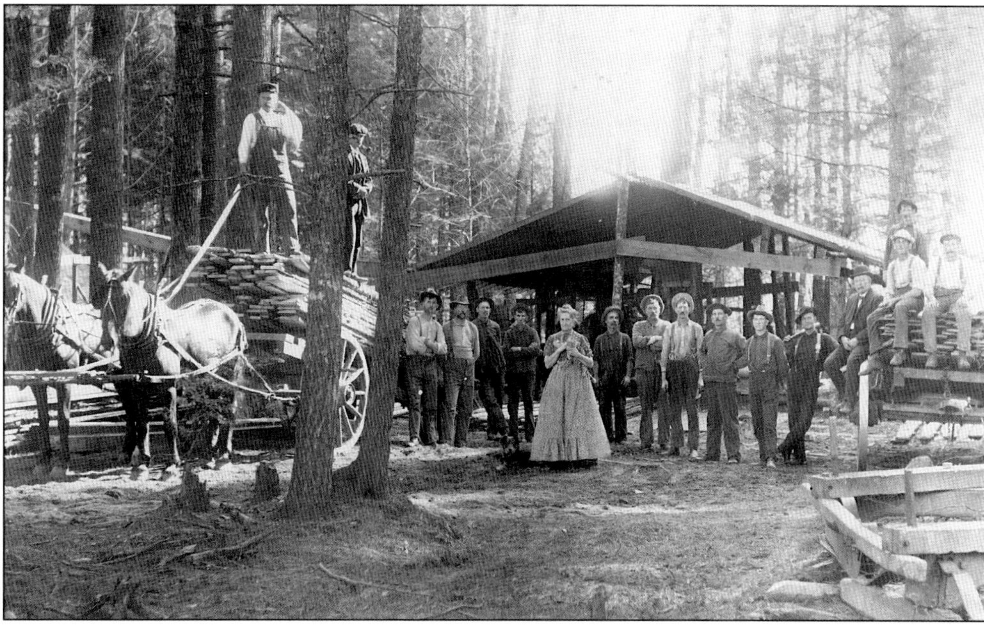

Lewis Knight's Portable Mill, c. 1895. Until after World War II at least, portable sawmills such as this one were operating on logging sites throughout Maine. The bulky logs were sawed into rough lumber, and then the lighter boards were transported to planing mills located on permanent sites. This is one of Lewis Knight's portable mills. He obviously employed a sizeable crew of cutters, sawyers, and teamsters.

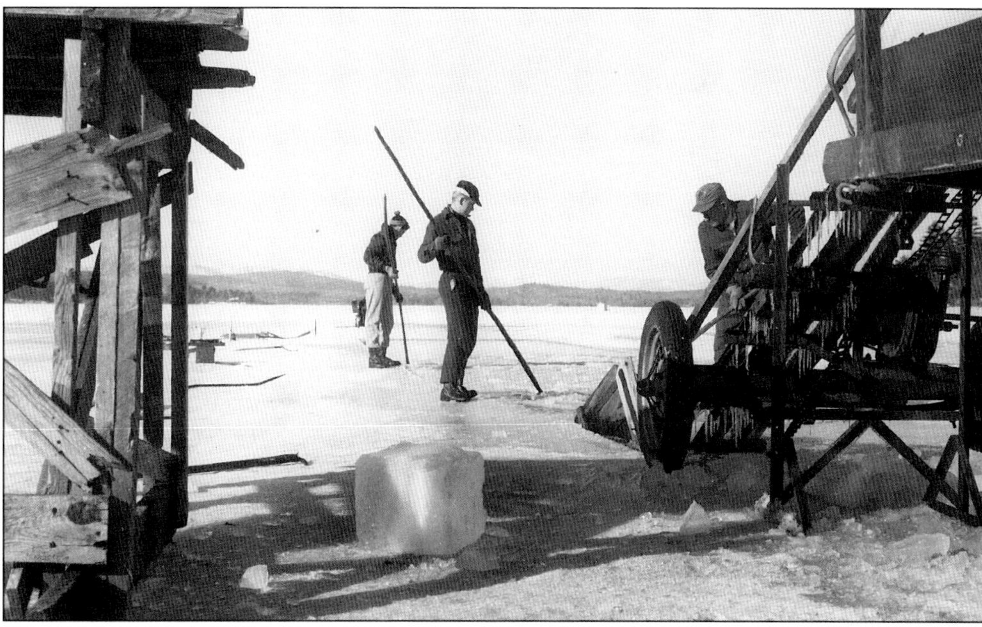

Harvesting Ice on Long Lake, c. 1938. Until the refrigerator replaced the ice box, harvesting ice in the winter was as important as harvesting logs and cordwood. By the time this photograph was taken by O.B. Dennison of Cornish, however, ice cutting was rapidly declining. Don Rogers may be doing the cutting, since he was the last person in Naples to cut ice. He averaged around 5,000 cakes a winter, each weighing about 140 pounds.

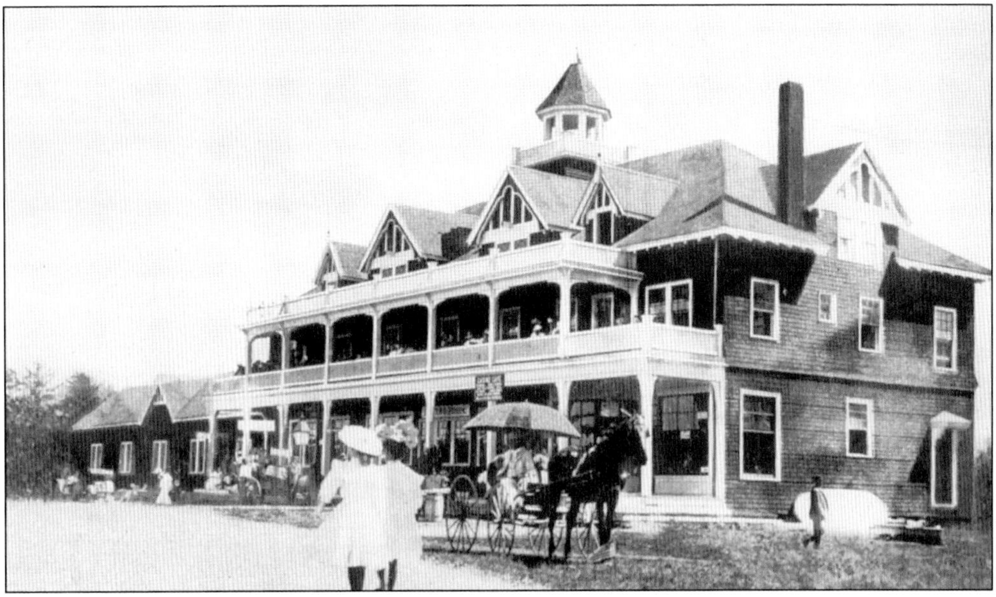

The Casino, c. 1905. The Casino on the Causeway greatly enhanced Naples as a summer amusement and recreational center. It was built in 1902 through the initiative of a local cooperation called the Longwood Real Estate Company. For the grand opening, Julian Eltinge, a famous "female impersonator," came up from Boston to perform. The first movies in town were shown here and for two summers the opera *Hansel and Gretel* was presented at the Casino.

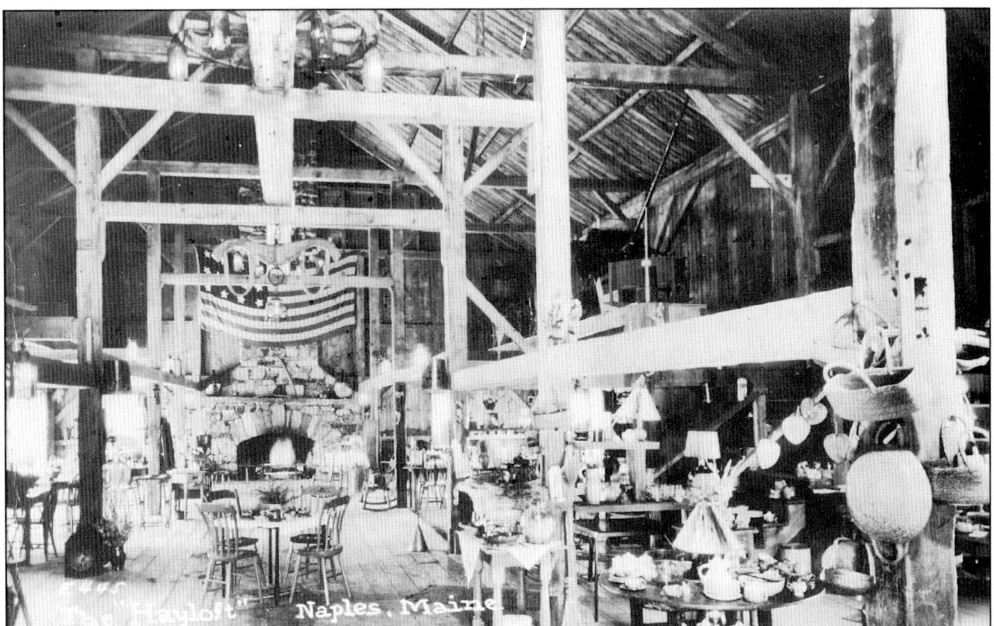

The Hayloft, c. 1927. Shortly after 1900, Mrs. Charles Soden purchased the large rambling farm buildings known as the White place and converted the barn into a tea room. All but the barn were destroyed by fire in 1951. Unfortunately, as a night club in the 1960s renamed Serenity Hill, it was anything but serene.

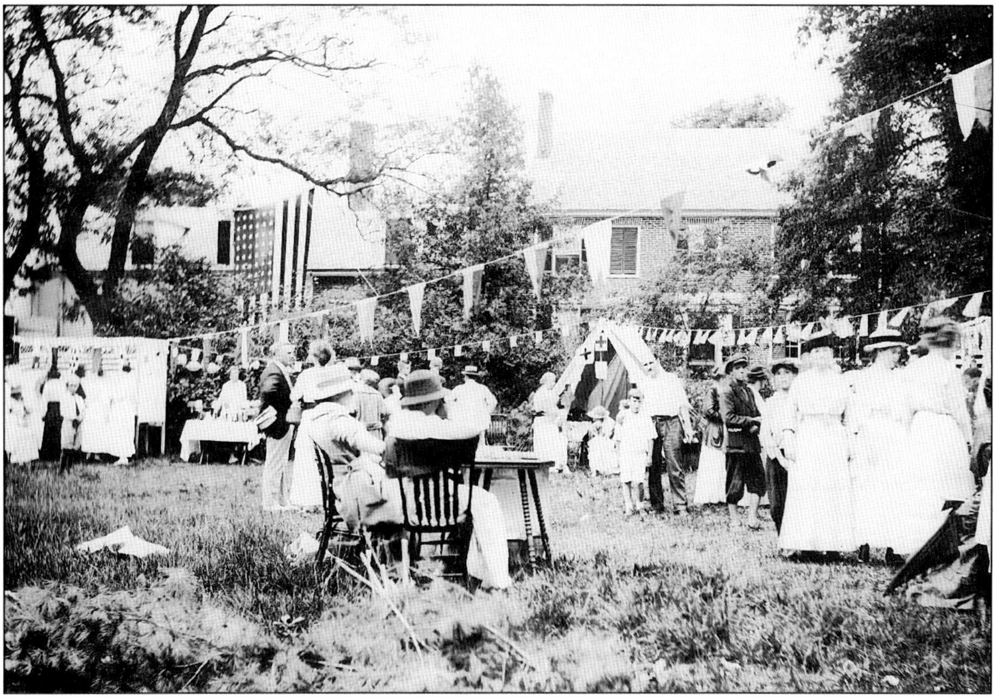

A Lawn Party at Louisa Robinson's, c. 1920. For many years lawn parties to raise money for the local library were an annual event held at Louisa Robinson's home directly across from the Lake House on the Lake House Road. The people here are a mixture of local and summer folks. For several years, beginning in 1909, a room in Mrs. Robinson's "Brick House" served as the local library. Over the years local and summer residents cooperated very closely in organizing various other types of social events and entertainment programs to raise money to purchase books and maintain a library in the community. Since 1939 the town has appropriated funds each year to support the library. It is presently located in Naples Village at the former Locust House, which for a number of years took in summer boarders and rented cottages on the premises.

NAPLES LIBRARY BENEFIT

MONDAY, AUGUST 5, 1912

PROGRAM

Sketch, "Our Aunt from California"

Vaudeville Act
By CAMP KINEO BOYS

Selections on Mandolin
By MR. DANIEL TEAGUE

Pantomime
Coached by MRS. GOUDY
Pine-o'-mine Tea Room

DANCING

A Naples Library Benefit, 1912. This varied program of evening entertainment also was a means of raising money for the Naples Library.

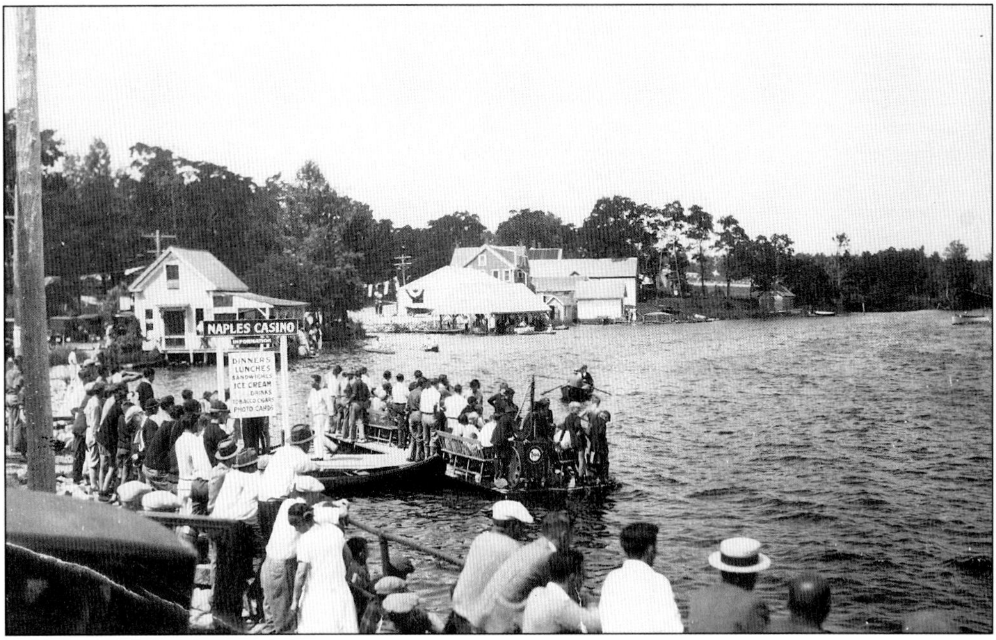

The Causeway, c. 1928. No place in the Sebago Lake area attracted more people on an average day throughout the summer months than the Naples Causeway, and this holds true even today. A major attraction here at the Casino wharf for a couple of summers in the early 1920s was a hydroplane, owned by a Mr. Loveitt of Portland and flown by a former Army pilot. For $5 one could be flown up Long Lake to Long Point and back.

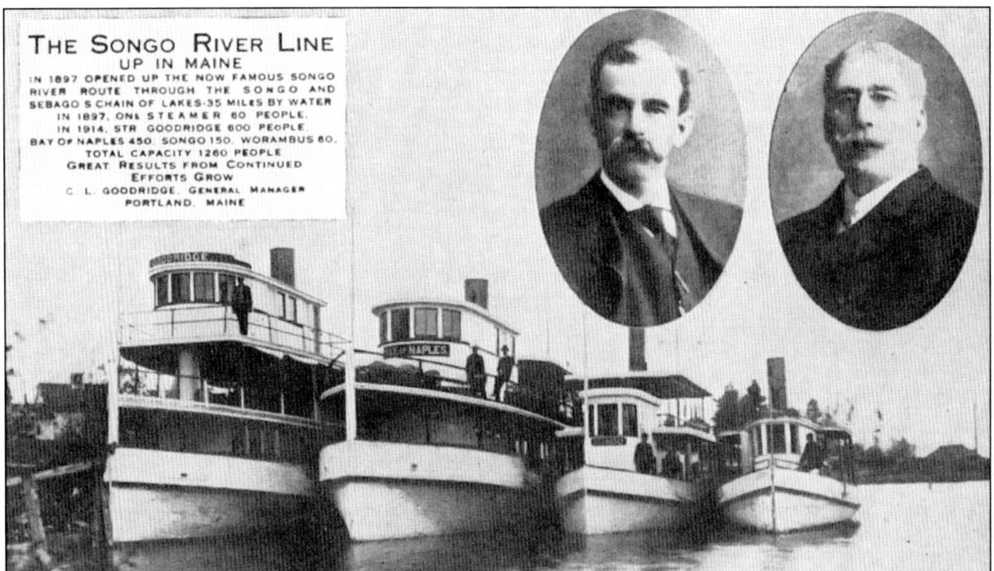

The Songo River Line, c. 1920. It was indeed an impressive sight when (from left to right) the *Goodridge*, the *Bay of Naples*, the *Songo*, and the *Worrambus* were secured side by side in the Bay of Naples. Charles L. Goodridge owned and operated the line from 1897 to 1917 when he sold out to C.W. Woodward and Captain S.W. Sawyer. In 1930 they sold the line to Captain H.W. Robinson of Machiasport, who ran it for another two years.

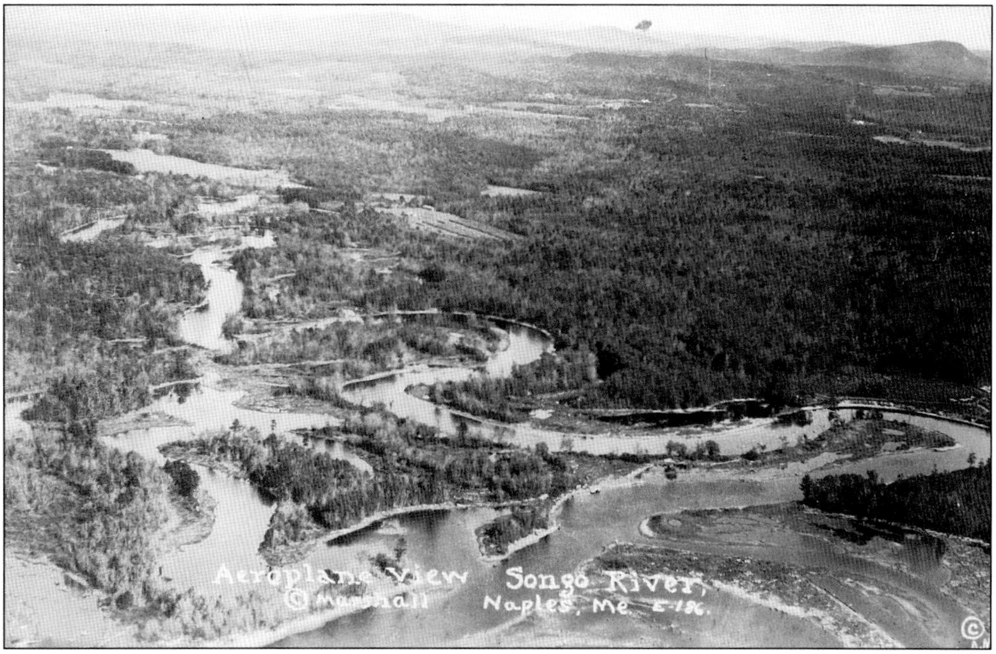

An Aerial View of the Songo River. The sinuous Songo River coils like a huge serpent for 6 miles between Brandy Pond and Sebago Lake, forming twenty-seven turns. Longfellow immortalized this scenic river when he wrote *The Songo* on September 18, 1875. In the opening stanza he states: "Nowhere such a devious stream/except in fancy or in dream/Winding slow through bush and brake/links together lake and lake."

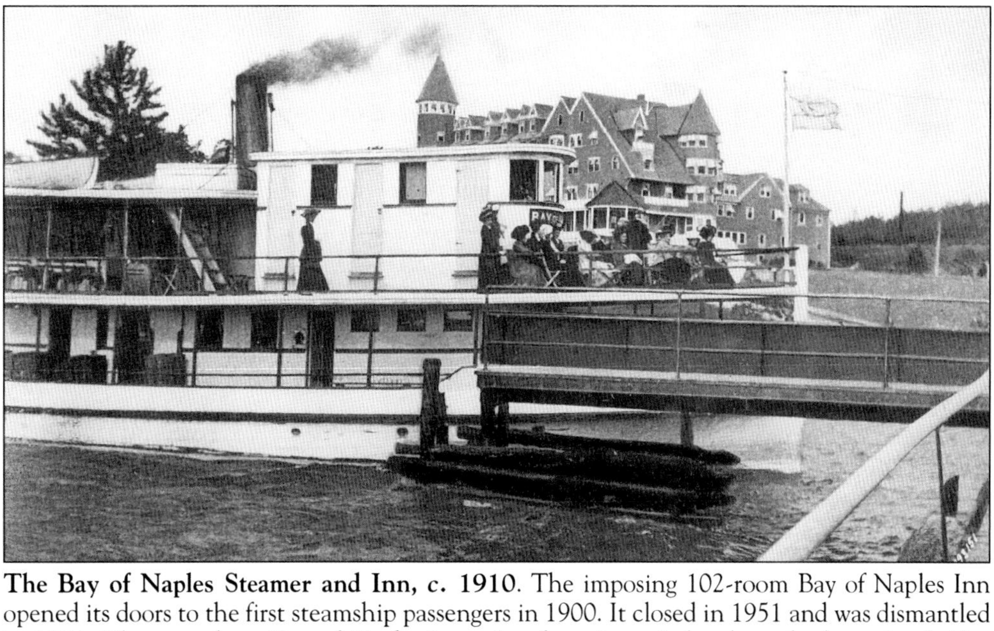

The Bay of Naples Steamer and Inn, c. 1910. The imposing 102-room Bay of Naples Inn opened its doors to the first steamship passengers in 1900. It closed in 1951 and was dismantled in 1964. The steamboat *Bay of Naples* is passing from Long Lake through the swing bridge spanning Chute's River and is headed down Brandy Pond and into Sebago Lake via the Songo River. It burned in the bay for which it was named in 1931.

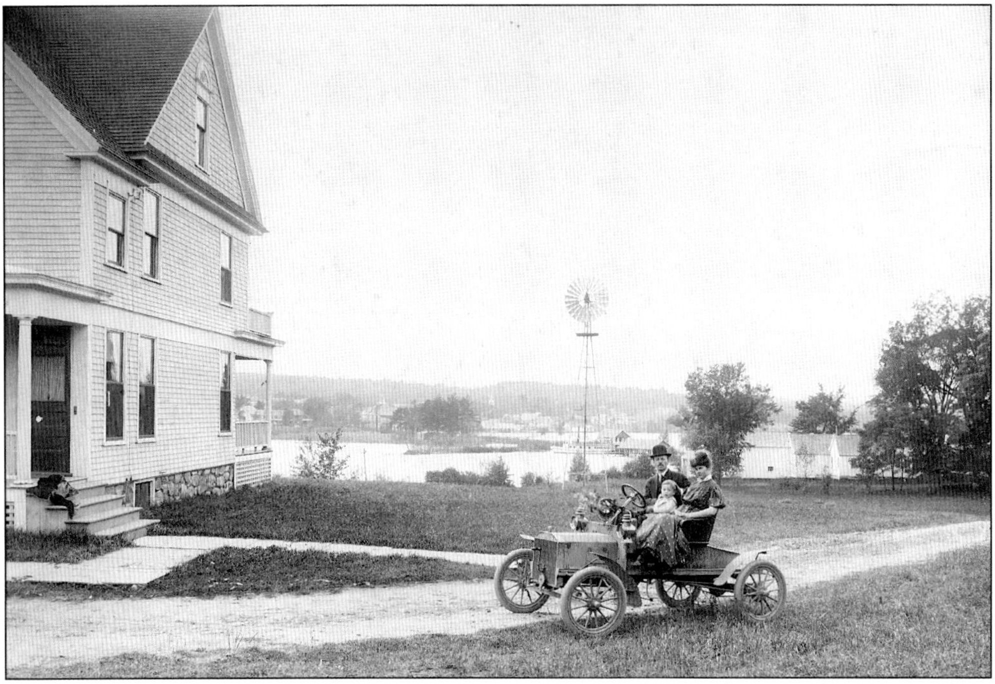

A Family Ride, c. 1906. Dr. Jerome Fickett is set to take his wife Electra and son Lewis for a ride in his new model-N Ford. Visible from the Fickett home is a portion of the Bay of Naples and Naples Village.

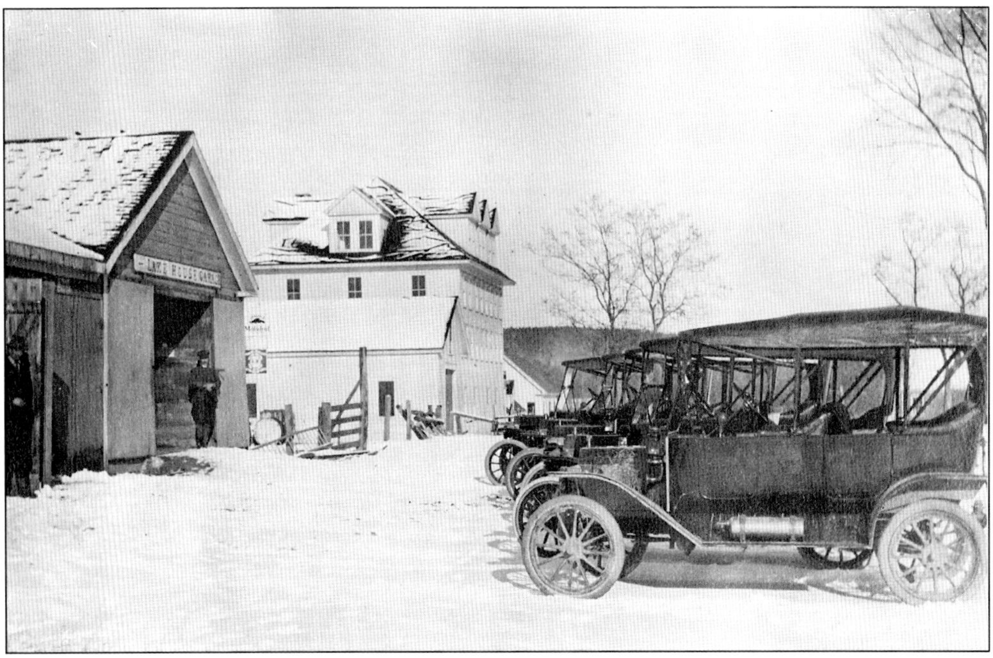

The Automobile Age, 1914. This handsome display of 1914 model-T Fords, three of which are touring cars, were for sale at Henry Teague's Ford Agency at the Lake House Garage. The automobile age had arrived, which would bring about rapid changes to Naples and other communities in the Sebago Lake area.

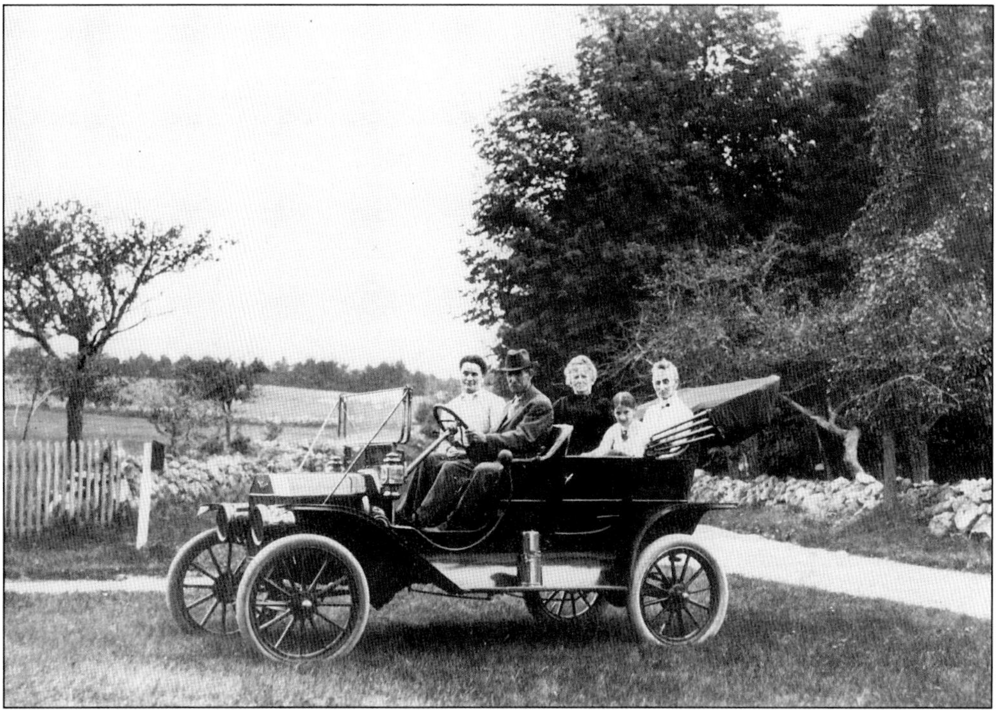

The Lambs Enjoy a Jaunt in the Country, 1909. The automobile was in an embryonic stage when Frank Lamb took several family members for a drive in his new 1909 model-T Ford with carbide headlights and kerosene sidelights. Seated in front is his wife, with Mrs. Henry Lamb (Alice), Rosalie Lamb (a niece), and Anna Lamb (his sister) in the back. The fields along the dusty country roads were still fastidiously manicured, as most of Naple's population was still bonded to the land.

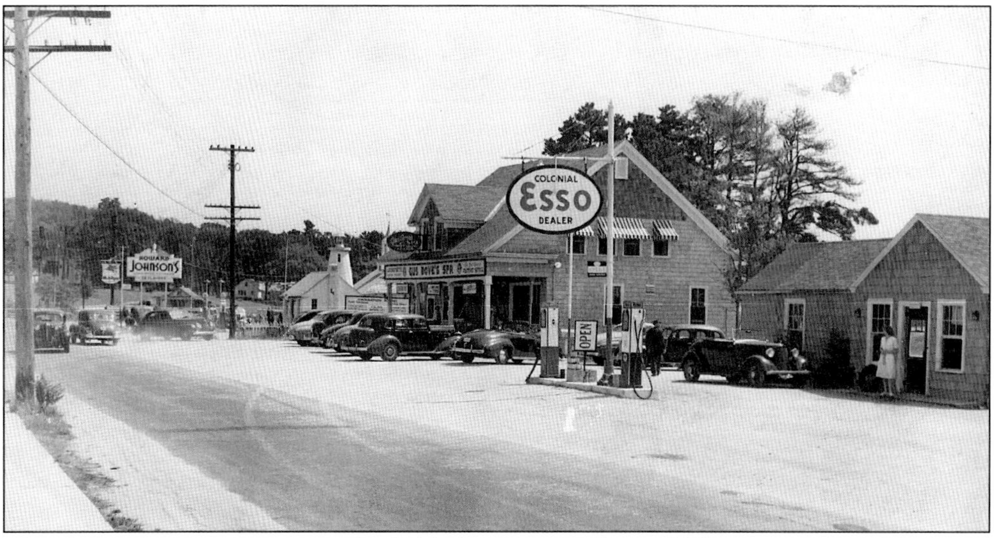

The Causeway in 1940. It is doubtful that the Lambs could have anticipated the rapid alteration of Naples three decades later, and that horse-drawn vehicles would have practically disappeared from our rural and village landscapes. By this time tourism was in high gear as the two gasoline stations and a Howard Johnson's testify.

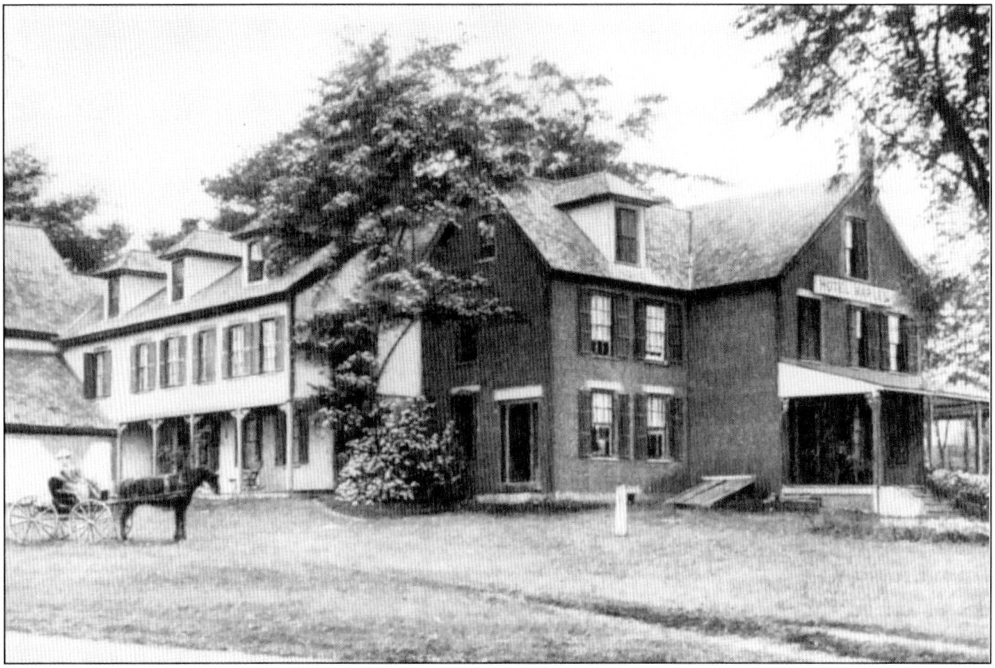

The Hotel Naples, c. 1890. Slipping back again to before the advent of the automobile age, this lovely brick structure on the corner of Routes 114 and 302 was one of the first places in Naples to accommodate summer visitors and traveling salesman. It was first operated by George Hall, a prominent local business man, who played a significant role in developing the local summer boarder trade. Room and board in the beginning was $3.50 a week. Today the present owners run a bed and breakfast here.

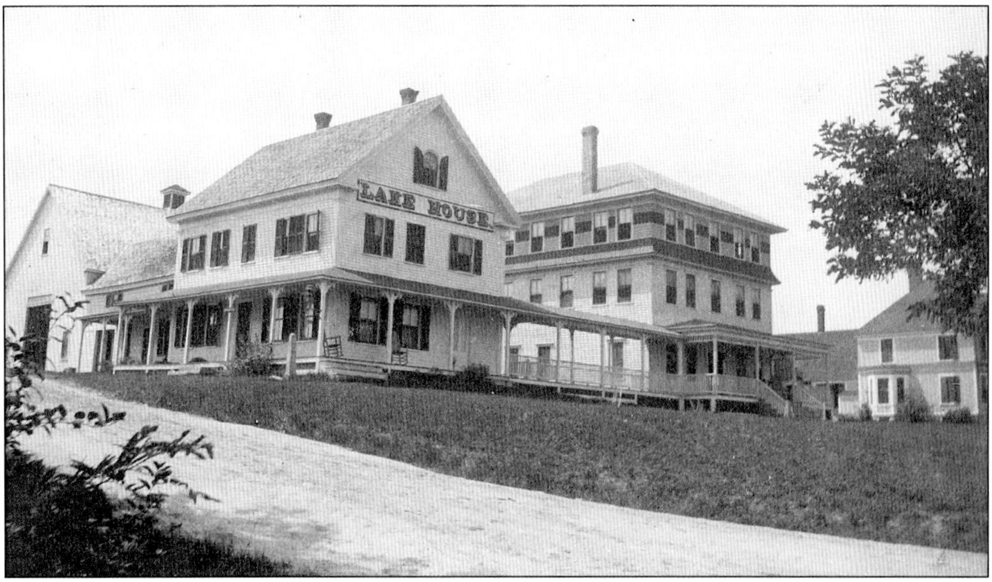

The Lake House and Annex, 1902. Not long after the opening of Hotel Naples, the Lake House was built and opened for business in 1890. Business increased so rapidly in just a few years that the owner, Stillman L. Wentworth, soon added the annex.

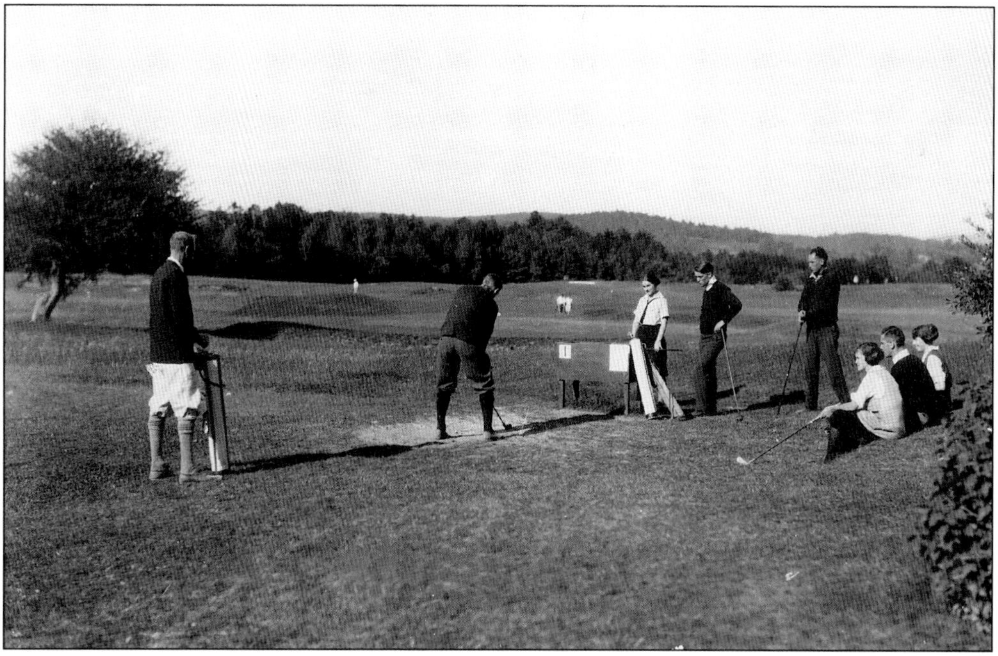

Teeing Off, 1929. A group of golf enthusiasts wait their turn to tee off at the Naples golf course, a few hundred yards from the Causeway on Route 114. It is very possible that after nine holes of golf, this group will head down to the Causeway for a bite to eat, perhaps at what was then the new Lou-Vic Restaurant. The Naples Golf and Country Club, Inc. was organized in 1921 exclusively for the summer residents. The Bay of Naples Inn also maintained a golf course.

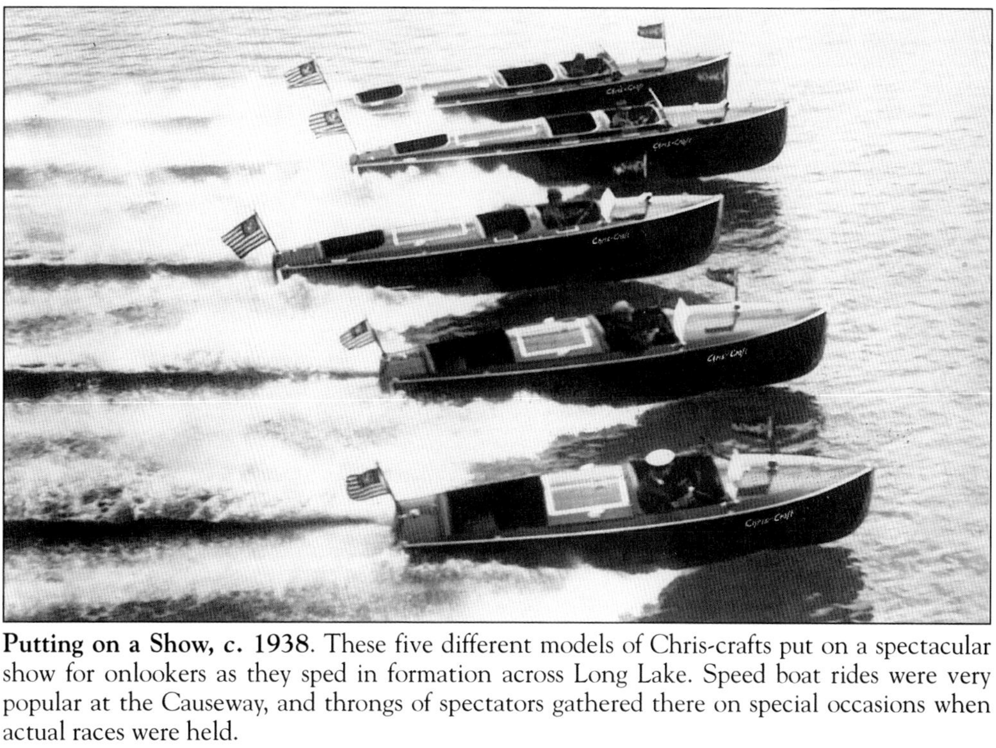

Putting on a Show, c. 1938. These five different models of Chris-crafts put on a spectacular show for onlookers as they sped in formation across Long Lake. Speed boat rides were very popular at the Causeway, and throngs of spectators gathered there on special occasions when actual races were held.

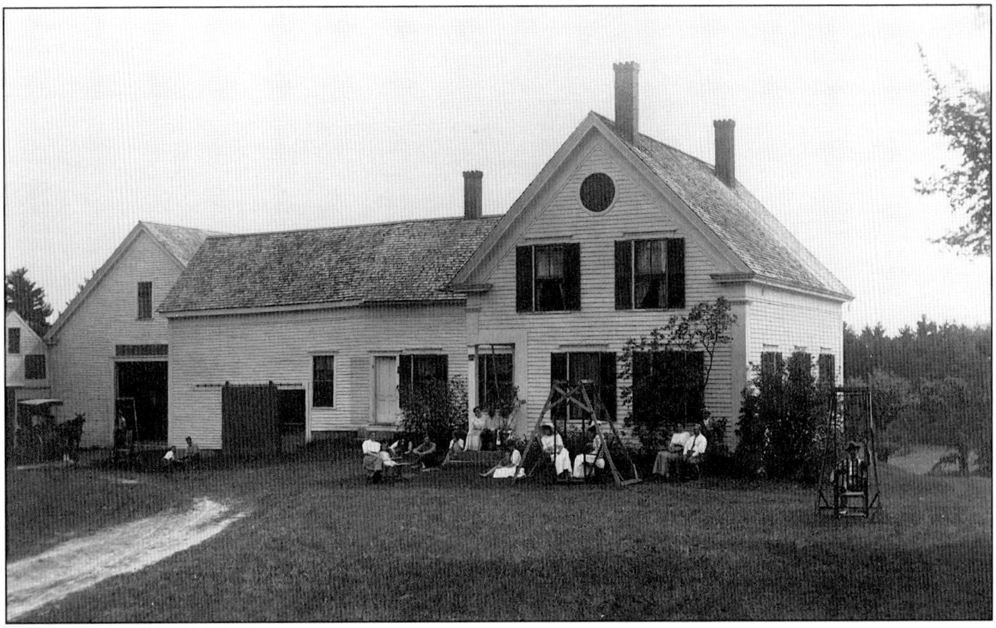

The Proctor House, c. 1915. The Proctor House, with its broad fields extending down to the shoreline of the Bay of Naples, was typical of the farms throughout the Sebago Lake region that began taking in summer guests. Charles and Bessie Proctor opened the door to guests in 1910. Eventually cabins, cottages, and another building were added. The Proctor House was taken down in 1977.

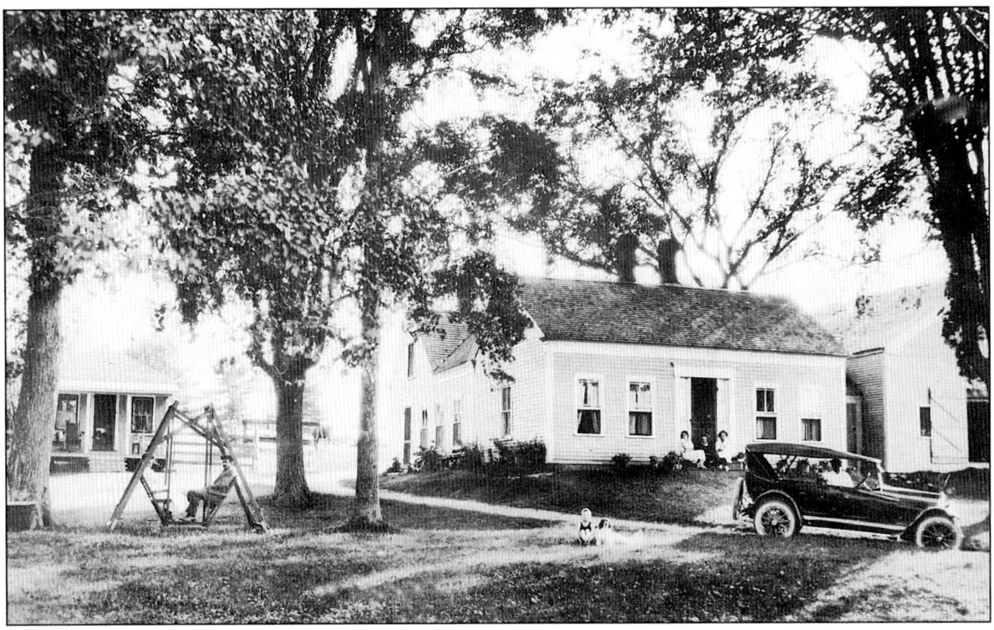

Chaplin Cottages, c. 1923. Where the Romah Motel is today at the junction of Routes 11 and 302, Perley and Nellie Chaplin built the first overnight cabins in the town of Naples at their elm-shaded farm. A family of tourists in what looks to be a 1922 or 1923 Packard have either just arrived or are pulling out to motor on to other places. The tourist era was gaining momentum.

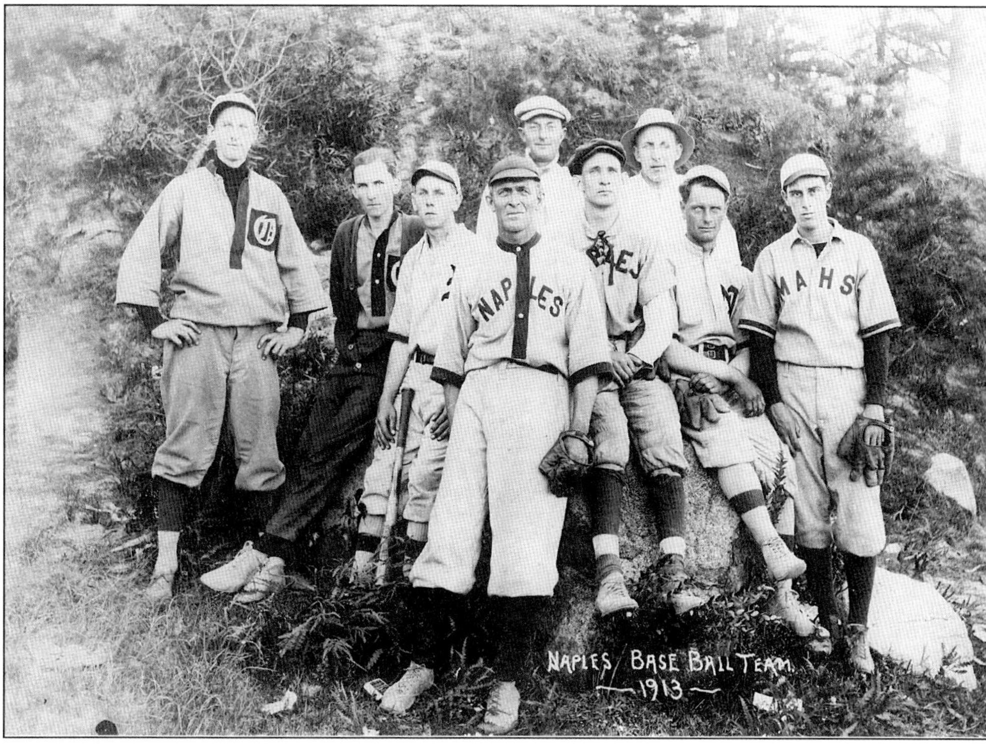

The Naples Town Team, 1913. Until a few decades ago, every town in Maine seemed to support at least one baseball team. Keen but usually friendly rivalries developed between towns such as Naples and Sebago, and in many instances between hamlets within a single town. Many a cow pasture was converted to a baseball field.

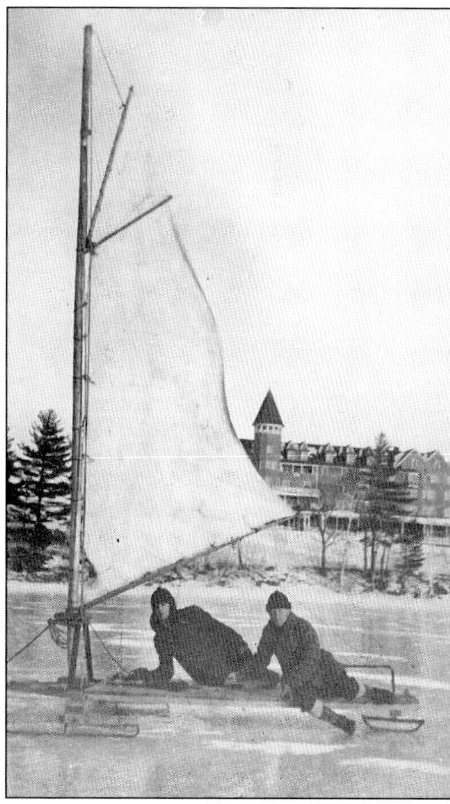

Ice Boating on Long Lake, 1920s. Until more recent years, winter in the Sebago Lake region belonged solely to the natives. Consequently the lakes and ponds were never crowded. Harold Welch (at the tiller) and a companion are enjoying ice boating on the clear black ice of Long Lake in the early part of winter as they glide by the Bay of Naples Inn—closed from early autumn to late spring.

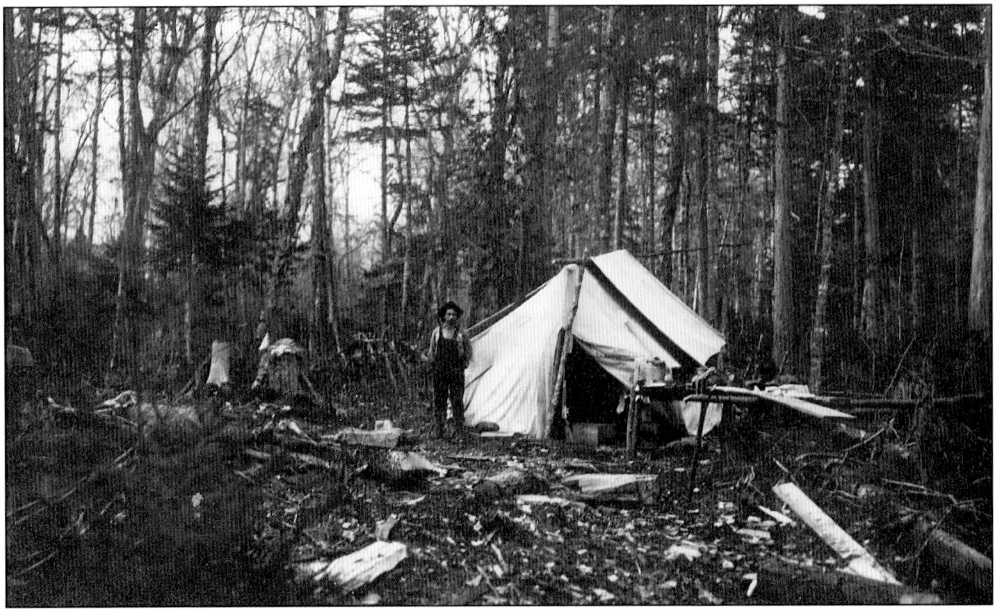

Roughing It, c. 1930. For the more rugged individuals, pitching a tent near some wooded stream or lake was preferable to an overnight cabin or cottage. Of course, it was ever so much more economical. Owners of overnight cabins often provided tenting grounds with outdoor fireplaces for those vacationers who preferred tenting out. Today, campers often travel with some sort of mobile camper or rent a permanent place in a privately owned or government park and leave their campers there from one season to the next.

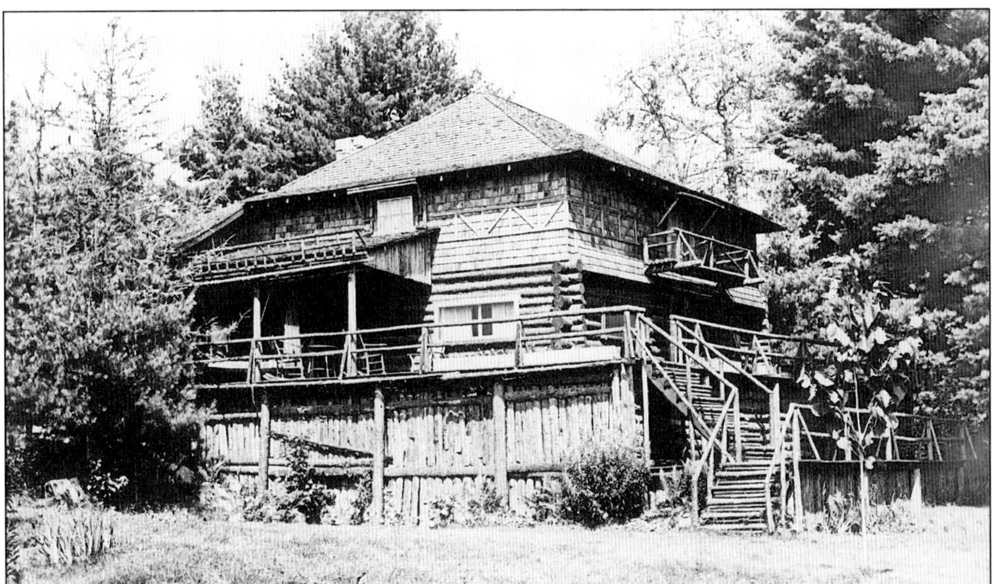

The Warne Cottage, c. 1925. By 1900 a few people were purchasing lots on the Sebago and Long Lakes and building camps and cottages. One of the more unusual ones was this log cottage built on the west shore of Long Lake by Edward and Augusta Warne. How perfectly it blends in with its sylvan surroundings.

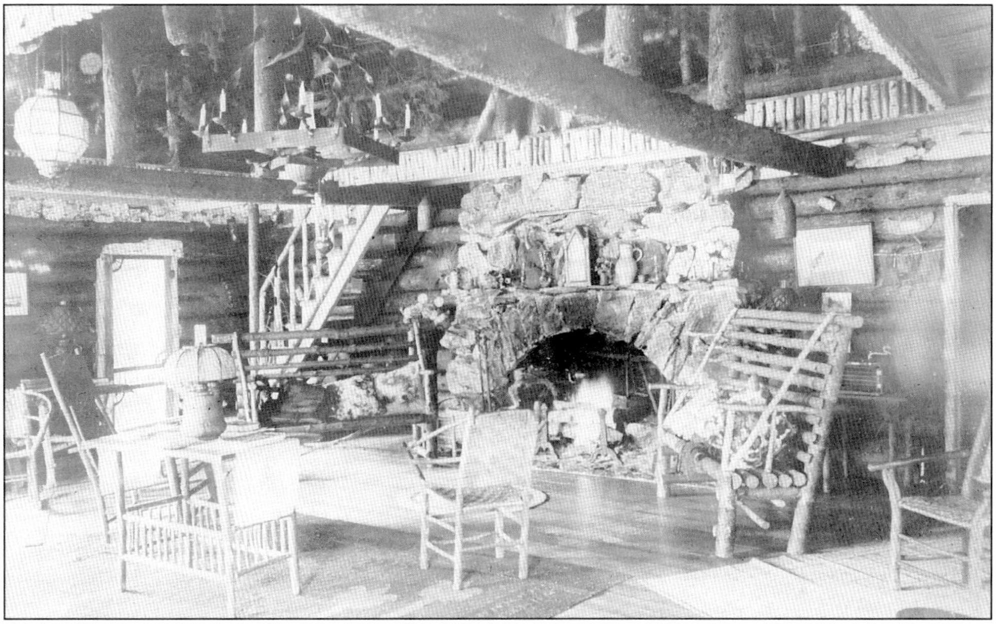

The Interior of the Warne Cottage. The interior of the Warne cottage with it huge fieldstone fireplace and its magnificent log beams exuded rustic comfort and was quite in keeping with the ambiance of forest and lake. As the chandelier hanging down from the center beam and the lanterns and lamps indicate, the Warnes had no electricity. Yet, mysteriously on a December night, the cottage went up in flames.

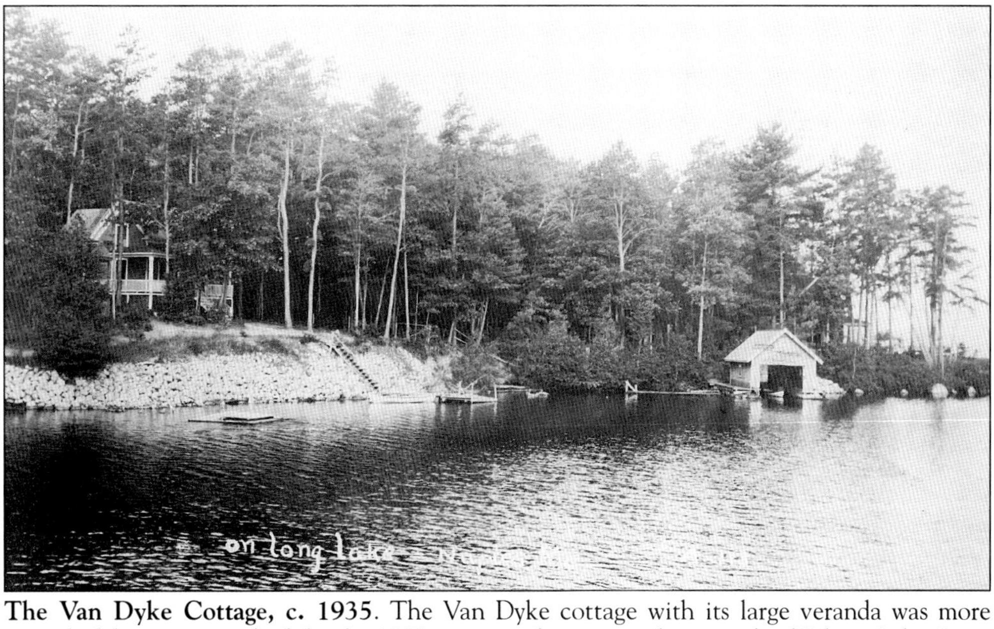

The Van Dyke Cottage, c. 1935. The Van Dyke cottage with its large veranda was more typical of the cottages which by the 1930s were mushrooming along much of Sebago Lake, Long Lake, and other bodies of water in the region. Those who had waterfront cottages often built a boathouse at the edge of the water, especially if they had some sort of large inboard motorboat such as a cabin cruiser. Those who seldom came to their cottages frequently either rented them out directly or through an agency to vacationers.

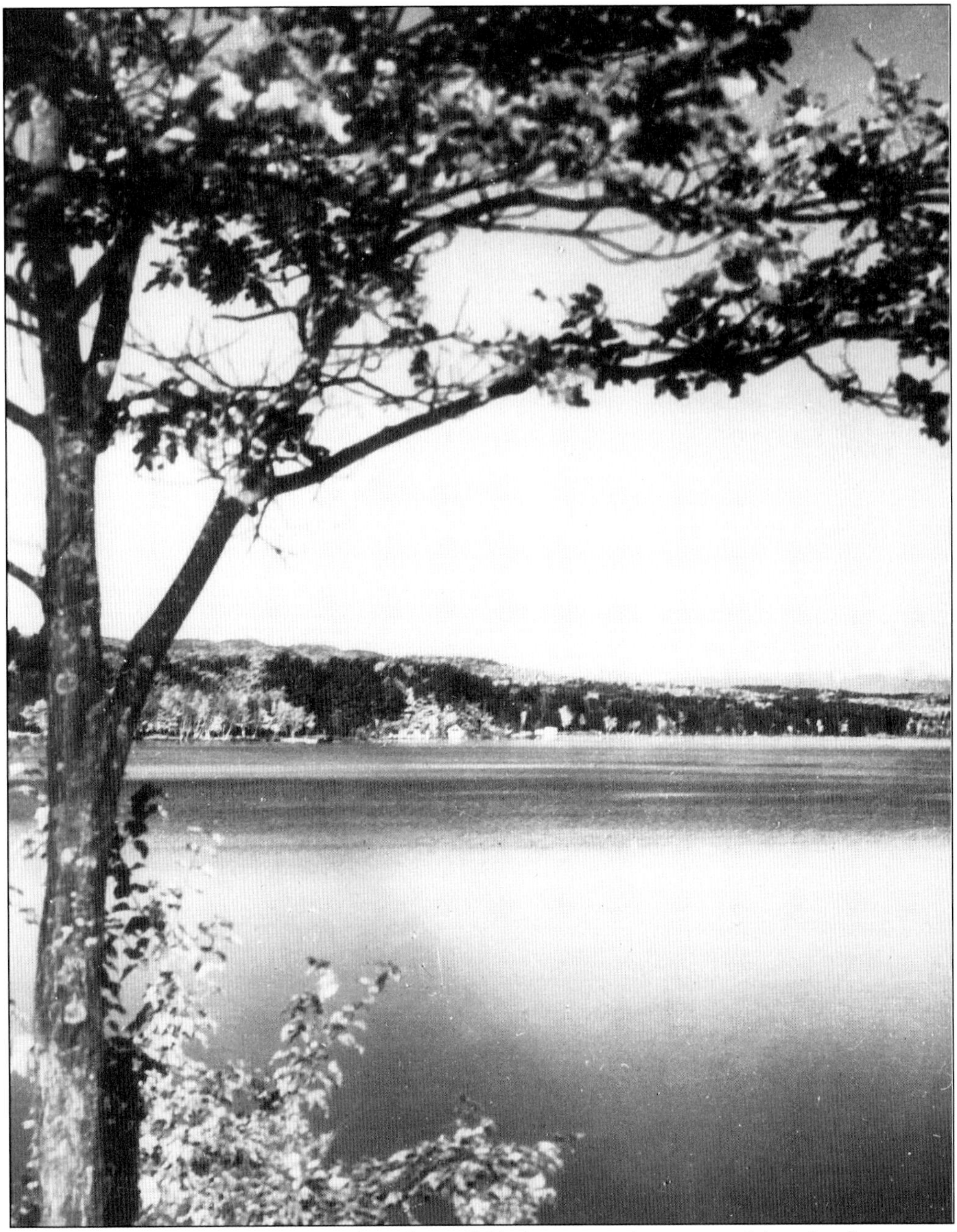

Long Lake in Early Autumn. With such ineffable beauty as this scene of the placid waters of Long Lake, viewed from the east shore overlooking the distant snow-capped White Mountains of New Hampshire, it is little wonder that there were those who referred to the Sebago Lake region as the "Switzerland of America." After Labor Day, most cottage owners closed up their summer places, and few tourists remained in the area. The lakes and ponds grew silent, except for the occasional cry of the loon or the liquid rhythmic sound of gentle waves washing against the shoreline. In more recent decades, however, the vacation season has been extended, and many people have winterized their cottages and now reside permanently on the shores of lakes and ponds.

Six

On the Water

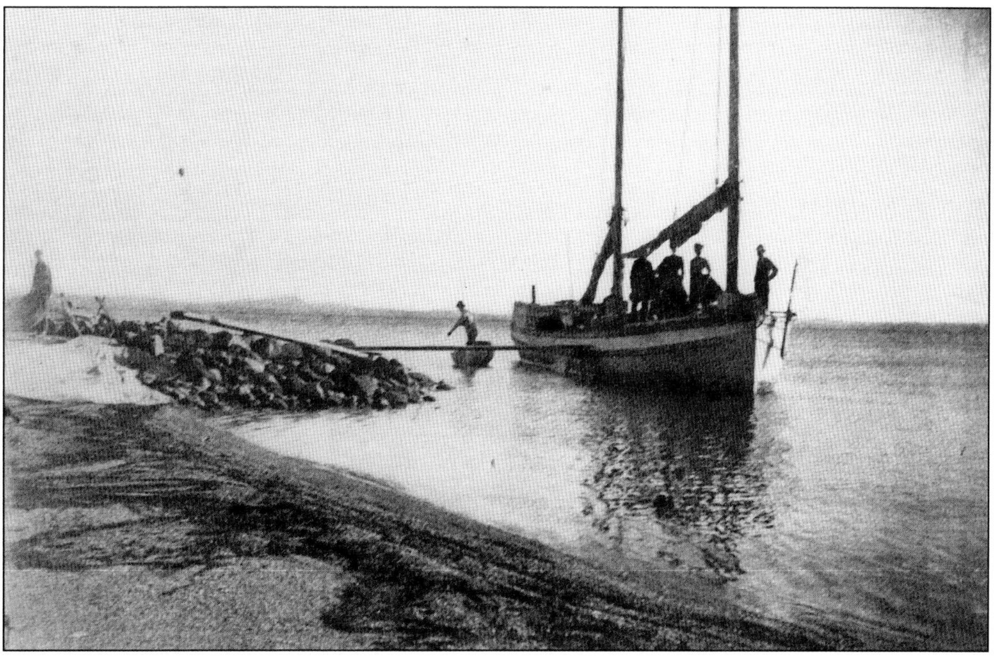

A Canal Boat on Sebago Lake, c. 1900. The *Bluebird*, a canal boat owned and operated by Captain Benjamin Knight of Raymond, was typical of the canal boats that once carried freight and passengers up and down the Cumberland & Oxford Canal between 1830 and 1870—a distance of 20 miles from the foot of Clark Street near the Portland Bridge to the Sebago Lake Basin at White's Bridge. A typical canal boat was 65 feet long, 10 feet at the beam, had a square stern and a rounded bow, and carried between 25 and 30 tons. The sails were for use on Sebago Lake, Brandy Pond, Long Lake, and Portland Harbor. When passing under a bridge, the masts—set in jaws—could be folded down like a jackknife. Sometime after the canal completely closed in 1872, Captain Knight installed a small steam engine.

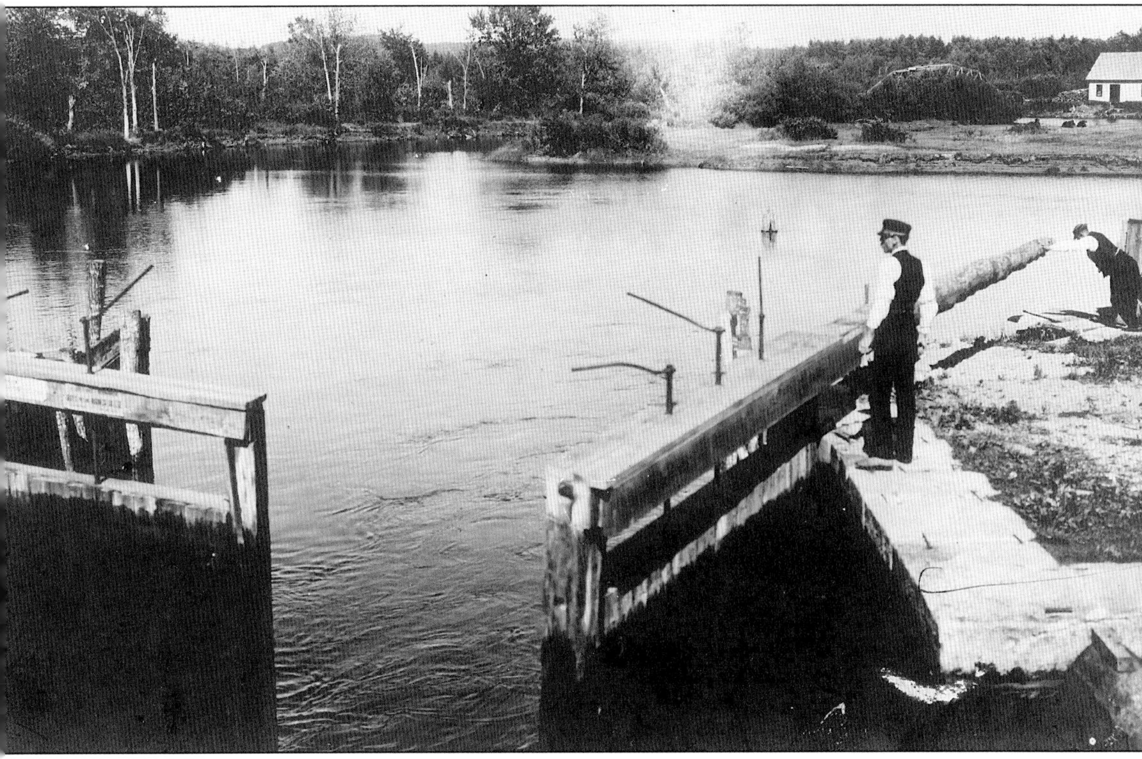

Opening the Songo Locks, c. 1915. The 20-mile Cumberland & Oxford Canal was dug mostly by Irish immigrants using picks and shovels. Since Sebago Lake is 264 feet higher than Portland Harbor, it was necessary to construct twenty-seven locks (each 80 feet long by 10 feet wide) along the canal, beginning with Lower Guard Lock at the entrance to Portland Harbor and ending with Upper Guard or Wescott Lock just before the canal joins Sebago Lake at the Basin. In order for canal boats to reach Long Lake via the Songo, it was necessary to add a twenty-eighth lock above the confluence of the Songo and Crooked Rivers, visible in this photograph. The lock in use here was constructed in 1911, replacing the original lock built in 1830, to meet the needs of larger freighters and steamers carrying passengers.

It was a 50-mile trip one way from Harrison at the end of Long Lake to Portland Harbor and normally took about three days. Canal boats used wind power on Long Lake and Brandy Pond. The sails were then lowered, and the boat's crew (usually consisting of a captain and two helpers) proceeded to pole the boats down the river by thrusting poles into the river bed and then walking the full length of the gunnel.

Once the boat entered Sebago Lake at the mouth of the Songo, the crewmen raised the sails and headed down the full length of Sebago Lake. Often the canal boats were pounded by ocean-like waves, but there is no record of any canal boat ever being sunk or wrecked.

Once the boats reached the canal, they were towed by a team of horses along the towpath. As the boat approached a lock, the captain would blow a horn to signal the lock keeper to begin opening the gates.

After the closing of the canal, many of the old canal boats continued to carry freight on Sebago Lake for several decades. From the 1870s to about 1932, steamboats carried passengers on round-trip excursions from Sebago Lake Station to the Bay of Naples. And the Songo Lock continued to raise and lower steamboats on route from lake to lake. Only the *Songo* remained to carry pleasure seekers for the next two decades. Since 1970, the *Songo River Queen*, a paddle wheeler powered by a diesel engine, has carried sightseers from the Bay of Naples through the Songo Lock and back to Naples.

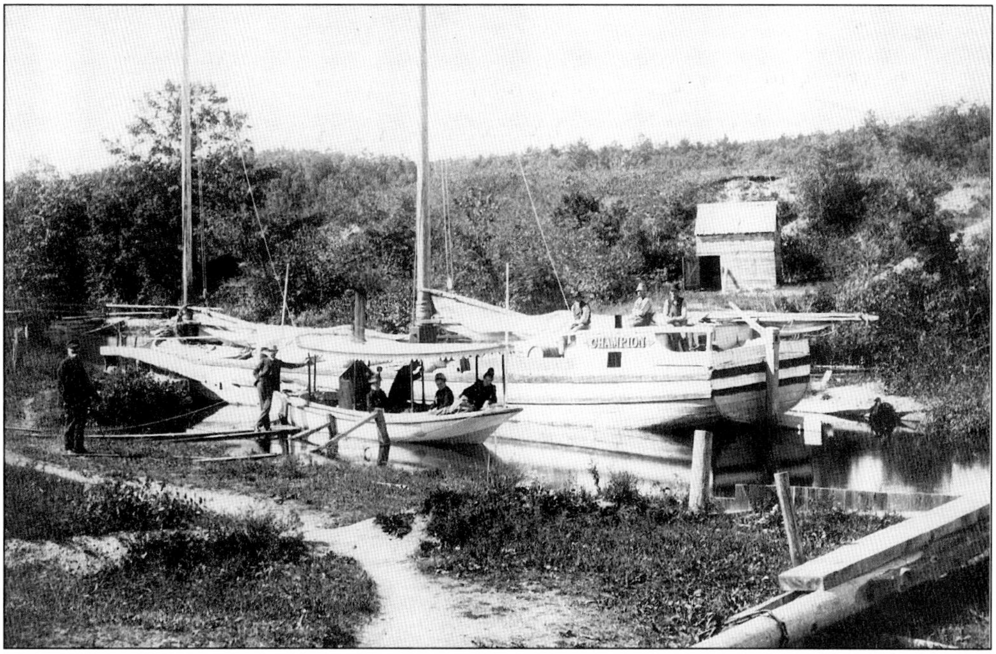

The *Champion* on the Canal, c. 1870. This early photograph of the canal boat *Champion*, along with a small steam launch, was taken at one of the locks on the canal. A typical canal boat cost about $500 to build, had a main and foresail, a flat bottom to pass freely over shallow waters, and two center boards instead of a keel to better enable the boat to hug the wind. The small but cozy cabin in the stern was where the three crewmen cooked their meals and slept. Generally the captain was paid $50 a month and each of his helpers $35.

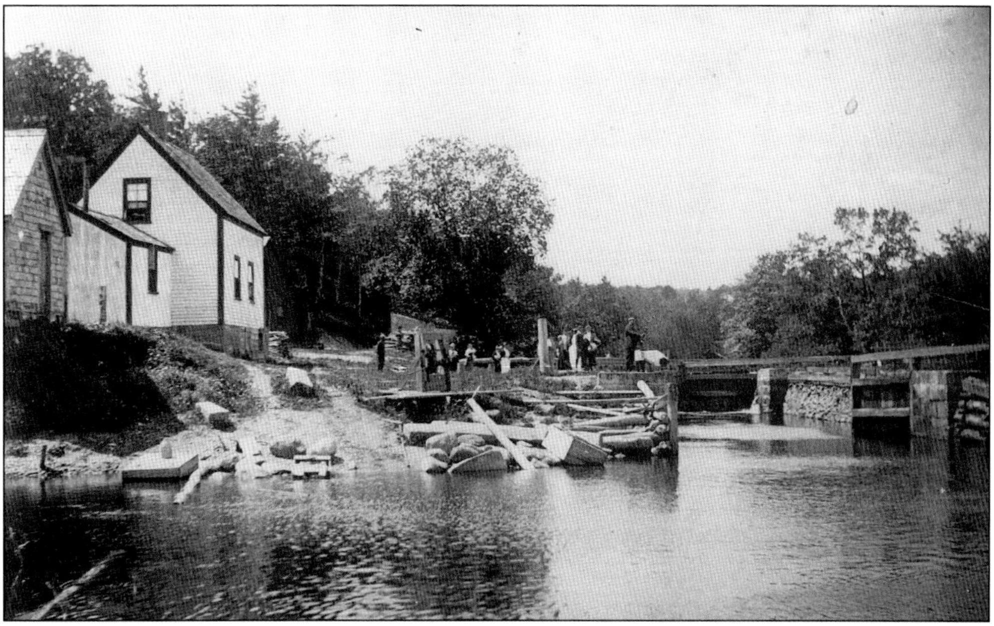

The Songo Lock, c. 1900. This looks to be the original lock before being widened in 1911. The upper gates in the direction of Brandy Pond and Long Lake are closed. The first canal boat passed through here in 1830. All of Songo River and the lock are located in the town of Naples.

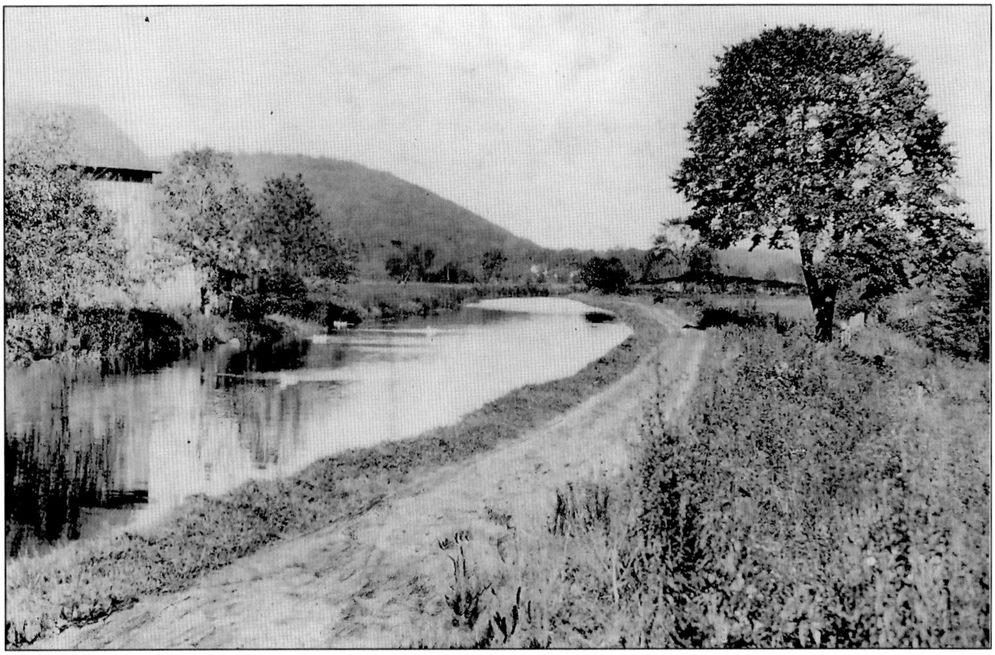

The Old Towpath. This halcyon scene of the well-trodden towpath somewhere along the Cumberland & Oxford Canal (possibly at Babb Bridge in Windham) was taken at a time when people and goods moved at a much slower pace. In fact, the Canal Company by-laws mandated that canal boats travel through the canal no faster than 4 miles per hour. One can almost hear the good-natured banter that passed between the teamsters towing the boats and the crewmen and the raucous laughter that followed the telling of an off-colored joke.

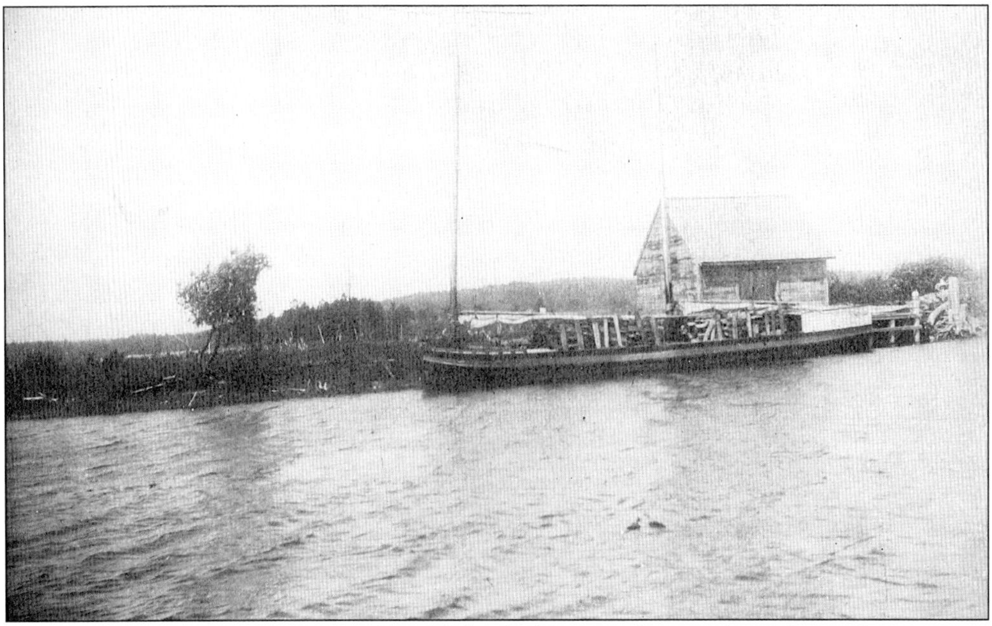

A Full Cargo. This canal boat with a full load of logs at the mouth of the Jordan River in Raymond was probably owned and operated by Captain Benjamin Knight. Canal boat such as this one could carry between 10 and 12 cords of wood, or 20,000 or so feet of lumber.

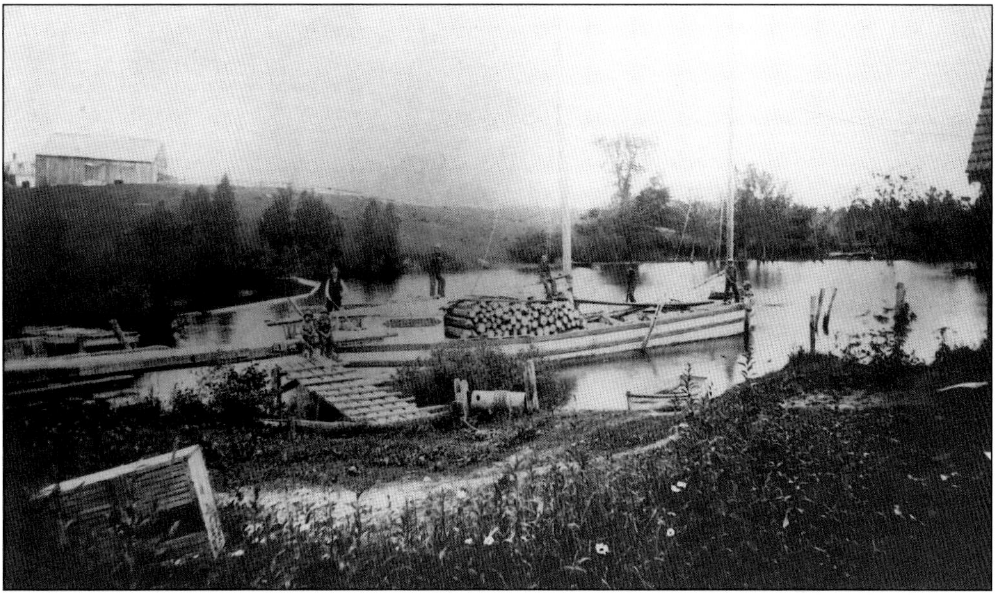

Freighting Pulp Wood Down the Songo. This appears to be an early photograph of a canal boat partially loaded with either pulp wood or cord wood at the lower end of Songo Lock where Crooked River empties into the Songo. Pulp and cord wood was often freighted from Long Lake down the canal to South Windham, Westbrook, and Portland. After the closure of the canal, wood and other products were unloaded at Sebago Lake Station and shipped to these destinations by rail.

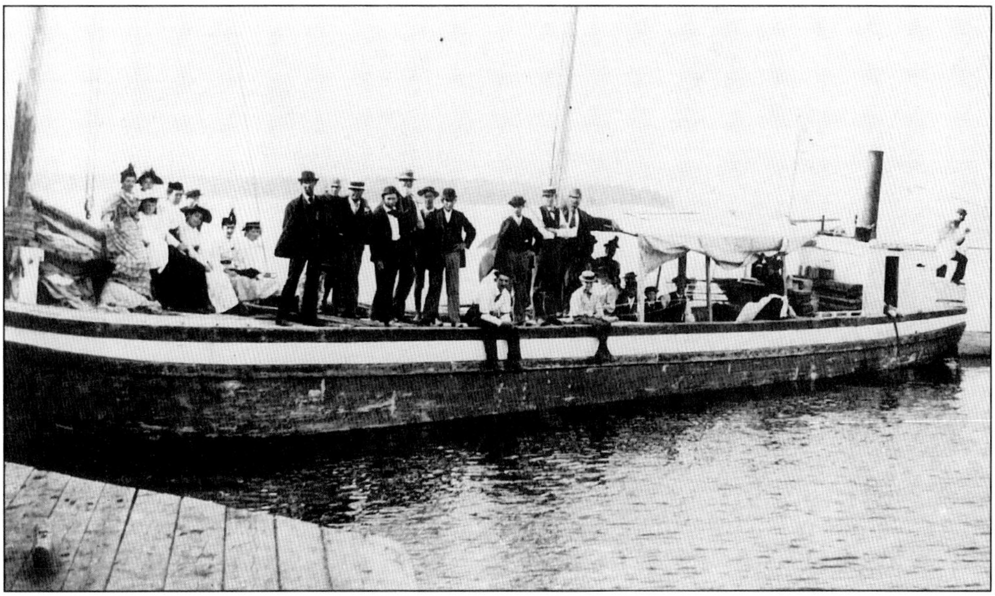

A Summer Outing on the *Bluebird,* c. 1890. This large group of either residents or borders from the Pine Grove Farm in Raymond seemed to be enjoying an outing at Sebago Lake Station aboard the canal boat *Bluebird,* owned and operated by Captain Benjamin Knight—the tall gentleman with the white beard. When the canal closed, Captain Knight continued to operate the *Bluebird* on Sebago Lake. The smoke stack near the stern indicates that he added a steam engine to enable him to navigate the lake more rapidly in calm weather.

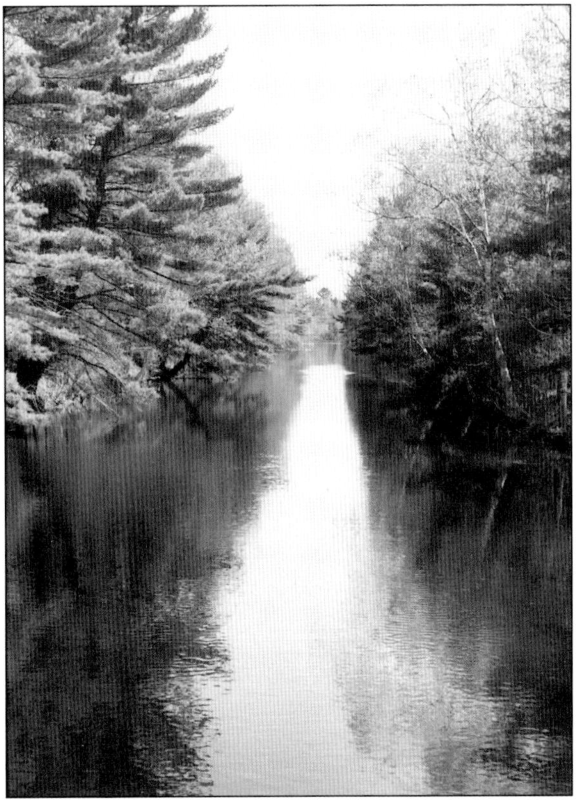

A View of the Canal, c. 1950. Deciduous and pine trees, arching gracefully like gymnasts, cast their reflections in the still waters of the long-abandoned Cumberland & Oxford Canal. This view, taken from the bridge on Route 35 (once the location of Eel Weir Lock) between Sebago Lake Village and North Windham, shows a portion of a mile-long stretch of the canal that has been preserved.

Wescott Lock, 1879. Little had changed at Wescott (or Upper Guard) Lock in the six years after the closing of the canal in 1873, when Captain Lewis P. Crockett of Naples and the *Arthur Willis* passed through these upper gates and entered Sebago Lake after making a final run down to Goff and Plummer's Mill at Middle Jam in Gorham. The granite stonework from Quarry Cove on the Raymond Cape still remains.

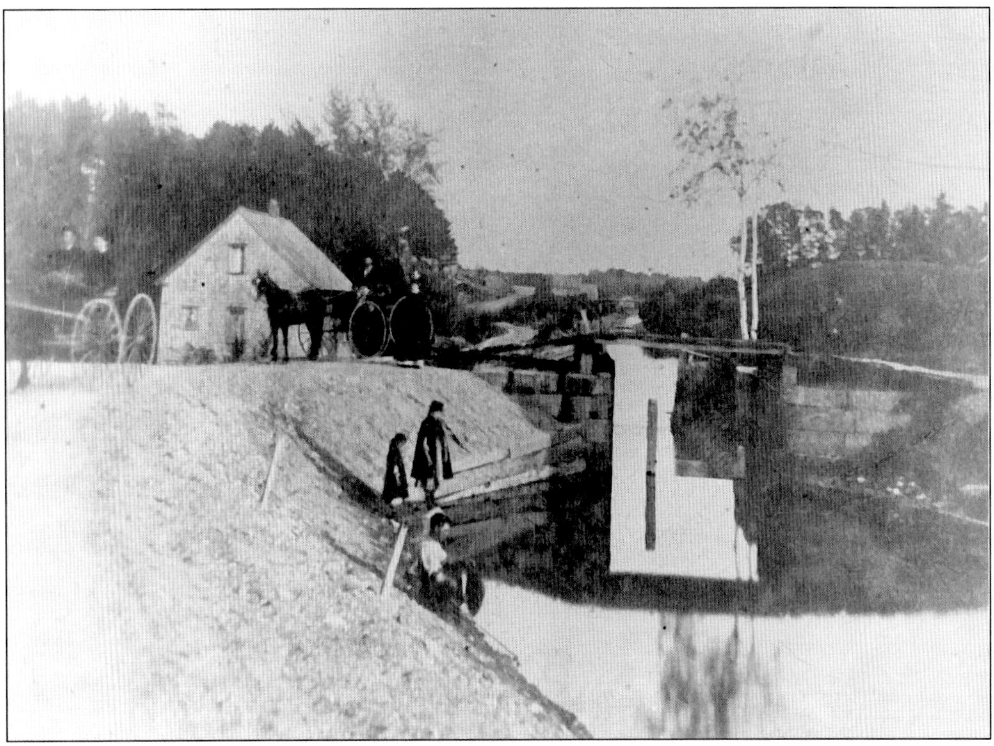

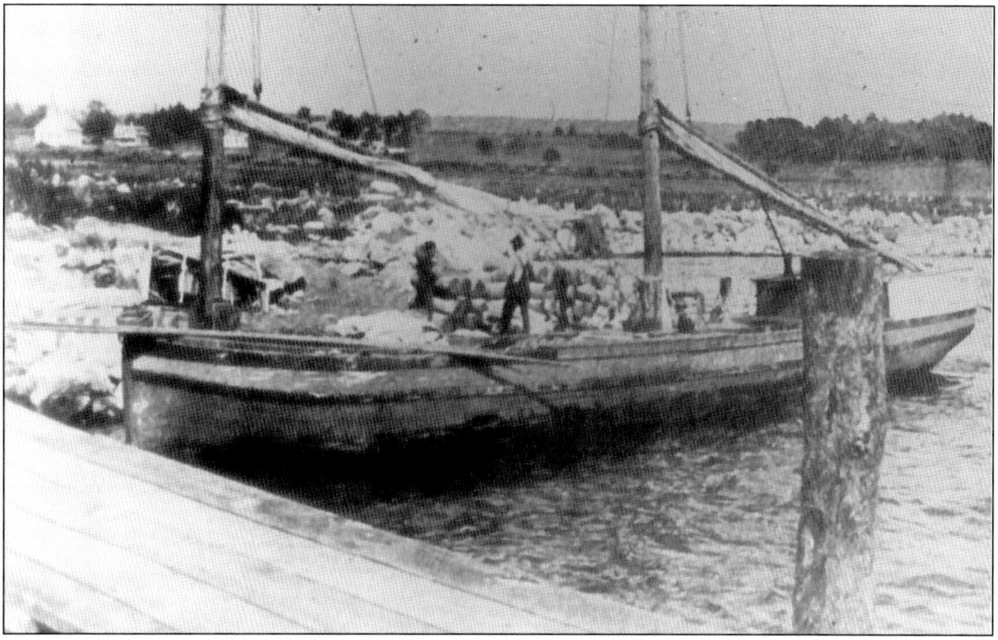

At Chadbourne Landing, c. 1870. The crew of an unidentified canal boat is either loading or unloading cargo at Chadbourne Landing in Standish at the foot of Lower Bay on Sebago Lake. The little Baptist church was torn down in 1875. Just out of view was the Chadbourne House, a popular stopover for both passengers and crewmen.

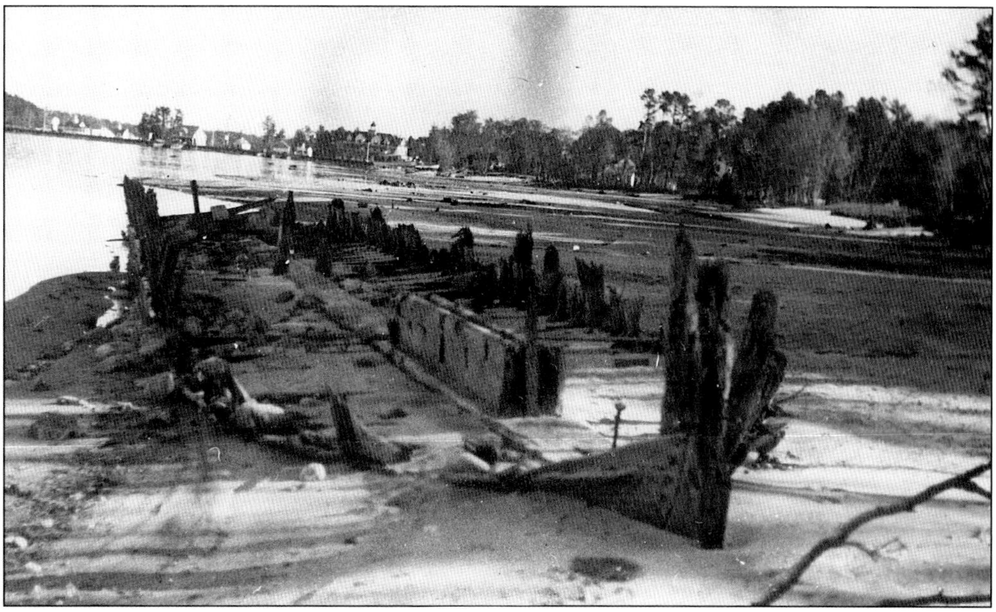

The Graveyard of the *Ethel*. Embedded in the sand at Brackett's Beach on Long Lake within view of the Naples Causeway lies the skeletal remains of the 60-ton freight boat *Ethel*, reputed to have been originally the *Ceres*. In 1894 it was purchased from the Crockett brothers of Naples by Lewis P. Knight and Mel Brackett of Naples, who together maintained a virtual monopoly of the water freight business from about 1900 to 1923, when trucks took over. The *Ethel* was abandoned in 1904.

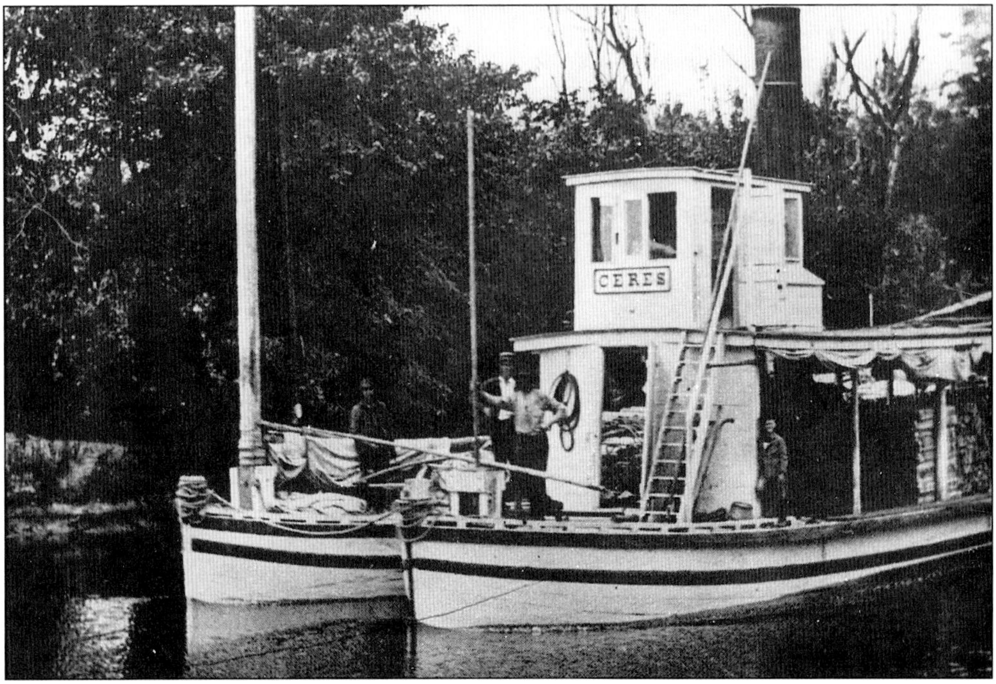

The *Ceres*, c. 1892. The freight steamer *Ceres*, loaded with pulp wood destined for Sebago Lake Station to be shipped by rail, very likely to S.D. Warren in Westbrook, is secured to a standard wind-driven freight boat. The *Ceres* was built and operated by the Crockett brothers of Naples, who—according to Robert Jordan Dingley, author of *The Story of Naples, Maine*—sold it in 1894 to Knight and Brackett, and it was then renamed the *Ethel*.

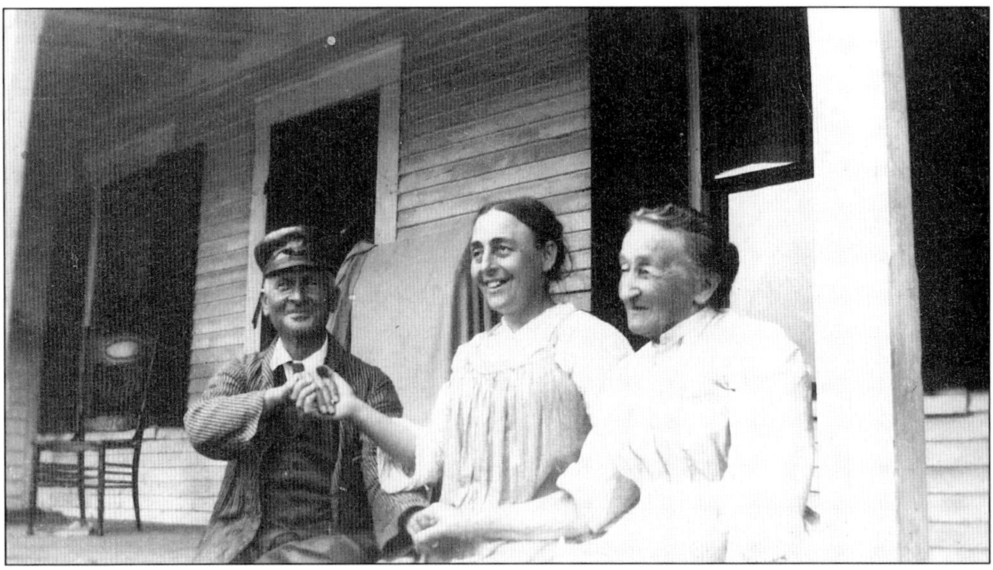

Kindred Spirits, c. 1900. Captain Ben M. Seaberry sits grasping the hand of Minerva ("Minnie") Brackett, the wife of Captain Mel Brackett of Naples. Captain Brackett's mother sits next to her daughter-in-law. "Minnie" Brackett was the only woman with an engineer's license. It can be said that she was Captain Mel's first mate on and off the water.

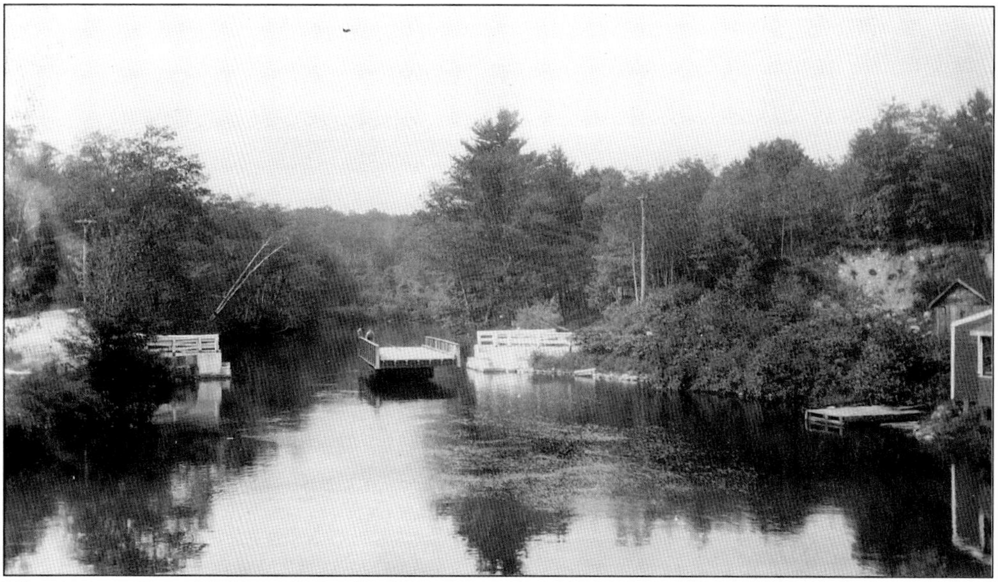

The Songo River Bridge. From late spring into October the attendant for this unique swing bridge just above Songo Lock is kept busy opening and closing this bridge. It is operated by inserting a bar into a slot and then walking around repeatedly in a circle as the bridge swings open and closed. A short distance around the bend toward Brandy Pond lies a well-preserved hulk of an old canal boat embedded in mud at the bottom of the river.

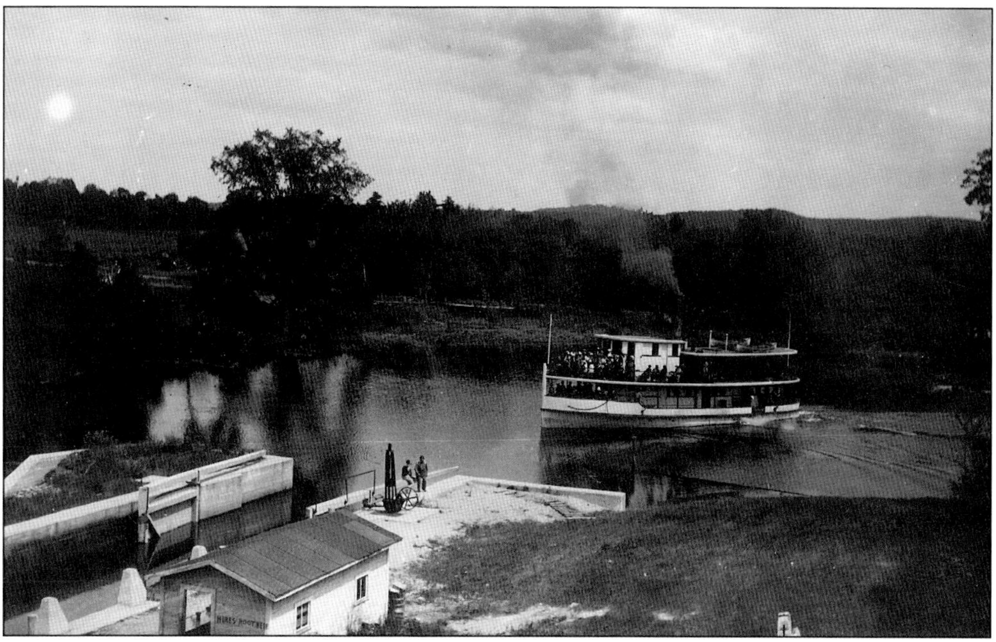

The *Bay of Naples* on the Songo, c. 1905. The *Bay of Naples*, with a sizeable number of sightseers on its decks, is arriving at Songo Lock from Sebago Lake Station. In 1892 the proprietor of the Bay of Naples Inn, Charles L. Goodridge, formed the Songo River and Bay of Naples Steamboat Company. The *Bay of Naples*, built in Muskegon, Michigan, was added to the fleet around 1902.

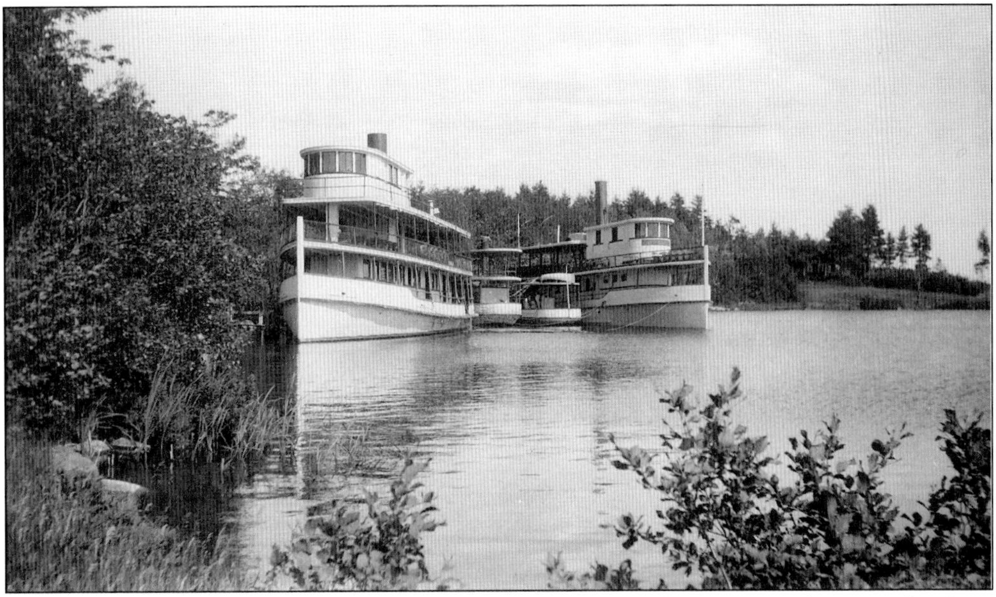

The Songo River Line, c. 1917. After two decades of successfully operating the steamship line, Goodridge sold out to Captain S.W. Sawyer and C.W. Woodward of the Coburn Steamboat Company at Moosehead Lake. In 1917 they formed the Songo River Line, Inc. This view of the *Goodridge*, the *Bay of Naples*, and what appears to be the *Hawthorne* and the *Longfellow*, was probably taken after the new corporation was formed.

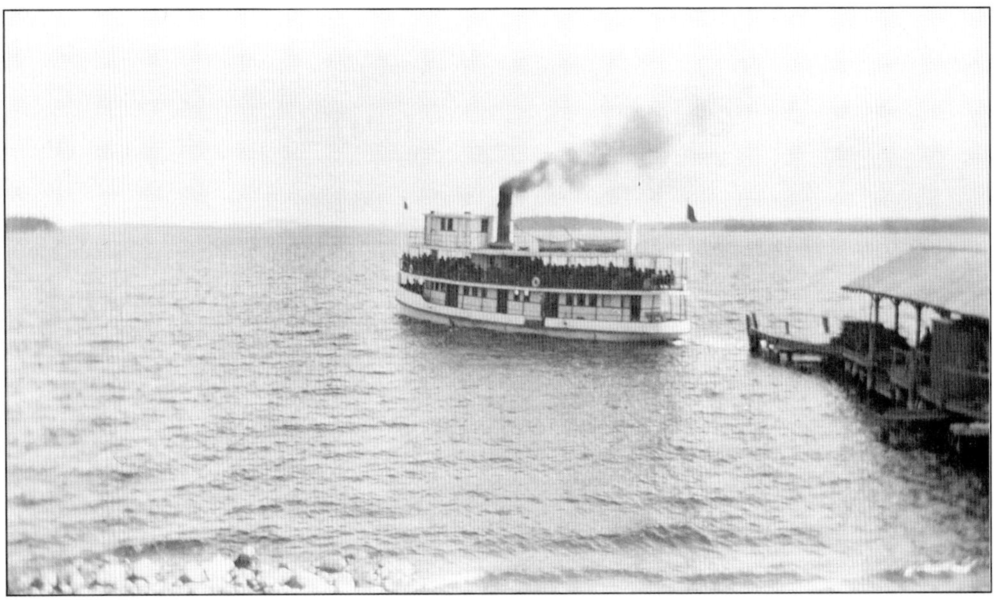

Heading up Sebago Lake, c. 1920. The *Bay of Naples*' twin decks appear to be filled to capacity (three hundred passengers), as it gets underway at Sebago Lake Station and heads up the 50-mile waterway. Chances are that the *Bay of Naples* was heading to rendezvous with a smaller steamer such as the *Worrambus* to transfer some of its passengers, mail, and luggage destined for points along the west shore of the lake.

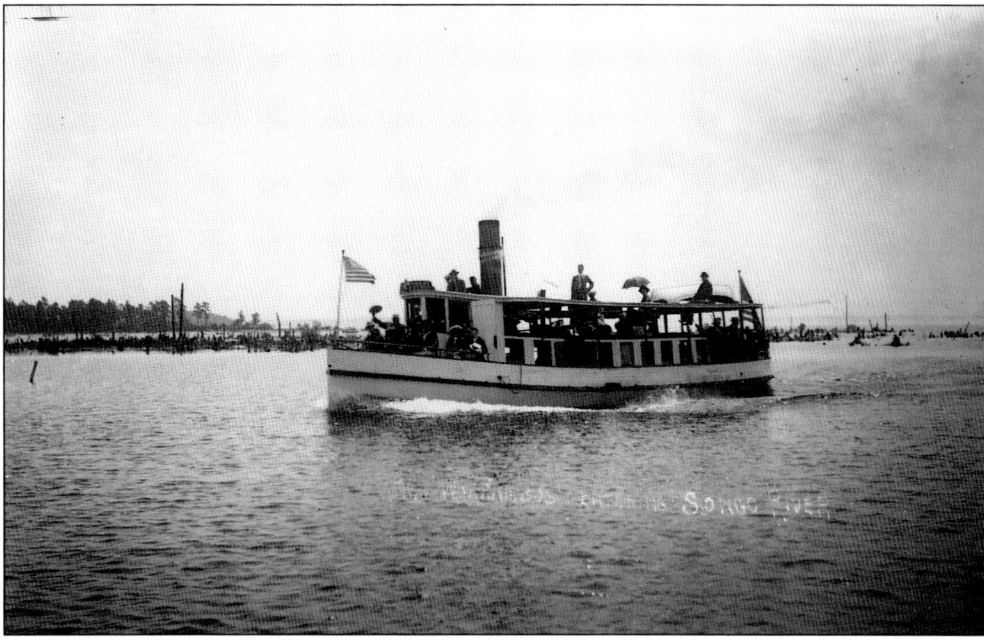

Crossing the Bar. This steamer, possibly the *Hawthorne*, seems to be having no trouble sailing up the sandy shallow channel at the mouth of the Songo known as the Songo Bar. Even though the bigger steamers such as the *Goodridge* and the *Bay of Naples* took only 3 feet of water, very often they would scrape the bottom. Consequently, their twin propellers had to be housed in tunnels for protection.

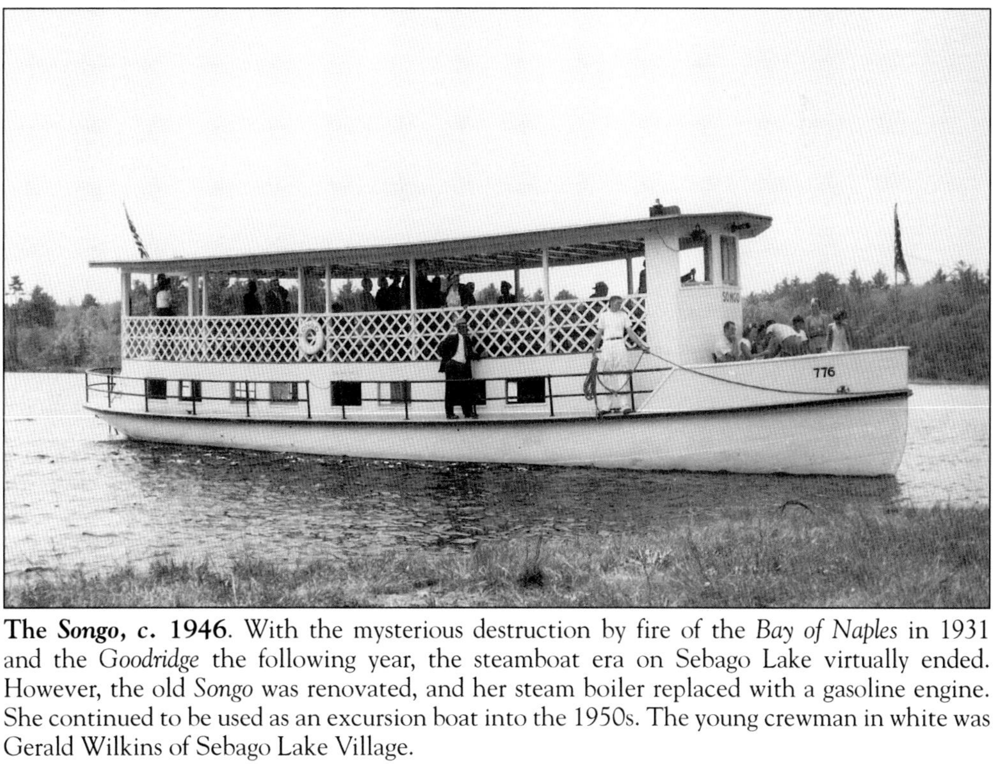

The *Songo*, c. 1946. With the mysterious destruction by fire of the *Bay of Naples* in 1931 and the *Goodridge* the following year, the steamboat era on Sebago Lake virtually ended. However, the old *Songo* was renovated, and her steam boiler replaced with a gasoline engine. She continued to be used as an excursion boat into the 1950s. The young crewman in white was Gerald Wilkins of Sebago Lake Village.

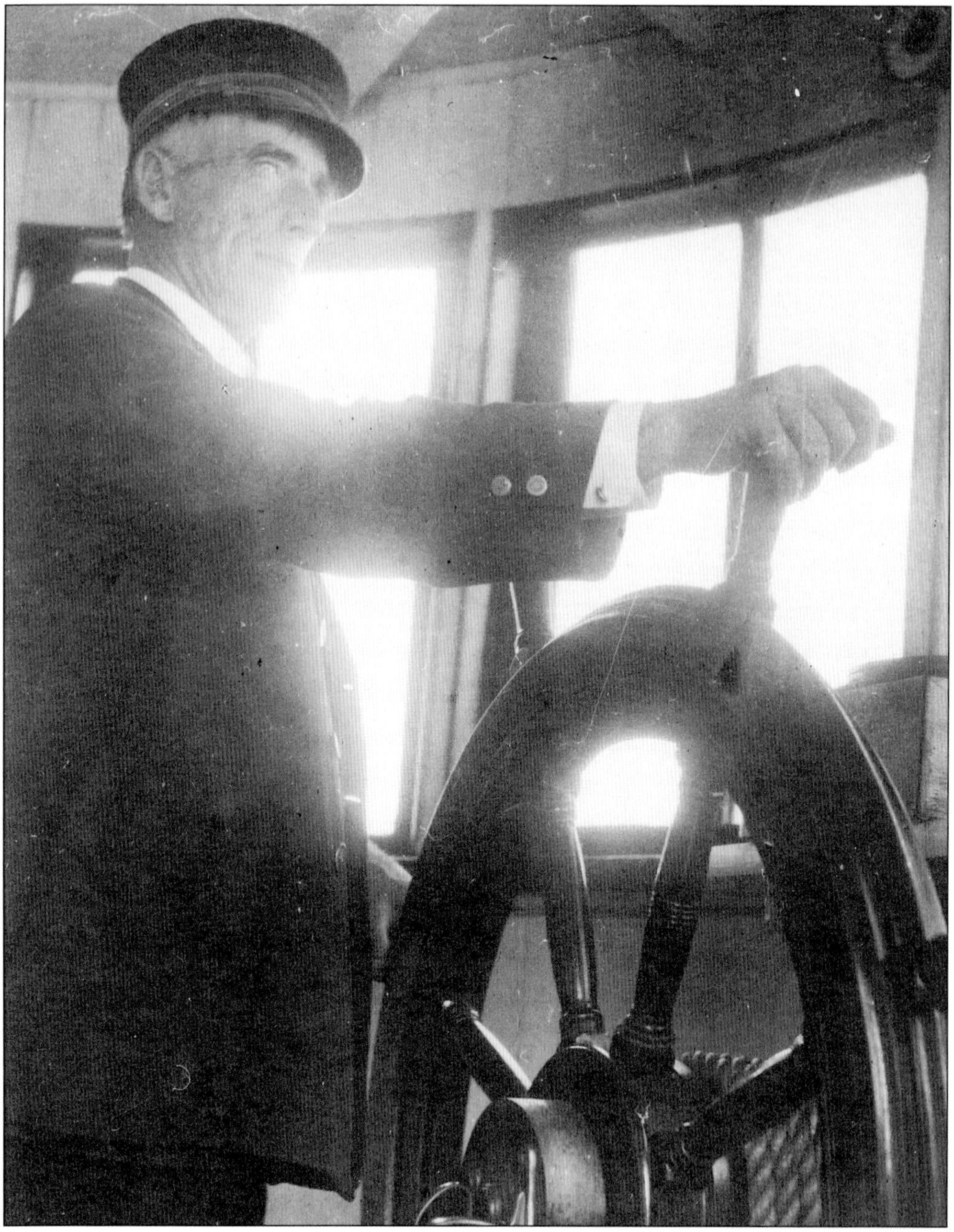

Captain Irving Mains at the Helm. Captain Irving Mains, seen here in the wheelhouse of the *Goodridge*, was one of the most distinguished steamboat captains during the colorful steamboat era. It was truly a challenge to negotiate the sinuous Songo River when this large vessel, constructed at the Bath Iron Works and designed to carry a maximum of six hundred passengers, often brushed against overhanging trees. Then there were the vagaries of crossing the Songo Bar.

Time and technology rendered the Cumberland & Oxford Canal obsolete, brought about the demise of the freight era on the lake a half century later, and ended the colorful steamboat days in 1932. All that remains to remind us of that time is a collection of old photographs.